Jennifer Stafford-Brown

edexcel
advancing, changing lives

Level 2 Higher Diploma

Sport and Active Leisure

A PEARSON COMPANY

Published by Pearson Education Limited, Edinburgh Gate, Harlow, Essex, CM20 2JE. Registered company number: **872828**

www.pearsonschoolsandfecolleges.co.uk

Edexcel is a registered trademark of Edexcel Limited

Text © Pearson Education Limited 2010
Designed by HL Studios
Original illustrations by ODI © Pearson Education 2010
Reuse illustrations © Pearson Education and Vicky Woodgate 2009
Index by Indexing Specialists (UK) Ltd

The author asserts her moral right to be identified as the author of this work

First published 2010

14 13 12 11 10
10 9 8 7 6 5 4 3 2 1

British Library Cataloguing in Publication Data
A catalogue record for this book is available from the British Library

ISBN 978 1 846 90764 7

Printed and bound in Great Britain at Scotprint, Haddington

Hotlinks
There are links to relevant websites in this book. In order to ensure that the links are up to date and that the links work we have made the links available on our website at www.pearsonhotlinks.co.uk. Search for this title **Level 2 Higher Diploma in Sport and Active Leisure** or ISBN **9781846907647**.

Disclaimer
This material has been published on behalf of Edexcel and offers high-quality support for the delivery of Edexcel qualifications. This does not mean that the material is essential to achieve any Edexcel qualification, nor does it mean that it is the only suitable material available to support any Edexcel qualification. Edexcel material will not be used verbatim in setting any Edexcel examination or assessment. Any resource lists produced by Edexcel shall include this and any other appropriate resources.

Copies of official specifications for all Edexcel qualifications may be found on the Edexcel website: www.edexcel.com

Contents

Acknowledgements

From the author, Jennifer Stafford-Brown

I would like to thank a number of people who have provided me with help in various different ways in researching and writing this text book. First of all my thanks go out to my husband Matt and children Ellie and Alex for their patience and encouragement throughout the writing process and to my parents, Ann and Brian, for all of their support and help over the years. I would also like to thank a number of subject specialists including Paul Butler, Phil Heslop, James Turner and Stuart White, all of whom have helped me with my research and contributed information for this textbook.

Finally I would like to say a big thank you to the Pearson Education publishing team, in particular Francesca Heslop and Katie Juden for all of their hard work and support throughout the duration of this project.

Photographs

The author and publisher would like to thank the following individuals and organisations for permission to reproduce photographs:

(Key: b-bottom; c-centre; l-left; r-right; t-top)

Alamy Images: Aflo Foto Agency 20, EPF commercial 8, Ted Foxx 49, Clynt Garnham 168, Les Gibbon 16, kpzfoto 123, Ilene MacDonald 26, Steve Skjold 38; **ArenaPAL:** Johan Persson 64; **Corbis:** James Leynse 140, Mika 216, Tim Pannel 207, PCN Photography / PCN 82, Ed Quinn 18, Peter Morgan / Reuters 88, Sean Aidan; Eye Ubiquitous 90; **Getty Images:** 145, 175, MARCEL MOCHET / AFP 174, PHILIP LITTLETON / AFP 171, Bill Baptist / National Basketball Association 165, Hamish Blair 143, Christof Koepsel / Bongarts 51, Gustavo Caballero 137, Brian Caissie 120, Phil Cole 201, Laurence Griffiths 46, 169, Simon Bruty / Sports Illustrated 86, altrendo images 208, Jupiterimages 203, LatinContent Editorial 195, Christopher Lee 118, Ian Walton 177; **iStockphoto:** 8/2, 76/4, 106, 138, 142, 151, 215, 224, 231, 232, AVAVA 113, Galina Barskaya 222, Phil Berry VI/2, Pamela Burley 173, Gene Chutka 110, Mike Dabell 98, Winston Davidian 230, DIGIcal 114, Martin Garnham 14, Oscar Gutierrez 199, Phillip Jones 147, Ryan Klos 163, Jim Kolaczko VII/2, Renee Lee 53, Rich Legg 74, David H. Lewis 104, 187, David H. Lewis 104, 187, Sean Locke 149, 167, Nancy Louie x, Brian McEntire VI, Paul Morton 81, Paul Prescott VI/3, Ranplett 109, Pali Rao 128, 184, Andrew Rich 64/3, Celso Pupo Rodrigues 8/3, Chris Schmidt 40, 124, 154, Alistair Scott 212, Eliza Snow 108, 117, Chris Tack 73, Bojan Tezak 223, Tony Tremblay 180, Frances Twitty 37, Scott Williams 87; **Katie Juden:** 64/4, 64/5, 65/2, 127, 127/2; **Pearson Education Ltd:** www.imagesource.com / Alamy 43, Mark Bassett 198, VII, Gareth Boden 4, 28, 30, Imagestate. John Foxx Collection 92, 225, Fancy. Veer. Corbis 181, 186, Digital Vision. Getty Images 4/2, Bananastock. Imagestate 115, Rob Judges 56, 76/2, 179, Businesswoman working on laptop 114/2, MindStudio 130, 156, 221, Digital Vision. Rob van Petten 162, Lisa Payne Photography 111, Tudor Photography 77/2, Photodisc. Photolink 12, 64/2, 76, Rubberball Productions 76/3, David Sanderson 7, 7/2, Jules Selmes XI, 227, Richard Smith 197, Stockbyte 65, 77, Photodisc. Karl Weatherly 23, Studio 8. Clark Wiseman 188; **Science Photo Library Ltd:** Matt Meadows, Peter Arnold Inc 15; **Thinkstock:** Jupiterimages 210, 211

Cover images: *Front:* **Pearson Education Ltd:** Roy Lawe. Alamy, Tudor Photography; **Shutterstock**

All other images © Pearson Education

Every effort has been made to trace the copyright holders and we apologise in advance for any unintentional omissions. We would be pleased to insert the appropriate acknowledgement in any subsequent edition of this publication.

INTRODUCTION TO THE QUALIFICATION

About the Diploma

Welcome to the Level 2 Higher Diploma in Sport and Active Leisure. The diploma is an exciting qualification which will give you the opportunity to explore and develop your understanding of the different sectors within the sport and active leisure industry through taking part in activities and working with sport and active leisure employers. The diploma in sport and active leisure covers four main areas – sport and recreation, health and fitness, the outdoors and play work. This qualification encompasses other sectors within the sport and active leisure industry such as youth work, caravanning, security, stewarding and grounds maintenance.

What you will cover

Your diploma is made up of three elements and you will have to pass all three of these elements to achieve your qualification.

* **Principal learning** – this is the main part of your qualification and is all to do with sport and active leisure. The units that you will be studying are shown in the table below. These units cover different aspects of the skills and knowledge required for working in the sport and active leisure industry.

Principal learning
Positive lifestyle choices and sport and active leisure
Encouraging participation in sport and active leisure
Science in sport and active leisure
Working in the local sport and active leisure industry
Businesses in the sport and active leisure industry
Media in sport and active leisure
Access for all in sport and active leisure

These are the units that you must study.

* **Generic learning** – During your course you will also be working on maths, English and ICT functional skills that will be vital in gaining skills required for work and for further education. You will also have the chance to develop your personal communication and thinking skills (known as personal, learning and thinking skills).

* **Additional and Specialist learning** – is the part of the qualification where you can either choose to broaden your knowledge outside of the sport and active leisure industry and study an unrelated qualification or choose a qualification which allows you to specialise even further within a sector or sectors within the sport and active leisure industry.

It also includes a project qualification (see pages viii–ix) and work experience (see pages x–xi). Your tutor will support you in achieving these aspects of your diploma.

Practical Work

As the principal learning in the diploma is taught through applied learning you will have the opportunity to take part in lots of practical work. Through taking part in practical activities you will gain an in-depth understanding of the subject area. Examples of these activities include carrying out fitness and health tests, using questionnaires to gain feedback from different people, assessing the lifestyle of an individual, taking part in a promotional campaign, and looking at how the media promote and support sport and active leisure.

About Your Assessment

How you will be assessed

Most of your diploma will be assessed through internal assessments. One unit of the higher diploma is externally assessed and takes the form of an examination paper.

Top Tips on preparing for assessment

Internal assessment

Your tutor will set you an assignment which consists of different tasks. You will need to provide evidence to answer the questions in each of the tasks and will be given a set time to complete each task. Whilst you are producing work that is going to be marked for the assessment you will be observed by your tutor or an employer from the sport and active leisure industry. This ensures that the work you produce is all your own work and clearly demonstrates your understanding of the subject that you are studying. Some of the tasks will require you to carry out research before you can complete the task. It is a good idea to complete this research as thoroughly and completely as you are able to as this will help to provide you with the information you need to answer the questions in the tasks. Your tutor may also give you trial tasks which will be similar to your actual assignment task to help you practise for the real assessment. Your tutor will be able to give you feedback on how you can improve your work in the trial or practice tasks which could help you to gain a higher mark when you are working on the real task.

For many of the internal assessments you will have the freedom to provide different types of evidence to meet the requirements of the task such as leaflets, posters and presentations. Your tutor will provide guidance as to which types of evidence are most suited to the task, however, if you have an idea for how you could produce your work, talk with your tutor first to make sure it meets the assessment requirements.

Some of your assessment will take the form of practical activities where your tutor or sport and active leisure employer will observe you carrying out the practical activity and give you marks based on what they have seen you do. These activities might assess how well you work in a team to come up with appropriate ideas for a specific topic, your ability to carry out fitness tests and measure and record data from these tests, your performance taking part in an interview for a job in sport and active leisure, or how well you are able to use leadership skills to assist in the delivery of a sport and active leisure activity etc.

External Assessment

Unit 1 is assessed through a paper-based exam. Make sure you understand each of the different topics covered in Unit 1 and ask your teacher or tutor to explain anything in more detail if you are unsure. Your tutor will probably give you practice exam questions to help to prepare you for the exam. Take time to complete these exam questions so that your tutor can mark them and give you feedback on your strengths and guidance on the areas in the topic that you need to improve on.

When you are revising for the exam, it is a good idea to use 'active' revision, where you read through your class notes and/or this textbook and write questions for yourself based on what you have read. Go back and answer these questions to test how much information you have remembered and, more importantly, how much you have understood.

Working in the Sport and Active Leisure Sector

When you are working in the sport and active leisure sector you will need to be able to work effectively by yourself and as part of a team. As part of your diploma you will be developing these skills through personal, learning and thinking skills (PLTS). The PLTS cover key skills in life and are important in helping you to pass this qualification and for helping you to follow your chosen career path.

Types of role

Each PLTS has been matched to a job in sport and active leisure in which that particular PLTS plays an important role. However, remember that, for each job, other personal, learning and thinking skills will also be used to some degree.

Team Worker
Leisure Centre Assistant

Achmed is still in education and attends a further education college. He works part time at the weekend and some evenings as a leisure centre assistant. This work requires him to work as a member of a team to get the sports hall ready for different sports. Some pieces of equipment, such as the trampoline, require more than one person to set them up, so teamwork is essential. Achmed has worked as a member of a team as part of his studies and has learnt that good communication skills are very important so that each member of the team knows exactly what they need to do and what is expected from them. Achmed has also learnt how to deal with any issues that come up whilst working with other people at college and at work so that different team members can work together effectively to meet their goals.

Independent Enquirer
Sports Journalist

Matt works as a sports journalist for a local paper. He spends time finding out about and going to local sports events so that he can write stories on sport and active leisure teams in his area. His job role requires him to carry out research and travel around his local area. He has to work out the themes or the focus of his articles based upon the sports teams performance and interviews with key players. He also takes photographs of the event and has to decide which photos, if any, are to be used in his articles.

Self-Manager
Personal Trainer

Kevin has always enjoyed going to the gym and exercise classes and is qualified as a health and fitness instructor. Whist in education Kevin was well organised and displayed good levels of initiative. He now owns his own business working as a personal trainer and is responsible for finding clients, designing fitness sessions for each client and organising the administration and financial side of his business. His role as a personal trainer means that he is responsible for his business and has to prioritise his time so that his business grows and his clients are happy with him and their workouts.

Reflective Learner
Sports Scientist

Cathy works as a sports scientist and specialises in exercise physiology. She enjoyed PE and science at school and went on to study sports science at university. In her role she carries out fitness tests on elite athletes to monitor their training. She uses the data from the fitness tests to provide feedback to the athletes about how they can change their training to improve their fitness levels further. Cathy has to keep up to date with current research in her area and is also carrying out her own research into an area of exercise physiology that she has an interest in.

Effective Participator
After School club manager

Rhian always planned to work with children and is now managing an after-school club for primary school-aged children. In the after-school club the children take part in different activities such as role play, board games, playing musical instruments and cooking. Rhian often finds joining in with these activities with the children helps them to stay focused and give them new ideas or skills to explore. At school Rhian enjoyed taking part in active learning and could be relied upon to fully participate which helped her with her learning and helped other students to get the best out of active learning.

Creative Thinker
Marketing for Sport and Active Leisure products

Arti has always been creative and really enjoyed assessments at college, which involved presenting work in a poster or leaflet format. She is now using her creativity in a job working in a sport and active leisure organisation to help to market their products. In this role her team have to think of imaginative ways of displaying information about the product which will appeal to customers and make them want to buy it.

Going out to Work

As part of your diploma course, you will have the chance to experience what it is really like in the working world. You will be spending at least 10 days on work experience, which will help you to gain a real feel for what working life is like and help you to decide which career you would like to aim for when you leave education.

Selecting your work experience placement

Although you don't have to carry out your work experience in the sport and active leisure industry, it is a good idea to try and find a placement in this sector as this experience will help you to understand and apply knowledge that you have gained from the principal learning units that you will be studying. The sport and active leisure industry is a very big sector which is continuing to grow so finding a placement is usually not difficult. There are a huge range of jobs within the sport and active leisure industry, some of which you may not even be aware of. Have a look at the list below which shows some of the different jobs available in the sport and active leisure sector:

* Coaching
* Officiating
* Sports development
* Sports administration
* Aerobics instructor
* Sports or active leisure facility management
* Before- and after-school child care, such as breakfast clubs
* Sport and active leisure holiday play scheme supervisor
* Referee or umpire
* Personal trainer
* Specialist health and fitness instructor
* Gym receptionist
* Children's play scheme coordinator
* Nursery nurse

* After-school play assistant
* Outdoor activity leader
* Caravan park manager
* Lifeguard
* Volunteer sports club coordinator
* Sport and exercise scientist
* Steward
* Sports grounds person
* Sports marketing
* Mountain leader
* Sailing instructor
* Sports journalism
* Sports therapist
* Sports nutritionist
* PE teacher
* Youth worker

Your work experience may take the form of a two week block in which you work for five days, have the weekend off (or other days if you are working shift work that requires weekend work) followed by a further five days, or you may find that your placement is for shorter periods over the course of your study.

Making Contact

How you make contact with your work experience provider will probably be determined by your school or tutor. Some schools or colleges have work placement officers who make the initial contact with work experience providers for you and then pass on their details for you to follow up. Others may give you the responsibility of selecting a work experience provider and getting in touch with them yourself. At some stage you will need to make contact with your provider and there are different ways of doing this. If you decide that you would like to visit the provider and take a more personal approach you should call the person that you need to meet beforehand to arrange a convenient time for you to talk.

You may decide that you would like to write to the provider in either an email or a letter. An email is an accessible and easy method of getting in touch with a person, if you know their email address. A letter is usually a more formal method of communicating and may be more appropriate for some organisations. Organisations that get a lot of requests for work experience may be more likely to respond positively to letters as it shows you have taken more time and effort.

However you approach your work experience provider, remember to always present yourself in a positive way and try to demonstrate your enthusiasm for the placement that you have chosen. If you are writing a letter or email make sure the spelling and grammar are correct and what you have said demonstrates why you want your placement with that provider and how they will benefit from having you with them. If you talk with a possible provider over the telephone, make sure your voice tone and expression convey a positive image and enthusiasm. An employer is much more likely to give a place to a student who has made an effort and appears keen and willing to learn.

You need to be prepared to receive a phone call, email or letter from your selected work experience provider saying they can't give you a place or you might not hear back from them at all as they may be very busy and not have time to get back to you. Don't take this personally and try not to let this put you off or stop you from applying to other work experience providers. Your tutor should be able to advise you on the best course of action for your circumstances and it is best to talk it over with them.

Hotlinks

Various links to relevant websites appear in Hotlink boxes throughout this book and in the 'useful links' of each unit's 'Assessment guidance' section. To ensure that the links work and are up to date we have made them available on our website www.pearsonhotlinks.co.uk. Search for this title
Level 2 Higher Diploma in Sport and Active Leisure
or ISBN **9781846907647**.

HOW TO USE THIS BOOK

This book has been divided into seven units to match the structure of the Level 2 Sport and Active Leisure Diploma qualification. Each topic is covered in its own clearly marked section. The final unit, Your project, gives guidance, ideas and advice on how to approach and do well in your project work.

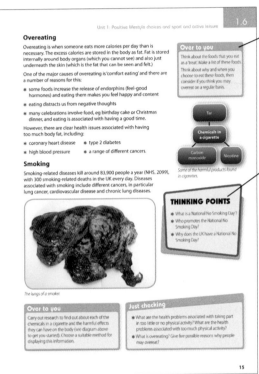

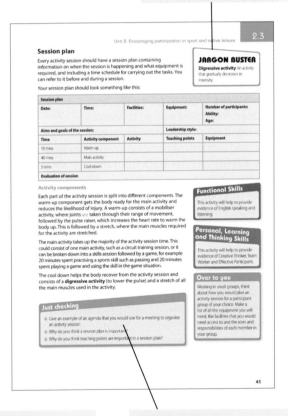

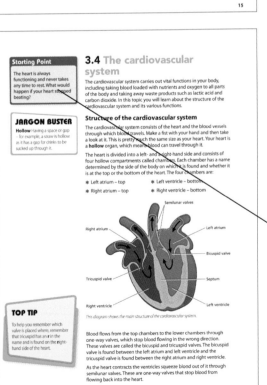

Over to you
These activities test your understanding and give you opportunities to apply your knowledge and skills.

Thinking point
To get you thinking further about the topic being covered.

Jargon busters
Key concepts and new words are explained clearly and simply to make sure you don't miss anything important.

Starting point
A discussion point or short activity that will introduce the key concepts and get you thinking about the topic.

Just checking
Summary questions focus on important points covered in each topic and check your understanding and knowledge.

Case study
Personalised case studies show the concepts covered in the book applied to real-world scenerios. Questions and activities will encourage you to push your understanding further.

Did you know
Fascinating facts to broaden and enhance your knowledge.

Top Tip
Tips to help you learn as you work through a topic.

Functional Skills
Functional skills features highlight opportunities to develop and practise your functional skills in English, ICT or maths. Remember, you will need a pass in all three functional skills to achieve the full diploma.

Personal, learning and thinking skills (PLTS)
These features highlight opportunities to develop your personal, learning and thinking skills (see pages viii–ix).

Hotlink
Hotlink boxes show you where certain websites may be useful for enhancing your studies. For instructions on how to access a full list of these sites, see page xi.

Diploma Daily
Newspaper-style features bring issues and topics to life.

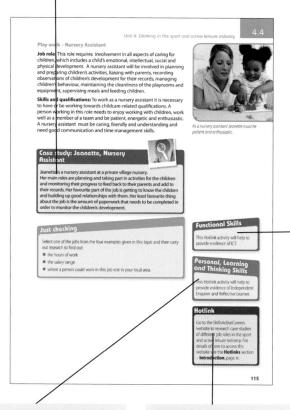

Unit 4: Working in the sport and active leisure industry

4.4

Play work – Nursery Assistant

Job role: This role requires involvement in all aspects of caring for children, which includes a child's emotional, intellectual, social and physical development. A nursery assistant will be involved in planning and preparing children's activities, liaising with parents, recording observations of children's development for their records, managing children's behaviour, maintaining the cleanliness of the playrooms and equipment, supervising meals and feeding children.

Skills and qualifications: To work as a nursery assistant it is necessary to have or be working towards childcare-related qualifications. A person working in this role needs to enjoy working with children, work well as a member of a team and be patient, energetic and enthusiastic. A nursery assistant must be caring, friendly and understanding and need good communication and time management skills.

As a nursery assistant Jeanette must be patient and enthusiastic.

Case study: Jeanette, Nursery Assistant

Jeanette is a nursery assistant at a private village nursery. Her main roles are planning and taking part in activities for the children and monitoring their progress to feed back to their parents and add to their records. Her favourite part of the job is getting to know the children and building up good relationships with them. Her least favourite thing about the job is the amount of paperwork that needs to be completed in order to monitor the children's development.

Just checking

Select one of the jobs from the four examples given in this topic and then carry out research to find out:
* the hours of work
* the salary range
* where a person could work in this job role in your local area.

Functional Skills
This Hotlink activity will help to provide evidence of ICT.

Personal, Learning and Thinking Skills
This Hotlink activity will help to provide evidence of Independent Enquirer and Reflective Learner.

Hotlink
Go to the SkillsActiveCareers website to research case studies of different job roles in the sport and active leisure industry. For details of how to access this website see the **Hotlinks** section – **Introduction**, page xi.

115

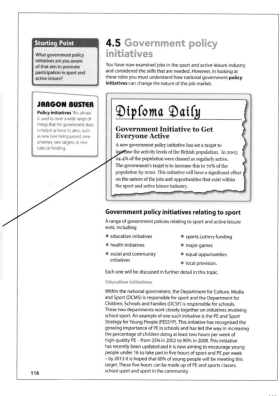

This type of lever is used in your lower leg when you stand on tiptoe – the ball of your foot acts as the fulcrum, the weight of your body is the load and the effort comes from the contraction of the calf muscle.

Standing on tiptoe: a second-class lever.

Third-class lever
A third-class lever has the fulcrum at one end, the effort in the middle and the load at the other end.

A third-class lever.

This type of lever is used to perform a bicep curl – the fulcrum is the elbow joint, the effort comes from the biceps contracting and the resistance is the weight of the forearm, plus any weight being held.

Performing a bicep curl a third-class lever.

Did you know?
The third-class lever is the most common type of lever found in your body.

TOP TIP
An easy way to remember the order of the levers is to use the term **FLE** to indicate which part of the lever is found in the middle:
* in a first-class lever the **F**ulcrum is in the middle
* in a second-class lever the **L**oad is in the middle
* in a third-class lever the **E**ffort is in the middle

80

Starting Point
What government policy initiatives are you aware of that aim to promote participation in sport and active leisure?

JARGON BUSTER
Policy initiatives This phrase is used to cover a wide range of things that the government does to help it achieve its aims, such as new laws being passed, new schemes, new targets, or new rules on funding.

4.5 Government policy initiatives
You have now examined jobs in the sport and active leisure industry and considered the skills that are needed. However, in looking at these roles you must understand how national government **policy initiatives** can change the nature of the job market.

Diploma Daily

Government Initiative to Get Everyone Active
A new government policy initiative has set a target to increase the activity levels of the British population. In 2003 24.4% of the population were classed as regularly active. The government's target is to increase this to 70% of the population by 2020. This initiative will have a significant effect on the nature of the jobs and opportunities that exist within the sport and active leisure industry.

Government policy initiatives relating to sport
A range of government policies relating to sport and active leisure exist, including:
* education initiatives
* health initiatives
* social and community initiatives
* sports Lottery funding
* major games
* equal opportunities
* local provision.

Each one will be discussed in further detail in this topic.

Education initiatives
Within the national government, the Department for Culture, Media and Sport (DCMS) is responsible for sport and the Department for Children, Schools and Families (DCSF) is responsible for schools. These two departments work closely together on initiatives involving school sport. An example of one such initiative is the PE and Sport Strategy for Young People (PESSYP). This initiative has recognised the growing importance of PE in schools and has led the way in increasing the percentage of children doing at least two hours per week of high-quality PE – from 25% in 2002 to 90% in 2008. This initiative has recently been updated and it is now aiming to encourage young people under 16 to take part in five hours of sport and PE per week – by 2013 it is hoped that 60% of young people will be meeting this target. These five hours can be made up of PE and sports classes, school sport and sport in the community.

116

POSITIVE LIFESTYLE CHOICES AND SPORT AND ACTIVE LEISURE

Introduction

People who lead a healthy and active life will usually look well, feel good and have a positive outlook. This unit explores the ways in which you can choose to lead a healthy lifestyle and the positive changes you can make to improve your overall **health** and **wellbeing**. Choosing a healthy lifestyle has clear benefits for society as a whole; this unit will also help you to explore those benefits.

What will you learn?

Over the course of this unit you will cover the following learning outcomes:

LO1: Know about healthy lifestyles
LO2: Know about influences on lifestyle choices
LO3: Understand the importance of participation in sport and active leisure
LO4: Understand how lifestyle choices impact on the health and wellbeing of individuals and society
LO5: Understand how lifestyle changes improve health and wellbeing

The following table shows how these five learning outcomes are covered by this unit.

Topic	Pages	Learning outcomes
1.1 Health and wellbeing	4–5	LO1
1.2 Positive lifestyle choices and their effects	6–7	LO1, LO4
1.3 Eating a healthy and balanced diet	8–10	LO1
1.4 Positive lifestyle choices: risk-taking activities and sleep patterns	11	LO1
1.5 Healthy lifestyle choices: **psychological** and **social** benefits	12–13	LO1, LO4
1.6 Negative lifestyle choices and their effects	14–17	LO1, LO4
1.7 Eating disorders	18–19	LO1, LO4
1.8 Influences on lifestyle choices	20–21	LO2
1.9 Encouraging participation in sport and active leisure	22–23	LO3
1.10 Different participant groups	24–25	LO3
1.11 Analysis of effects of lifestyle changes	26–27	LO5
1.12 Improving an individual's health and wellbeing	28–29	LO5

THINKING POINTS

* Do you think you lead a healthy and active lifestyle?
* What sort of things in your lifestyle do you think are healthy?
* What sort of things in your lifestyle do you think are not healthy?

Functional Skills

Personal, Learning and Thinking Skills

This unit offers various opportunities to develop functional skills and personal learning and thinking skills. Where appropriate, different activities are signposted with the relevant skills that you can develop.

Diploma Daily

A healthier lifestyle saves lives

Cancer, coronary heart diseases, stroke and mental illness are the killers for almost three quarters of the UK population before the age of 75. Thousands of people die from these conditions each year but research proves that there are things you can do to keep these diseases at bay. Healthy living has been shown to help to prevent or reduce the impact of these killers. The government are investing money in initiatives to help our nation stop smoking and increase our exercise levels. They are providing more information on healthy eating and suggested diet changes in hospitals and Doctors' surgeries up and down the country. Time will only tell if these initiatives can turn the health of Britain around and stop these killers in their tracks.

1 Carry out research and list the ways in which people in your school and local area are encouraged to:

* increase their participation in sport and active leisure

* improve their diet

* stop smoking.

2 Produce a spider diagram that has 'healthy lifestyle' in the centre and then all the ways in which a person can try to lead a healthy lifestyle stemming off from it.

3 Carry out research to describe the current problems associated with British health today.

How you will be assessed

For this unit you will be assessed by an externally set paper covering all of five of the unit learning outcomes. There will be a mixture of short answer and longer questions. As part of the paper you will be asked to interpret information from tables and case studies about information relating to a lifestyle.

The paper will be sat under controlled conditions and you will be given 1 hour and 30 minutes to complete it.

Case study: Claire's lifestyle choices

Claire is 16 years old and enjoys taking part in street dance activities. She has been with her dance group for 3 years and they are now looking to take part in competitions. However, Claire's friends at school have recently started to smoke and are trying to encourage Claire to join in. Claire knows the harm that cigarettes can do to her body and that smoking will affect her fitness levels and her dancing. She does wants to loose weight though and thinks that smoking may help her to stop snacking. She is a size 10 but thinks she is the biggest girl in her dance group. She has now started missing meals to try and loose weight.

1 What positive lifestyle choices has Claire selected?

2 What negative lifestyle choices has Claire selected?

3 What are the problems associated with missing meals and worrying about being overweight?

4 What advice would you give to Claire about smoking?

Unit links

This unit links closely to Level 2, Unit 2: Encouraging participation in sport and active leisure and Unit 3: Science in sport and Active leisure.

JARGON BUSTER

Health The state of physical, emotional and social wellbeing.

Wellbeing People feeling good about themselves.

Psychological To do with the mind.

Social To do with life with other people.

What is 'healthy'?

Think about what the term 'healthy' means to you. What sort of things would you look for in a healthy person? What do you think 'unhealthy' means? Give examples of the sort of things you would find in an unhealthy person.

Do you think the person in the photo above is healthy or unhealthy? What about the person below? What influenced your decision?

1.1 Health and wellbeing

In this topic you will learn about health and wellbeing and what it actually means to be healthy. You will also learn about some basic health checks which help to determine if a person is healthy.

What is health?

There are a number of definitions to describe what health is – one of the most popular is 'The state of complete physical, emotional and social wellbeing and not merely the absence of disease.' World Health Organization (WHO).

Physical health

Physical health can be assessed in different ways. Two of the key things to look at are blood pressure and body composition.

Blood pressure

Your heart pumps blood around your body – the force of this blood being pumped around your body is called 'blood pressure'. Blood pressure needs to be in a certain range for you to remain healthy.

There are always two values given for blood pressure measurements. The first measures the force when the heart is pumping blood out (systole) and the second reading is when the heart is relaxed (diastole). For a healthy adult, a resting blood pressure reading should be 120/80 mmHg. As a person gets older their resting blood pressure will start to increase.

Having a high blood pressure puts extra strain on the heart and, if left untreated, it could lead to a stroke or heart attack. A reading of 140/90 would be considered as having high blood pressure (hypertension).

Did you know?

Around 15–25% of British adults have been diagnosed as having a high blood pressure (known as hypertension).

Body Composition

Body composition means what your body is made of. The main components of your body are:

* bone (males: 15%, females: 12%)*

* muscle (males: 45%, females: 36%)*

* fat (males: 15%, females: 27%)*

*All figures given are averages. Figures from McArdle W, Katch F and Katch V – *Exercise Physiology: Nutrition, Energy and Human Performance* (Lippincott Williams and Wildins, 1996)

When you measure body composition, the main thing to consider is the amount of body fat a person has. You need some body fat to be healthy but too much can result in health problems.

Body Mass Index (BMI) is a popular method of measuring body fat.

Formula to work out a person's BMI:

BMI = Weight in kg/ (height in m²)

For example, for a female who is 75 kg and 1.7m tall:

BMI = 75/(1.7 × 1.7)
   = 75/2.89
   = 25.6

In this case, the person's body mass index is **25.6**. Use the table below to work out if this person has too much, too little or just the right amount of body fat.

Classification	BMI
Underweight	less than 18.5
Normal	18.5-24.9
Overweight	25-29.9
Obese I	30-34.9
Obese II	35-39.9
Extreme obesity	40 or higher

For people who have a lot of muscle, such as body builders, the BMI test would be unsuitable. When you have a lot of muscle tissue you carry more body weight and, as the BMI test does not distinguish between body fat and body muscle tissue, a muscular person will often fall into the overweight or obese category!

What is 'wellbeing'?

Your wellbeing is related to your mental and emotional state, and is a contented state of being happy and healthy. Self-esteem, confidence and sociability are all key factors involved in wellbeing and can be improved through positive lifestyle choices. Self-esteem is best explained as the ability to appreciate your own worth and is something that usually takes time to develop. If you have high self-esteem you will have a positive attitude, be confident in your abilities and feel in control of your life. High self-esteem helps you to to make independent choices and decisions and not bow down to peer pressure.

If you have high levels of self-esteem you are likely to be self-confident. Self-confidence is the belief that you can manage your life and that you have faith in your own abilities. Benefits associated with having self-confidence include being more productive, more assertive, increased courage, a greater ability to help friends and contribute to society, and the ability to learn from mistakes.

Sociability is related to feeling at ease and enjoying the company of other people. Most people feel the need to be involved in a variety of social groups in which they can have friendships, fun, learn from each other and seek support. Without a social network, people can feel lonely and are more prone to depression and other mental illnesses.

Over to you

Follow these steps to work out your own body mass index:

1 work out and record your height in metres

2 find out your weight in kg

3 then carry out the BMI calculation as shown above.

In which classification does your BMI fall into? From this information do you think you need to gain weight, lose weight or stay just as you are?

Just checking

∗ Research lifestyle analysis questionnaires on the internet. Working in a small group, choose five lifestyle areas covered by the questionnaires – such as smoking, diet or exercise.

∗ Discuss potentially positive and negative influences on people's lifestyle choices in these areas.

∗ Suggest ways in which people can make healthy lifestyle choices.

1.2 Positive lifestyle choices and their effects

Every day you are faced with decisions about how you lead your life and, where possible, you should try to make positive lifestyle choices. Exercise and regular activity is essential for your body to stay fit and healthy. This topic explores the amount of physical activity that people should take part in and the benefits associated with doing so.

Participation in regular exercise and physical activity

A number of organisations research how much physical activity and exercise you should do to maximise health benefits. In Britain in 2004, the Department of Health recommended that children aged 5–17 should participate in at least 60 minutes of **moderate exercise** per day. This 60 minutes can be spread out over the day and can include things like walking or cycling to school. They also suggested that children in this age group should aim to include at least two weekly sessions of activities that will increase flexibility, for example stretching, and improve muscle and bone strength, for example resistance-based exercise.

Effects of participation in physical activity

By taking part in a range of different types of exercise and physical activity you can help to ensure that your body is fit and healthy.

Cardiovascular fitness

Aerobic exercises such as swimming, jogging and cycling for periods of 20 minutes or longer three times per week help to improve cardiovascular fitness. Your cardiovascular system includes the heart, the blood vessels, through which your blood travels, and your lymphatic system.

As the heart is a muscle, it responds to aerobic exercise by getting stronger.

Exercise increases the number of blood vessels supplying the heart and muscles with blood, which increases the supply of nutrients and oxygen and helps to reduce blood pressure. Cardiovascular exercises also act to lower **cholesterol** levels in the body.

Cardiovascular fitness is good for your health and allows you to take part in sports and complete everyday activities without undue tiredness.

Muscular endurance

Muscular endurance is the ability for muscles to work for prolonged periods without tiring. Examples include jogging for three miles, doing 30 sit-ups or completing a number of repetitions using a piece of resistance equipment. Muscular endurance exercises help to tone up your muscles, giving them a more defined appearance and allow you to carry out everyday activities without tiredness.

JARGON BUSTER

Moderate exercise
Exercising at a certain level so that the activity raises your heart rate but you are still able to carry on a conversation, ie you are not out of breath!

Cholesterol
Cholesterol is produced naturally by the body and is in some of the foods we eat. Having too much cholesterol in the body is not good for us as it sticks to the insides of our blood vessels. This reduces the space for blood to flow through, which results in an increase in blood pressure.

Personal, Learning and Thinking Skills

This activity will help to provide evidence of Independent Enquirer and Self-manager.

Over to you

The American College of Sports Medicine (ACSM) researches how much and what types of exercise adults should perform in order to help improve and maintain health. Research the ACSM guidelines and put together an example of a weekly programme for:

* an adult
* an older adult (over 65).

Muscular strength

Strength is the amount of force a muscle can produce. On average, males are stronger than females because they have more muscle tissue. However, if you were to remove the same amount of tissue from a male and a female and test the amount of force that it can produce, they would be identical!

Flexibility

Flexibility is the range of movement available at a joint – the more flexible you are the greater the range of movement at your joints. Some flexibility is required for normal everyday living, such as reaching up to a cupboard, and sporting activities, such as lunging for a shot in badminton. If you are not flexible or have limited flexibility you are more prone to injuries like sprained ligaments.

Improving posture

Posture is the way you stand and hold your body. Many people adopt a slouched body posture, where shoulders are forwards, stomach is relaxed and the upper back is arched. Bad posture is not good for your appearance and can result in several health complications, including back aches, back pain, migraines and increased risk of slipping a disc in your back. Someone with a good posture will have their back straight, shoulders pulled back, back and head looking forwards.

Bad posture.

Good posture can help you to look slimmer, taller and more confident. Exercises to strengthen the back muscles will help to pull shoulders back and hold the back straight and in correct alignment. Abdominal exercises help to improve posture by helping to support the spine.

Body weight

Physical activity plays a significant role in helping people to lose excess body weight or to maintain their current weight. Taking part in physical activity requires energy. This energy is gained from either the food we eat or fat stored in the body.

Good posture.

* For people wishing to maintain their current body weight, exercise participation helps to burn off any excess calories that have been eaten, rather than storing this excess as body fat.

* If a person wants to lose weight they must eat fewer calories than they burn. If they exercise and eat a restricted diet, their body will take energy from their fat stores and they will lose body weight.

Just checking

* List five different types of physical activity.
* Describe one physical benefit of taking part in each of these five types of activity.

Example: *physical activity:* aerobics exercise class, *physical benefit:* improvement in cardiovascular fitness.

1.3 Eating a healthy and balanced diet

Most people in Britain today can choose from a huge range of different foods. Some of these are healthy and provide you with all of the nutrients needed to help your body to grow, repair itself and remain in a state of good health. However, there are also plenty of unhealthy foods on offer. A balanced diet needs to consist of the right quantities of the main nutrients – carbohydrates, proteins and fat – with plenty of water to prevent **dehydration**.

Carbohydrates

Carbohydrates are mainly used as an energy source by your body. They come in two main forms, simple and complex. Simple carbohydrates are found in foods that taste sweet, such as jam, sugar and fruit. These provide you with a quick supply of energy. Complex carbohydrates do not taste sweet and include bread, rice, pasta, cereals and potatoes – these supply your body with a slow release of energy for a long period of time.

Protein

Protein is required in your diet for growth and repair of body tissue. Taking part in sport and exercise, particularly resistance exercises, causes your muscle tissue to tear – these tears are microscopic (tiny) but act as the stimulus to make muscles grow.

The majority of protein-rich foods come from animal sources and include meat, chicken, fish, eggs, milk and cheese. Soya and tofu are vegetable-based foods that contain high levels of protein.

Fat

While it is true that too much fat in your diet is bad for you it does serve a purpose and some fat should be included as part of a balanced diet. Fat provides energy, insulates the body and protects internal organs. Some vitamins are stored in your body fat and these are used in the production of hormones.

The main types of fat are saturated and unsaturated. Eating too much saturated fat can cause health problems – it is found in dairy products such as cream, and 'junk food' like biscuits and the fat found in and around meat. No more than 10% of the fat you eat should be saturated. Unsaturated fat is usually found in plant products such as olive oil, fish oils and nuts.

Some examples of carbohydrate-rich foods.

Some examples of protein-rich foods.

Some examples of foods that contain high levels of fat.

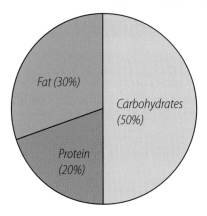

This pie chart shows the proportion of carbohydrates, fat and protein you should include in your diet

Vitamins and minerals

Your diet should also include the right amounts of vitamins and minerals to help your body to function. The tables below show the main vitamins and minerals, which foods you will find them in and their main function.

JARGON BUSTER

Dehydration When a person does not have enough water in their body.

Did you know?

Did you know that two thirds of your body is made up of water? Medical professionals suggest that a human can live for up to six weeks without food but only three days without water.

Vitamins: sources and functions

Vitamin	Food sources	Function
A	Carrots, apricots, liver, dark green vegetables, mackerel	Helps to maintain good eye health and vision and helps maintain the function and production of skin.
B	Wholegrains, milk, nuts, meat, Marmite, cereals, liver, yeast, eggs, beans	Helps to break down food to produce energy and helps with the function of the nervous system; helps with the formation of red blood cells.
C	Citrus fruits – oranges, lemons, grapefruit, most fresh fruits and vegetables	Helps our immune system to fight infection; maintains healthy skin and gums and helps wounds to heal.
D	Oily fish, eggs, sunlight	Helps to build strong bones and teeth.
E	Vegetable oils, nuts, seeds, dark green leafy vegetables	Acts as an antioxidant which helps prevent damage to cells.
K	Leafy green vegetable, dairy products and meat	Helps blood to clot.

Minerals: sources and functions

Mineral	Food sources	Function
Iron	Liver, lean meats, eggs, dried fruits, nuts, chicken	Helps with the formation of red blood cells.
Calcium	Milk, cheese, yogurt, fish bones, green leafy vegetables	Helps to build strong bones and teeth and helps blood to clot.
Sodium	Salt, seafood, processed foods, celery	Helps to maintain fluid and electrolyte balance in cells; helps in muscle contraction.
Potassium	Bananas, meat, shellfish	Works with sodium to maintain fluid balance, aids muscle contraction, maintains blood pressure.
Zinc	Milk, cheese, eggs, shellfish, meats	Encourages tissue growth and repair and helps the immune system to fight infection.
Iodine	Shellfish, seaweed	Helps with the maintenance of basal metabolic rate.

Make a copy of the table below (with more rows). Now examine the following foods and place them into the correct category in your table – decide if each food is classifed as a carbohydrate, fat or protein.

Jam	Fish	Oranges	Margarine	Sausages
Rice	Potatoes	Cereal	Bacon	Apples
Cream	Bread	Olive oil	Pasta	Chips
Chicken	Cheese	Crisps	Beef	Ice cream

Carbohydrate	Fat	Protein

Case study: Amy's diet

Amy is in her school cross country club. She has a 5 km county race coming up and wants to ensure that she is eating the right foods to help her prepare for the race.

Amy doesn't usually have time for breakfast in the morning so just grabs a snack from the vending machine in her first school breaktime, such as a bag of crisps or a chocolate bar. Amy has a cooked lunch at school and tries to only have chips three times a week. On other days she will have a jacket potato with cheese or a tuna filling, pizza or a white ham salad bagette.

For dinner, Amy has one takeaway a week (either curry or a Chinese), a full roast dinner one night a week, pasta-based meals, such as spaghetti bolognese, or lighter options, such as beans on toast.

She snacks on crisps and chocolate but occasionally eats a piece of fruit. She drinks lots of water and sometimes has a fizzy drink.

1 What do you think of Amy's diet?

2 What sort of things does Amy eat that you think are healthy?

3 What things does Amy eat that are not healthy?

4 What sort of foods should Amy eat to help her with her long distance running?

5 How could Amy improve her diet?

Just checking

Make a list of everything you ate today and yesterday, then place the food items into the correct categories in a copy of the table below (add as many rows as you need). An example of how you might fill the table in is given here.

Meal/snack	Carbohydrate		Fat		Protein
	Simple	Complex	Saturated	Unsaturated	
Breakfast	Jam	Bread	Butter		Eggs

Now examine the vitamin and mineral tables above then make a list of the vitamins and minerals you have eaten over the last few days. From the information you have put into this table and from your vitamin and mineral assessment, explain whether you think you ate healthy and balanced diet.

Hotlink

There is more information on a healthy diet on the British Nutrition Foundation website. For details of how to access this website see the **Hotlinks** section – **Introduction**, page xi.

1.4 Positive lifestyle choices: risk-taking activities and sleep patterns

Positive lifestyle choices include what you choose to do with your time in the day, as well as how much time you give yourself to recover. By taking part in positive activities that carry some risks you can help to make the most of your abilities and improve your self-confidence. However, your body and mind also need time to relax and this is best achieved through sleep. Both the quantity and quality of your sleep play a crucial role in keeping your body and mind working at their best.

Positive risk-taking activities

Positive risk-taking activities are those that take you outside your comfort zone and positively challenge you. Good examples of positive risk-taking activities include outdoor and adventurous activities, such as abseiling or potholing. These sorts of activities are perceived as dangerous and those taking part in them will usually feel afraid, sometimes to the point where they may almost fear for their life. However, with all the safety precautions in place, these fears are usually unfounded. By completing an activity that is seen as challenging and dangerous, you will feel pleased and proud for overcoming your fear and this can lead to an increase in self-esteem and confidence.

Sleep

The amount of sleep you get plays an essential role in maintaining good mental and physical health. Therefore, it is very important to get enough sleep and to make sure you have a regular sleep pattern. There are a range of problems associated with not getting enough sleep, including:

* inability to concentrate
* forgetfulness
* skin problems, eg acne
* impatience
* less able to fight infection
* more prone to depression.

At different ages, your body requires different amounts of sleep. As a baby you would have probably spent about three-quarters of your day asleep. As a teenager activities such as doing homework, socialising or part-time work may stop you from getting to bed early enough, and you may not get enough sleep. Teenagers should aim to have between 8 hours 30 minutes to 9 hours 25 minutes sleep per night, although this will vary from individual to individual.

Personal, Learning and Thinking Skills

This activity will help to provide evidence of Independent Enquirer and Reflective Learner.

Starting Point

Can you think of other examples of positive risk-taking activities?

What sort of positive risk-taking activities have you taken part in?

How did you feel both before and then after completing the activity?

Do you think you would like to take part in more positive risk-taking activities?

Explain your answer.

Over to you

Design your own sleep diary and write in it every day for at least a week to track your sleeping pattern.

You will need to include:

* time of going to bed
* time of waking
* how you felt when you woke up – refreshed or still tired
* if you slept all night without any interruption.

Now look through your sleep diary and answer the following questions:

* Do you get enough sleep each night?
* Do you have a regular sleep pattern? If not, why not?
* Could you improve your sleep pattern? If so, how?

Just checking

Carry out research:

* to find out about the psychological benefits of ensuring that you have sufficient quantity and quality of sleep.
* to find out if sky diving is really as risky as you think. Try going to the British Parachute Association website. To access this site, see the **Hotlinks** section – **Introduction**, page xi.

Starting Point

How do you think taking part in sport and exercise improves your social life?

How do you feel after you have taken part in a sport or active leisure session?

1.5 Healthy lifestyle choices: psychological and social benefits

Making and participating in positive lifestyle choices improves physical health and provides psychological benefits, as well as benefits to society.

Psychological benefits

When you take part in physical activity your body releases endorphins into your blood stream. These endorphins help to relieve feelings of pain that may be felt whilst exercising, and have the added benefit of improving mood – this is sometimes known as 'the runner's high'. In cases of mild depression, exercise participation may be prescribed by a GP to boost a patient's mood.

Making the positive lifestyle choice to take part in physical activity can help to improve self-confidence and self-esteem. Setting and then achieving fitness goals, such as running a half-marathon or learning new basketball skills, will leave you feeling confident in your own abilities. Physical activity participation is also an excellent way of socialising, making new friends and improving your sense of belonging. You might join a five-a-side football team or take part in an exercise class and get to know the class members.

Other psychological benefits of taking part in physical activity include:

* increased motivation, stamina and **mental resilience**
* reduction of anxiety and stress
* improving awareness of personal limitations and your ability to judge risks.

JARGON BUSTER

Mental resilience The mental ability to cope with stress and recover from disappointments.

Developing new skills

Playing sports such as basketball, hockey and volleyball can teach you how to work well in a team, as well as improving your organisation and communication abilities. The skills you pick up when you are playing team games like these can also be put to good use in other areas of your life, for example when you complete group projects at school or college, or work as a team in your part-time job.

Playing team sports can also teach you leadership skills. For example, being appointed team captain, or simply observing others in this role, can help you to learn basic leadership skills and see that there are different types of leadership style.

Playing a team sport allows you to pick up new skills, such as leadership and improved organisation.

Over to you

What team and leadership skills have you learnt through taking part in team sports?

How does participation in sport and physical activity affect your social life?

Personal, Learning and Thinking Skills

This activity will help to provide evidence of Reflective Learner, Team Worker and Effective Participator

Benefits to society

Increasing your participation in sport and active leisure can bring a number of benefits, not only for yourself, but also for society in general.

Reducing anti-social behaviour

Participation in sport and active leisure helps to reduce anti-social behavior in a number of ways.

∗ Anti-social behaviour can be caused by boredom. Being involved in a regular activity or becoming a member of a sports team gives people something purposeful to do and can help to build routine.

∗ In most sports there will be lots of opportunites to train and compete – this can help to get young people off the streets and make them less likely to turn to petty crime, drug-taking and excessive alcohol consumption.

∗ As participation in sport and active leisure helps to increase confidence and self-esteem people are less likely to take part in bullying. Bullies are usually people who lack self-confidence and try to make themselves feel better by picking on others' weaknesses.

Reduced burden on the NHS

By leading a healthy lifestyle and making positive lifestyle choices you are less likely to suffer from long-term illnesses such as diabetes and heart disease. Both of these illnesses require substantial treatment and medication from the NHS over prolonged periods of time, which costs the NHS a lot of money.

Community involvement

People who choose to lead a healthy lifestyle are more likely to have a sense of community spirit and take part in voluntary activities, such as volunteering to help run charity events, help out at youth clubs or coach children's sporting activities.

Contribution to education

People who lead healthy lifestyles are more likely to have a good attendance at school or college and are therefore more likely to do well in exams and coursework.

Personal, Learning and Thinking Skills

This activity will help to provide evidence of Reflective Learner, Team Worker and Effective Participator.

Just checking

Carry out research to find out

∗ the psychological benefits of taking part in physical activity

∗ how participation in sport and active leisure is encouraged in order to try to reduce anti-social behaviour

∗ how participation in sport and active leisure can reduce the likelihood of young people taking drugs and/or consuming alcoholic drinks.

Starting Point

What sort of things do you think would count as 'negative lifestyle choices'?

Do you make any negative lifestyle choices and if so why do you think you make these choices?

Personal, Learning and Thinking Skills

This activity will help to provide evidence of Reflective Learner and Creative Thinker.

Over to you

Think about all of the new devices used to help with housework (and our lifestyle in general) which reduce the amount of physical activity in our everyday lives – automatic washing machines, cars etc.

Draw a spider diagram that highlights how our lifestyle has become less active.

1.6 Negative lifestyle choices and their effects

The negative choices you make are things that are not beneficial to your health and wellbeing, and may even be harmful. Making negative lifestyle choices can affect physical and mental health, as well as having an impact on society.

Low participation in physical activity

You know the benefits that physical activity can have on your body, but are you aware of the problems associated with not taking part in enough physical activity? There are a wide range of physical and mental problems associated with lack of physical activity, including:

* obesity
* coronary heart disease
* type 2 diabetes
* depression and low self-esteem
* high blood pressure
* illnesses relating to body image.

A typical British lifestyle involves little physical activity – people drive rather than walking or cycling, video games are very popular and people choose TV over physical activities. Household chores now require very little physical exertion and shopping can now be carried out in front of a computer!

Those following this kind of lifestyle are encouraged to examine their routine and find ways to build in daily physical activity – you could cycle or walk rather than drive and try to make time for specific exercise sessions, such as going to the gym or swimming regularly.

Over-participation

A number of people take physical activity participation to extremes and become addicted. This is partially explained by the 'feel good' hormones that are released during exercise (endorphins). A person who is addicted to exercise will typically take part in some sort of physical activity session every day and finds the thought of missing a session very distressing. They will even exercise when injured and in pain. They may miss social events and neglect school or work commitments to make time for exercise. Their bodies suffer as they do not give themselves time to relax and recover. Health problems associated with over participation include:

* overuse injuries, eg tendonitis, shin splints, stress fractures
* decreased immunity
* insomnia
* feelings of inadequacy – comparing themself to other performers.

Over-participation can increase your potential for injury.

Overeating

Overeating is when someone eats more calories per day than is necessary. The excess calories are stored in the body as fat. Fat is stored internally around body organs (which you cannot see) and also just underneath the skin (which is the fat that can be seen and felt.)

One of the major causes of overeating is 'comfort eating' and there are a number of reasons for this:

* some foods increase the release of endorphins (feel-good hormones) and eating them makes you feel happy and content

* eating distracts us from negative thoughts

* many celebrations involve food, eg birthday cake or Christmas dinner, and eating is associated with having a good time.

However, there are clear health issues associated with having too much body fat, including:

* coronary heart disease
* type 2 diabetes
* high blood pressure
* a range of different cancers.

Smoking

Smoking-related diseases kill around 83,900 people a year (NHS, 2099), with 300 smoking-related deaths in the UK every day. Diseases associated with smoking include different cancers, in particular lung cancer, cardiovascular disease and chronic lung diseases.

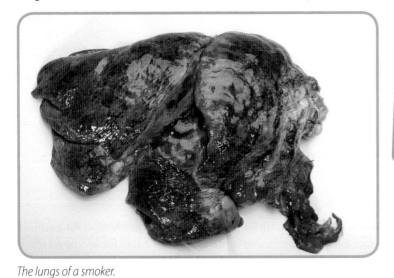

The lungs of a smoker.

Over to you

Think about the foods that you eat as a 'treat'. Make a list of these foods.

Think about why and when you choose to eat these foods, then consider if you think you may overeat on a regular basis.

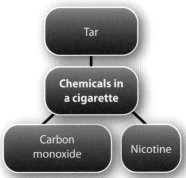

Some of the harmful products found in cigarettes.

THINKING POINTS

* What is a 'National No Smoking Day'?
* Who promotes the National No Smoking Day?
* Why does the UK have a National No Smoking Day?

Over to you

Carry out research to find out about each of the chemicals in a cigarette and the harmful effects they can have on the body (see diagram above to get you started). Choose a suitable method for displaying this information.

Just checking

* What are the health problems associated with taking part in too little or no physical activity? What are the health problems associated with too much physical activity?
* What is overeating? Give five possible reasons why people may overeat?

Personal, Learning and Thinking Skills

This activity will help to provide evidence of Reflective Learner.

THINKING POINTS

* Do you or your friends drink alcoholic drinks?
* What are the problems associated with drinking alcoholic drinks?
* Why do you think people under the legal age drink alcoholic beverages?

Drinking an excessive amount of alcohol can seriously damage your health.

Excessive alcohol consumption

Alcohol is a legal drug in the UK and may be bought and consumed by people aged 18 years and over. However, according to the Institute of Alcohol Studies (IAS), 84 % of children aged 12–17 have had an alcoholic drink and, in the UK, people aged between 16–24 are the heaviest drinking group in the population.

Alcohol consumption causes serious short- and long-term health problems.

Short-term effects

* Alcoholic drinks affect the brain so mood may be altered and judgement compromised.
* Drinking alcohol can lead to a loss of inhibitions, blurred vision, slurred speech and anti-social behaviour.
* Physical coordination is affected by even small amounts of alcohol – this can lead to accidents.
* In 2008, one in seven people admitted to Accident and Emergency departments across the UK for alcohol-related health issues were under 14 years old – this increases the burden on the NHS.
* Alcohol is a poison and, if too much is consumed, it can lead to coma and even death.
* A study of 14–17 year olds found that the most commonly reported unsafe behaviour whist under the influence of alcohol included: regretted sexual experiences, injury through accidents and fighting, and walking home alone.

Long-term effects

Excessive long-term alcohol consumption can lead to ill health. The IAS state that excessive alcohol consumption is the third leading cause of disease and injury, resulting in almost 10 % of all health problems and premature deaths in Europe. Alcohol-related diseases include: cirrhosis of the liver; cancer of the mouth, oesophagus, liver, breast, bowel and larynx, and mental health problems like depression. Drinking too much can also cause social problems, such as relationship breakdowns and work problems.

Recommended intake

In the UK, the recommendation for alcohol consumption for adults is no more than two to three units of alcohol a day for women and three to four units for men, with at least two or three alcohol-free days per week. However, there are no recommendations for children and young people as it is illegal for them to consume alcohol.

It takes around an hour for the adult body to get rid of one unit of alcohol. However, it takes longer for young people.

Over to you

How much is a unit?

Find out how many units of alcohol are in the following:

* a pint of beer
* a bottle of strong beer (5%)
* an alcopop
* a shot of vodka
* a small glass of wine.

For more information about alcohol go to the Institute of Alcohol Studies website. For details of how to access this website see the **Hotlinks** section – **Introduction**, page xi.

Drugs

There is a wide range of illegal drugs available in Britain; you may have heard of some of them. All illegal drugs are extremely dangerous to your health and taking them can result in death.

The spider diagram below shows some of the most common types of illegal drug, along with their 'nicknames'.

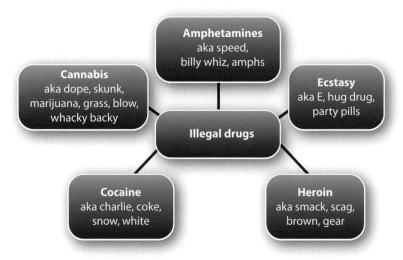

This table shows the immediate effects of taking these illegal drugs and the short- and long-term health problems that they can cause.

Drug	Immediate effects	Short- and long-term health problems
Cannabis	More relaxed Heightened senses Very hungry Giggly	**Paranoia;** serious mental illnesses; if smoked can lead to lung diseases and cancers
Cocaine	Exhilaration Increased confidence Increased mental alertness	Nasal damage; heart problems; breathing problems; depression; paranoia
Ecstasy	Increased energy levels Increased confidence Increased sociability	Anxiety; paranoia; depression; heart disease; liver damage; kidney damage
Heroin	Increased confidence Altered mood Drowsiness	Vomiting; heart disease; liver disease; breathing problems; diseases from infected needles, eg HIV
Amphetamines	Increased heart rate Increased mental alertness	Exhaustion; aggression; mental health problems; heart disease

Social effects

Taking illegal drugs also has a number of social effects. For example, taking drugs may lead to anti-social or out-of-character behaviour or could affect someone's ability to get or hold down a job.

Personal, Learning and Thinking Skills

This activity will help to provide evidence of Reflective Learner, Creative Thinker and Independent Enquirer

Over to you

Why do you think people take illegal drugs?

Carry out research to find out how society is affected by people who take drugs.

JARGON BUSTER

Paranoia Excessive anxiety and suspicion.

Just checking

What are the health problems associated with:

∗ smoking   ∗ excessive alcohol consumption   ∗ taking illegal drugs?

Why do you think people make and participate in these negative lifestyle choices?

Why do you think females aged 15–25 are the most common age and gender to be affected by eating disorders?

Why do you think more young males are starting to suffer from eating disorders?

1.7 Eating disorders

The National Institute of Health and Clinical Excellence guidelines on eating disorders estimate that around 1.6 million people in the UK are affected by eating disorders. There are two main types of eating disorder: anorexia nervosa and bulimia nervosa. Someone may suffer from the two disorders at the same time. Both of these disorders can be extremely harmful to health and around 10% of sufferers will die as a result of their eating disorder.

Usually, a combination of factors is responsible for eating disorders. These can include low self-esteem, problems with family or friends, lack of confidence or abuse. An eating disorder is often thought to give sufferers a form of control in their life. They are classed as psychological conditions and are treated through psychological intervention.

Any person, regardless of age, gender or culture, may be susceptible to having an eating disorder. However, females aged 15–25 are the most common group to be affected. Yet recently, there has been an increase in the number of young males suffering from eating disorders.

Anorexia nervosa

This eating disorder is characterised by a form of self-starvation – this may start out as a crash diet which is then continued for a prolonged period of time.

The signs and symptoms of anorexia are:

* extreme weight loss
* dizziness/fainting
* downy hair on the body (lanugo)
* distorted perception of body image
* weakened immune system
* lethargy
* heart failure
* depression
* dehydration
* loss of periods (in females)
* mood swings
* a yellowish skin tone
* tooth decay
* low blood pressure
* kidney failure.

The body needs energy to survive. If it is not getting enough food, it will start to break down its own body tissue in order to get the energy it needs. The heart muscle and other muscles are broken down in this process, which can lead to heart damage and possible heart failure.

Bones are also affected by anorexia, they become less dense when insufficient minerals are consumed, making them more likely to break. This bone condition is called osteoporosis.

If a person suffering from anorexia does not receive treatment they will become extremely ill and may die.

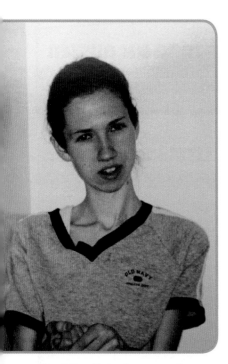

This girl is suffering from anorexia nervosa.

Did you know?

Osteoporosis is a condition that cannot be reversed even when someone has recovered from anorexia.

Bulimia nervosa

This eating disorder is characterised by a person consuming large quantities of food (binge eating) followed by the use of laxatives, self-induced vomiting and/or excessive exercising in order to try to rid the body of this excessive calorie intake. A person suffering from bulimia may well have a normal body weight and this condition can go unnoticed for prolonged periods of time. However, there are serious health problems associated with bulimia. These include:

* kidney and bowel problems from excessive use of laxatives
* mouth ulcers
* sore throats (from vomiting)
* frequent fluctuations in weight
* heart and kidney failure
* lethargy
* a loss of or irregular periods (in females)
* skin problems
* tooth decay (from vomiting)
* anxiety and/or depression
* choking
* low blood pressure.

People suffering from bulimia will suffer from severe health problems, including heart failure, if the disease is left untreated.

Negative perception of body image

Body image is the way that you view your body and overall physical appearance. People suffering from an eating disorder will also usually have a negative perception of their body image. However, this problem can also affect people without eating disorders.

When a person is not comfortable or happy with their body it can lead to low self-esteem and feelings of worthlessness and depression. This in turn can lead to eating disorders and health problems. Many people with a negative body image have a distorted view of their body – they see it in a different way to anyone else. They often view themselves as being very overweight when, in fact, they may be extremely underweight with unhealthily low levels of body fat.

Over to you

There is a huge pressure on both girls and boys to look good – the media promote images of impossibly perfect models whose bodies have been **airbrushed** in order to attain this perfection.

How does the media portray the perfect female body?

How does the media portray the perfect male body?

What size are most models in fashion magazines and on the catwalk?

How do you think this affects people's perception of their own bodies?

Why do you think young males are becoming more affected by eating disorders than in the past?

JARGON BUSTER

Airbrushed Using computer technology to improve the way someone looks in a photograph.

Just checking

* What is the difference between anorexia and bulimia?
* What sort of illnesses are anorexia and bulimia classed as?
* What are the health problems associated with anorexia?
* What are the health problems associated with bulimia?

Hotlink

More information about eating disorders can be found on the 'beat' website.

For details of how to access this website see the **Hotlinks** section – **Introduction**, page xi.

Case study: Standing up to peer pressure

John is 14 years old and plays basketball at county level. Recently his school friends have started smoking and are teasing John for not joining in. He knows smoking is bad for his health and could decrease his fitness levels, affecting his basketball skills. However, he wants his friends to stop making fun of him so is seriously thinking about smoking when he is with them.

1 How is peer pressure affecting John? What could he do to stand up to this peer pressure?

2 How would smoking affect John's ability to play basketball and his long-term health?

1.8 Influences on lifestyle choices

Although you largely make your own choices about your lifestyle – whether positive or negative – we can all be influenced by people around us and the culture in which we have been brought up.

People influences

Family

From an early age the main influence on your lifestyle choices is your parents or guardians. As children you observe your parents' lifestyle choices and learn from these. For example, children whose parents eat a healthy, balanced diet are more likely to do so when they become adults.

Peers

Peer pressure is where a group of 'friends' encourages a person to change their behaviour or morals to 'fit in'. It is common among young people but can occur in later life, eg workplace bullying. Peer pressure often leads to negative lifestyle choices, but can have positive effects, like peers encouraging one another to join a sports team.

Role models

Generally, role models are people you look up to who can positively influence your behaviour. There are many sporting celebrities people admire, such as David Beckham. They act as positive role models and encourage participation in sport. However, some role models could be seen to encourage negative lifestyle choices, such as footballers who carry out deliberately dangerous tackles.

Many sporting celebrities, like Rebecca Adlington, are seen as positive role models.

Over to you

* Which role models influence you?
* Do these role models encourage positive lifestyle choices, and if so how?
* Name two sporting role models. How do they encourage negative choices?

Image and the media

The media portray many role models as impossibly perfect-looking. Photos in magazines are often airbrushed, making females appear slimmer and males more muscly. Plastic surgery is used by many celebrities, and some models use drugs to stay slim. This obsession with image and achieving the 'perfect body' is thought to have played a significant role in the increase of drug misuse and eating disorders in young people today.

Cultural influences

Culture refers to the set of shared attitudes, beliefs, values, goals and practices belonging to different groups of people. Examples of cultures include:

✱ ethnic groups ✱ countries or regions people come from ✱ religions

Within a culture people may also be classified into certain groups based on factors like age, gender, income and whether they have a disability. There are clear differences in how culture, and these classifications like age or gender, affect participation in sport, both at elite and recreational levels.

Barriers to participation

People don't all have equal access to sport and active leisure opportunities. For some people, access to sport or physical activity can be very difficult. Examples of barriers include:

✱ **time** – one of the most commonly stated reasons for not exercising.

✱ **access to and location of facilities** - facilities are not evenly spaced; some people will be very close to a leisure centre, others will have to travel a long way.

✱ **ability** – new participants may be embarrassed as they lack ability/ have low fitness levels.

✱ **cost** – buying sports equipment and paying for activities can be offputting.

✱ **illness and health problems** – people with health conditions will need a medical professional's clearance before exercising. However, most people will benefit from some form of physical activity.

New kinds of interactive computer games, such as the Wii fit, have helped people to overcome some of these barriers – they can exercise in the comfort of their home, do not have to travel, and can take part whenever it is convenient. These games can motivate and engage people of all ages.

Medical advice/guidance

A GP or other medical professional can play a significant role in encouraging a healthy lifestyle. A person may know that their lifestyle is unhealthy but choose to ignore this until they have a check-up or develop a health condition. The medical professional will then provide them with evidence that their health is suffering and recommend healthy lifestyle choices for them to adopt.

Did you know?

Research conducted by Sport England found that people of Pakistani origin have the lowest participation rates in sport.

Functional Skills

This activity will help to provide evidence of English speaking.

Personal, Learning and Thinking Skills

This activity will help to provide evidence of Creative Thinker, Independent Enquirer and Team Worker.

THINKING POINTS

In small groups consider the following questions:

✱ How often are female rugby games shown on TV?

✱ How many disabled swimmers can you name?

✱ How many professional footballers over the age of 40 can you name?

✱ Why do golfers tend to be from wealthy families?

Just checking

✱ How do people influence your lifestyle choices?

✱ In the 2008 Olympic Games, what was the ethnic origin of the following gold medallists:

– 100 m male sprinter
– 400 m female freestyle swimmer
– 800 m wheelchair racing.

Try to explain how their culture, ethnic origin and any disabilities may have influenced their participation in their chosen sport.

✱ Explain what barriers to participation are – which could affect you?

Starting Point

Do you think the British public are healthy? What stories have you heard in the news that help to justify your answer?

1.9 Encouraging participation in sport and active leisure

The British Government has identified that the health of the nation is not as good as it could be. Too many people are eating an unbalanced, unhealthy diet and not exercising enough, resulting in a range of health conditions that require medical attention. As a result, there are a huge range of initiatives, part-funded by national and local governments, to improve the nation's health.

Traditional methods

Various traditional methods are used by leisure centres, teachers and coaches to encourage people to take part in sport and active leisure.

Taster sessions give you a taste of the activity to see if you like it, eg an afternoon or drop-in session at a club or centre where people can have a go at a particular sport. These sessions are often free or low priced. Those who enjoy the activity can then get involved more regularly.

Junior development programmes are designed to help improve young peoples' ability in a range of sports. Where children are showing an interest and ability in a particular sport, programmes have been set up around the country to try to improve their skills and help them to reach their full potential.

Club trials are used to spot talent and recruit new players. Many different sports have local clubs that train people of different ages and enter them for competitions. The higher the ability of the player, the more dedication is required, and participants may find that they have to commit to weekly training sessions and weekend competitions.

School visits to different sport and active leisure environments help introduce learners to new sports that are not part of the national curriculum or are not accessible at school. Outdoor pursuit activities are a popular choice and students may be introduced to a range of different sports such as windsurfing, canoeing or climbing. Learners can try these activities out with their friends, usually at little or no cost, which may then encourage them to pursue the sport in the future.

Over to you

Carry out research to find out about different initiatives that try to increase participation in sport and active leisure, eg Change4Life or Fitter Families. Select one and describe the main methods employed by the organisation to try to increase participation.

THINKING POINTS

Appealing to different people

Think about how the following factors might affect someone's choice of physical activity:

* level of formality/informality
* amount of time and commitment required
* setting – is it safe? Is it easy to get to?
* flexibility of timing – fixed timetable or 'drop in'?
* whether the activity is supervised/instruction is provided
* cost – for activity? For equipment/clothing?
* whether you will have someone else to go with
* effect of taster sessions
* which groups of people may be specifically attracted or put off by each of these factors? eg, a businessman working long hours may not be able to spare much time.

Club membership for active leisure may encourage participation through schemes that offer members reduced fees and other perks, such as money off sports equipment. Another incentive is to challenge people to complete a certain number of activities in a given period, for example 'swimming the channel in a month'.

Innovative methods

Innovative methods are relatively new ways of introducing and encouraging people into sport and active leisure.

Formal settings and play include such places as schools and pre-schools which have specified areas and times for sport and play activities to take place.

Informal settings such as parks or village greens, allow spontaneous play or participation in sport and active leisure.

Drop-in sessions allow you to take part in an activity without having to book ahead – the venue, day and timings of this activity are advertised and you just turn up to take part.

Street games take place in the street so there is no need to hire a sports hall or pitch – they are very accessible.

Flexible timing is usually used when a facility is in high demand. For example, there is an ice hockey team in the UK that hire an ice rink at 3 am in the morning for their practice sessions as the costs are lower.

Unusual venues are places intended to be used for other things that have become venues for sporting activities. For example, a Tesco car park in the south of England is hired out and used regularly by young people for sport and active leisure.

Case study: Scott takes up mountain biking

Scott used to spend his free time surfing the internet and watching TV. However, he started to realise that he never got out or did anything active. He hasn't got much money and isn't keen on fixed routines. But he has a great sense of adventure and loves to try new things. He knows a few friends who mountain bike so decided are used to spot talent and recruit new players. to take it up. So far he is really enjoying it …

1 Why do you think mountain biking is well-suited to Scott?

2 What do you think encouraged him to take it up over other activities?

Just checking

Carry out research in your local area to find out how people are encouraged to take part in sport and active leisure. For example, are there any taster sessions at your local leisure centre? Is your school planning any school trips to introduce you to new sports activities?

Draw a spider diagram of all of the different initiatives in your local area that try to encourage participation in sport and active leisure. List the initiatives that are:

✱ traditional

✱ innovative.

* What sort of activities do you like to take part in?
* Why do you enjoy these activities?
* Do you mix with lots of different people when you take part in these activities or are any of them restricted to a certain type of person, eg male, female, elite athlete, etc?

Over to you

Select a sport of your choice. Think about how you could run an activity session for your selected sport and how you would adapt it for:

* a beginner
* an intermediate participant
* an elite participant.

Functional Skills

English

Develop your English speaking and listening skills by discussing the following questions in small groups.

Which gender:

* do aerobics classes usually appeal to?
* does circuit training usually appeal to?
* does participation in football usually appeal to?
* does participation in competitive swimming usually appeal to?

Explain each of your answers.

1.10 Different participant groups

Physical activity is essential for maintaining health and wellbeing. Different people will have specific requirements and may be more suited to particular types of physical activity.

Different ability

The type of exercises included in an activity session depend on whether you are experienced or a new starter.

Beginners may have lower levels of fitness so will need a longer warm-up. They will need plenty of time to practise new skills and require lots of instruction. The activities should have a large 'fun' element so that beginners enjoy the activity and are keen to continue.

Intermediate ability participants will require less skill instruction and usually spend more time practising in game or competition situations. There should be some fun elements but at this level participants have demonstrated their commitment to the activity.

An **elite participant** will need very specific feedback to help improve their performance and tailor-made training programmes to increase their fitness in line with their sport. The elite participant is focused on doing their best in their sport.

Gender

Males and females can and do take part in the same sports and physical activities. However, for most competitive sports, males and females do not compete against each other.

Specific populations

Different groups of people have different needs that may affect their ability to participate in sport and active leisure activities.

Older people need to be active as physical activity can reverse or slow the effects of ageing. Someone aged 50 plus is classed as an 'older person'. However, your body starts ageing from around 35, when you start to lose muscle and bone mass, tendons and ligaments weaken and you may gain body fat.

A programme incorporating resistance exercise (to maintain or build muscle mass), plus cardiovascular work (to keep the heart and vascular system healthy) is ideal. Muscle strength and endurance exercises help maintain good posture and balance exercises can reduce the risk of falling. Low impact exercises like walking or swimming are suitable as they place less strain on the joints.

Children and young people need activity sessions that take into consideration their age and physical development. Sport sessions designed for learning should incorporate a play element so that children enjoy the activity and want to continue taking part. Activities for both children and young people should be at sufficient intensity levels to increase heart rate but must have frequent break periods for recovery and relaxation. Care needs to be taken to ensure that an activity does not negatively affect physical growth, particularly bone and muscle development.

Obese people should take part in physical activity to help them to lose body fat. A GP will need to ensure that an obese person is sufficiently healthy to take part in physical exercise. An exercise programme that incorporates cardiovascular, resistance and flexibility training is advisable. The programme should start at low levels of intensity and largely include non-weight-bearing and low-impact exercises, like swimming. Walking is a good choice as this can be incorporated into a person's everyday life.

People with health conditions may become seriously ill from exercising. If a **PAR-Q** identifies someone as having a health condition, they will need to be cleared by a GP before starting an exercise programme. Generally, warm-up and cool-down periods will be longer, and exercises or activities must be appropriate for their particular condition. For example, a person with arthritis should exercise later in the day when their joints have warmed up.

People with injuries will need to take part in rehabilitation exercises that do not affect the site of the injury. For people with leg or foot injuries, for example, non-weight-bearing exercises like aqua aerobics will help to keep the person active but will not place undue stress on their injury.

People from different cultures or religions may be restricted in the way they dress for sport and active leisure, and the types of activities they can take part in. For example, some cultures will not allow males to see females in swimsuits. Therefore, centres must provide female-only swimming sessions with female lifeguards. Signs and promotional material should be available in a range of languages so that everybody can access information.

People with physical or learning disabilities may require different types of equipment to help them to take part in sport and active leisure sessions. Staff need to be appropriately trained so that they know how to meet the needs of all their customers. For example, staff who know how to operate the hoist to lift people from their wheelchair into the swimming pool should always be available.

People from different socioeconomic backgrounds may find taking part in sport and active leisure activities costly. It may be necessary to pay for sports clothes, equipment and facility hire. Many local authorities are aware of this and offer lower cost or even free participation in sports centres for various activities for those with a low income.

Over to you

Visit one sport and active leisure centre and find out about its provision for one participant group. Compile a report that describes:

* how it meets the needs of the participant group
* what sort of activities are available to encourage participation from the group
* how could the centre improve its provision for this group of participants?

JARGON BUSTER

PAR-Q This stands for 'Physical Activity Readiness Questionnaire' and consists of a list of questions with 'yes' or 'no' answers that ask about someone's health. If a person answers 'yes' to any question they may need to visit a doctor and get their authorisation before exercising. See page 233 for an example of a PAR-Q questionaire.

Just checking

List a range of activities or sports that would appeal to the following specific populations and explain your selections:

* young people
* females
* older people
* obese people
* males.

Starting Point

* Have you carried out or been involved in any health and fitness tests?
* Which tests were they and what were they measuring?

1.11 Analysis of effects of lifestyle changes

A number of methods are available to determine how your health and fitness can be improved through positive lifestyle changes. The main ways to identify how someone has responded to leading a healthier lifestyle are:

* fitness tests
* body composition tests
* health tests
* lifestyle diaries
* psychological questionnaires to assess mood and attitude before and after introducing a healthy lifestyle programme.

Fitness tests

Participation in physical activity will usually result in an increase in overall fitness levels. The following tests are appropriate for most people with no underlying health issues and can be used for overall fitness assessments. Different types of tests are used depending on the aspect of fitness being measured.

Examples of tests to measure:

* **cardiovascular fitness** include: multistage fitness test (also known as the bleep test); Cooper's 12-minute run; Harvard step test; arm **ergometer**.
* **muscular endurance** include: one-minute sit-up test; one-minute press-up test.
* **flexibility** include: sit and reach test; shoulder flexibility test.
* **muscle strength** include: hand grip dynamometer; one rep max test.

Results of each test taken before and after the healthy lifestyle programme will identify physical fitness improvements, and tables of 'norms' will help to indicate whether you need to improve or just maintain the different components of fitness (see Unit 3 – pages 90–96).

Adapted fitness tests

The tests listed are not appropriate for everyone and, in some cases, need to be adapted so they do not cause undue stress or over-exertion. An elderly person might carry out the six-minute walk test – an adapted version of the 12-minute Cooper run that tests their **functional fitness**. People with disabilities may need to use specially adapted equipment, such as a treadmill designed for wheelchair users.

The sit and reach test.

Personal, Learning and Thinking Skills

This functional skills activity will help to provide evidence of Reflective Learner, Team Worker and Effective Participator.

Functional Skills

Maths

Take part in a range of different fitness tests to assess your overall fitness. Work out which areas of your fitness are within the normal or good ranges and which areas you need to try to improve – see Unit 3, pages 72–73.

JARGON BUSTER

Ergometer A piece of exercise equipment designed to measure the amount of work performed by a muscle or a group of muscles.

Functional fitness The ability to carry out everyday tasks such as bending to tie shoelaces or walking to the shops.

Personal, Learning and Thinking Skills

This activity will help to provide evidence of Self Manager and Effective Participator.

Over to you

Carry out research to find out about tests adapted for older people that would measure their:

* cardiovascular fitness
* flexibility
* muscular strength
* muscular endurance.

Health tests

One of the main tests used to assess a person's health is a blood pressure reading. A healthy diet and exercise help to avoid high blood pressure and will make you less prone to heart disease. Resting heart rate can also be measured as this is a good indicator of cardiovascular fitness levels. The average heart rate for an adult male is 70 beats per minute, and slightly more for a female.

Body composition tests

A combination of healthy eating and physical activity will usually reduce body fat and increase muscle tissue. Therefore, a body composition test such as **Bioelectrical Impedance Analysis** carried out before and after the healthy lifestyle programme should help assess body composition changes and indicate whether fat has been lost. Excess body fat can lead to long-term health problems like type 2 diabetes, heart disease and some forms of cancer.

Over to you

A diary is another good method of assessing a person's lifestyle. Record:

* what foods you have eaten
* how much physical activity you have taken part in
* how much sleep you have had (including timings of going to bed and waking up)
* any negative lifestyle choices.

You could use a copy of the table given in the 'Just checking' table on page 10.

Now use your diary to assess which areas could be classed as healthy and which areas you need to improve. Write a report explaining what you could do to modify your lifestyle so that you can improve your overall health and wellbeing.

Just checking

Emma took part in an eight-week healthy living programme – she exercised regularly and ate a healthy diet. Take a look at her 'before' and 'after' healthy living programme test results:

	Before healthy living programme	After healthy living programme
BMI	28	25
Blood Pressure	125/85 mmHg	120/80 mmHg
Resting heart rate	75 bpm	70 bpm
Sit and reach test	15 cm	20cm

Compare the 'before' and 'after' results and explain how the healthy living programme has affected Emma's health and fitness levels. What other tests could have been used to help assess her health and fitness levels?

Functional Skills

Maths

In this activity you will measure your resting heart rate. You will need a stopwatch. Lie down for no less than five minutes and relax. After at least five minutes, find your pulse point on either your wrist or neck (remember not to use your thumb to take your pulse). Once you have found your pulse, start the stopwatch and count how many heart beats you feel in one minute. If your resting heart rate is under 70 beats per minute, you have good cardiovascular fitness.

Did you know?

Elite athletes such as cyclists in the Tour de France may have resting heart rates of fewer than 30 beats per minute!

JARGON BUSTER

Bioelectrical Impedance Analysis This measures body composition by sending a low-level electrical current through the body – the current will encounter resistance when passing through fat tissue. This level of resistance can be used to calculate a body fat percentage.

Personal, Learning and Thinking Skills

This activity will help to provide evidence of PLTS Reflective Learner, Team Worker, Self Manager, Independent Enquirer and Effective Participator.

* What sort of positive
  lifestyle choices do your
  family and/or friends make?

* What sort of negative
  lifestyle choices do your
  family and/or friends make?

* What sort of things could
  your family and/or friends
  do to improve their
  lifestyles?

Did you know?

Research shows that making positive changes, such as increasing activity levels, can provide significant long-term benefits, including a reduced risk of developing:

* coronary heart disease

* type 2 diabetes

* some forms of cancer

* osteoporosis

* depression

* obesity.

Positive changes can also provide benefits to society as a whole, such as reducing anti-social behaviour and the burden on the NHS.

1.12 Improving an individual's health and wellbeing

Most people know that some aspects of their lifestyle could be improved. This section provides ideas on how to adapt everyday activities and limit negative choices in order to become healthier.

Positive impacts of lifestyle changes

A healthy lifestyle involves making positive lifestyle choices and incorporates:

* regular physical activity, in line with ACSM guidelines (see page 6)

* eating a healthy and balanced diet

* taking part in positive risk-taking activities

* getting sufficient good-quality sleep

* maintaining a sensible work-life balance.

Being healthy also involves limiting negative lifestyle choices, such as smoking and drinking alcohol.

Changing your lifestyle to make it healthier can bring immediate, short-term benefits such as:

* decreased, healthier levels of body fat
* weight loss
* improved confidence
* better sleep patterns.

Making positive lifestyle choices

There are a number of positive lifestyle choices that you can make to improve your lifestyle.

Increasing physical activity

Physical activity can be incorporated into your daily life. For example, you could walk or cycle to school rather than going by car or bus. If it is too far, walk to the next bus stop not your nearest one. Joining a sport and active leisure centre or a club team will help increase fitness levels and provide social benefits.

Increasing your activity levels provides a number of psychological and health benefits, such as improved self-esteem, reduced risk of developing certain cancers and better-quality sleep.

Healthy diet

What you eat has a significant effect on your immediate and long-term health and on your body composition. Here are a few of the simple modifications you can make to your usual diet to make it healthier.

Physical activity can be incorporated into your daily life.

* Try to incorporate enough fruit and vegetables into your diet (at least five a day). Snack on fruits and vegetables between meals rather than eating unhealthy snacks.

* Take care over how you prepare foods. For example, a potato is healthy when baked but chips contain a lot of fat.

* Think about the timing of your food intake. Do you skip breakfast and then eat lots in the evening? Always start the day with a healthy breakfast, as this will keep you going until lunch and may stop you snacking on unhealthy foods between meals and later in the day.

Sleep

Sleep is important for your physical and psychological wellbeing. The quantity and quality of your sleep is important, so you should aim to have a fixed sleep pattern with regular bedtimes and getting up times.

Work-life balance

Many people today spend a large proportion of their time working. With devices like BlackBerrys and netbooks people can access work-related information at all hours. Everyone needs time off work to dedicate to themselves and pursue leisure activities. If a person does not maintain a good work-life balance with sufficient 'me time' they risk becoming stressed and affecting relationships with friends and family members.

Increasing positive risk-taking behaviour

By setting yourself challenges and goals through positive risk-taking behaviour you will help to improve your confidence and self-esteem, which play a major role in your wellbeing and social life. For example, you might challenge yourself to try rock climbing or abseiling.

Decreasing negative lifestyle choices

There are a number of things you can do to limit your negative choices.

Reducing alcohol intake

Keeping a drinking diary of how many units are consumed, and when, can help people to ensure that they are sticking to recommended limits. Making changes such as diluting alcohol with non-alcoholic drinks can also help people to limit the number of units they consume.

Stopping smoking

A person can try to stop smoking through a variety of different methods, including:

* slowly reducing the number of cigarettes smoked per day

* totally stopping smoking and using nicotine replacement therapy

* seeking support from a GP or the NHS Stop Smoking campaign.

Personal, Learning and Thinking Skills

This activity will help to provide evidence of Reflective Learner.

Over to you

Make a list of ways in which you can:

* increase your physical activity levels as part of your normal lifestyle

* improve your current diet.

In both cases, use the examples given here to start you off but also try to think of some of your own improvement ideas.

Did you know?

People become addicted to smoking because of the nicotine in cigarettes and the psychological addiction to the act of smoking, which makes stopping very difficult.

Just checking

* What are the benefits of taking part in regular physical activity?
* What are the benefits of having regular sleep patterns?
* What are the problems associated with eating an unhealthy diet?
* Carry out research to find out how organisations, such as the NHS, work to encourage people to stop smoking and reduce their alcohol consumption.

Case study: Freddy, Personal trainer

Freddy's job

Freddy is a personal trainer and works freelance for a range of different clients. One of the main focuses of his job is on encouraging his clients to take part in sport and active leisure so that they can improve their health and wellbeing. Most clients are keen to improve their body image by losing weight and toning up.

A number of clients who are in very demanding jobs have been encouraged to increase their activity levels as a means of dealing with stress. Freddy also has clients referred to him by medical professionals in the hope that increasing their activity levels will decrease their BMI score, lower their blood pressure and improve their overall health. Clients are sometimes referred to him with mild cases of depression, as physical activity participation is recommended as one way of helping to treat this condition.

Freddy's role as a personal trainer is not just to encourage physical fitness, but also to improve his clients' lifestyle choices. He educates them on what a healthy diet is and will have consultations to analyse a client's diet and find ways to improve it without making too many drastic changes.

A new client

Freddy has just met with a new client, Leroy. Freddy asks Leroy what he would like to get out of his personal training sessions and Leroy tells him that his goals are:

* to improve his level of fitness
* to lose body weight
* to stop smoking
* to reduce his alcohol intake
* to meet new people
* to improve his diet.

Freddy then asks Leroy some questions about himself and his lifestyle and finds out the following information.

* Leroy is a 28-year-old single male.
* He works long hours and commutes into London every day.
* He mainly eats takeaways for his evening meal and has at least three curries and two pizzas a week.
* He goes to the pub most nights after work and usually consumes around 25 units of alcohol a week.
* He smokes between 10 and 20 cigarettes a day.

1 If you were Freddy what sort of physical activity participation would you suggest for Leroy and why?

2 How could Leroy incorporate physical activity into his everyday life?

3 What methods could you suggest to help Leroy to:

   a reduce his alcohol consumption?   b give up smoking?
   c improve his diet?

For your project

This unit explores what a healthy lifestyle is and how people can make positive lifestyle choices in order to help to improve their lifestyle. Helping British people to understand what a healthy lifestyle is and how to lead a healthy lifestyle has become a huge focus for the national and local governments. Statistics have shown that, as a nation, the British public has some serious health concerns which can be dealt with through living a healthy lifestyle.

The following diagram gives some ideas for what you might decide to do your project on, based on the content of this unit.

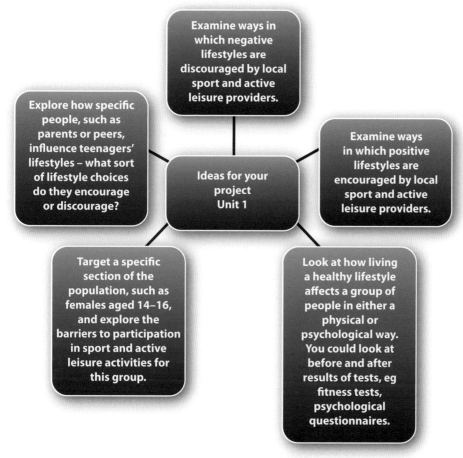

Possible project titles

∗ Does a healthy living programme improve a person's confidence?

∗ Does taking part in 60 minutes of activity a day improve a person's health?

∗ Does physical activity participation decrease anti-social behavior?

∗ What are the psychological effects of taking part in positive risk-taking activities?

∗ What is the best method of giving up smoking?

∗ How does the media encourage positive lifestyle choices?

∗ How does the media promote negative lifestyle choices?

Assessment guidance

This unit is assessed by an external test of 1 hour and 30 minutes. The questions in this test will consist of short answer and longer answer questions. The majority of the questions will require you to read some information, such as case studies or tables of data, and then demonstrate that you can apply your knowledge of the subject in your answer. You will complete the examination under supervision and will not be able to communicate with anybody except an invigilator. The examination will cover all the learning outcomes of the unit – see table opposite.

Time management

* The external test is set under timed conditions so you must be able to write your answers within a time limit. Therefore it is a very good idea to practise writing answers to examination questions so that you are prepared for the external test.

* Your teacher will probably give you examination-style questions after teaching parts of the unit content and you may well have a mock examination, which is a trial exam of the whole unit content, to help to prepare you for the real thing. Make sure you complete these practice tests and have them marked by your teachers so that you can see how well you are progressing and if there are any areas that you need to spend more time studying.

* It is a good idea to set time aside to revise your work at set intervals throughout the delivery of this unit, rather than waiting until the unit is finished. By ensuring that you understand and remember each section of this unit you will be able to build on this knowledge and gain a much fuller understanding of the subject area.

* Make your revision sessions active by writing questions as you progress through each section, then test yourself at the end of your revision session to make sure you have retained all of the relevant information.

Useful links

There are many television programmes that examine different aspects of healthy lifestyles, including both positive and negative lifestyle choices. Try to watch any documentaries that are examining these subject areas. If you watch news broadcasts, you will also see that there are often stories linked to the health of the nation and government initiatives to try to encourage the British public to make positive lifestyle choices.

Visiting organisations connected with sport and active leisure, and having discussions with employees in these sectors, will allow you to find out about what sort of things they do in order to try to help increase individuals' positive lifestyle choices.

The Active People survey conducted by Sport England will provide you with valuable information on sport and active leisure participation by the British public, barriers to participation and current initiatives to try to increase participation.

There are lots of useful websites that will help you with your research for this unit. For details of how to access these sites see the **Hotlinks** section – **Introduction**, page xi.

How you will be assessed

For your Unit 1 assessment, you need to make sure that you can meet all of the assessment criteria for the five learning outcomes, as shown in the table below.

Learning outcome	Assessment criteria
LO1: Know about healthy lifestyles	**1** Identify the key indicators of good health and wellbeing. **2** Identify positive lifestyle choices. **3** Identify negative lifestyle choices. **4** Describe eating disorders related to negative body image.
LO2: Know about influences on lifestyle choices	**1** Describe influences on lifestyle choices.
LO3: Understand the importance of participation in sport and active leisure	**1** Explain the reasons why different methods of participation may appeal to different groups.
LO4: Understand how lifestyle choices impact on the health and wellbeing of individuals and society	**1** Explain the effects of lifestyle choices or eating disorders on individuals. **2** Explain the benefits to society of regular or increased participation.
LO5: Understand how lifestyle changes improve health and wellbeing	**1** Analyse the effects of lifestyle changes on the health and wellbeing of individuals. **2** Suggest lifestyle changes to improve the health and wellbeing of individuals. **3** Justify suggested lifestyle changes to improve the health and wellbeing of individuals.

Introduction

Participation in sport and active leisure is beneficial to health and wellbeing. Various initiatives are in place to encourage increased participation in sport and active leisure activities. This unit covers the benefits to individuals and society of regular participation. You will learn about different leadership styles that can be used for different participant groups and how to plan and support the delivery of activity sessions. This unit also helps you to assess the ways in which the sport and active leisure industry encourages participation in the different sectors and explain how activity sessions can be improved.

What will you learn?

In this unit you will cover the following learning outcomes:

LO1: Know the benefits of participation in sport and active leisure to individuals and society
LO2: Understand how leaders in sport and active leisure encourage participation
LO3: Be able to plan sport and active leisure participation activities
LO4: Know how risks are managed in sport and active leisure
LO5: Be able to use leadership skills to support the delivery of participation activities in sport and active leisure
LO6: Understand the effectiveness of sport and active leisure activities in encouraging participation

The following table shows how these six learning outcomes are covered by this unit.

Topic	Pages	Learning outcomes
2.1 The benefits of participation for different groups in sport and active leisure	36–37	LO1
2.2 Leadership and motivation in sport and active leisure	38–39	LO2
2.3 Planning a sport and active leisure activity	40–41	LO3
2.4 Activities to encourage participation in sport and active leisure	42–43	LO3
2.5 Use of media to promote sport and active leisure activities	44–45	LO3
2.6 Dealing with conflict in sport and active leisure activities	46–47	LO3
2.7 Managing risks in sport and active leisure	48–49	LO4
2.8 Supporting the delivery of activities in sport and active leisure	50–53	LO5
2.9 Reviewing the effectiveness of encouraging participation in sport and active leisure	54–56	LO6

THINKING POINTS

* Have you ever led part of a sport and active leisure session?
* What skills do you think a leader needs to run a sport and active leisure session?

Functional Skills

Personal, Learning and Thinking Skills

This unit offers various opportunities to develop functional skills and personal, learning and thinking skills. Where appropriate, different activities are signposted with the relevant skills that you can develop.

Diploma Daily

Dancing craze hits the nation!

Everybody's doing it – from ballroom to street dance, from hip hop to salsa; people of all ages are getting down and boogying! TV shows such as Strictly Come Dancing and Got to Dance are encouraging the nation to get off their sofas and put on their dancing shoes. With obesity levels hitting a new high, the timing couldn't be better for this dance craze to sweep the nation and get the British public moving on the road to a healthier lifestyle.

1 Why do you think dancing has become such a popular physical activity?

2 Carry out research and list at least ten different types of dance style.

3 Using your research, explain what age groups each type of dance tends to appeal to.

4 Do you think dancing appeals more to females or males? Explain your answer.

How you will be assessed

This unit will be assessed by one main assignment, which requires you to support the delivery of a group active leisure activity. You will need to present evidence of the following in your assignment:

✱ A signed observation record form completed by your tutor or an employer in the sport and active leisure industry. They must have witnessed your discussion with team members or colleagues in which you planned a sport or active leisure participation activity.

✱ An activity plan that describes how you will use your leadership skills to support the delivery of a sport or active leisure activity.

✱ A risk assessment for your planned activity.

✱ A signed observation record form completed by your tutor or an employer in the sport and active leisure industry. They must have witnessed you using your leadership skills to support the delivery of your planned sport or active leisure activity.

✱ A review of the strengths and weaknesses of two different sport and active leisure participation activities from at least two different sport and active leisure sectors, with an explanation of how these activities could be improved.

Unit links

This unit links closely to Level 2, Unit 1: Positive lifestyle choices and sport and active leisure, Unit 4: Working in the local sport and active leisure Industry and Unit 7: Access for all in sport and active leisure.

Case study: Samantha's activity sessions

Samantha is 18 and enjoys aerobics and step aerobics. She also does some martial arts to help her keep fit. She would like to work with children and has recently qualified as a children's fitness instructor. She knows many sport and active leisure centres are trying to encourage children to be more active and hopes to soon be able to lead activity sessions for children in one of these centres.

1 Why do you think the sport and active leisure industry is trying to encourage children to take part in activity sessions?

2 What sort of skills do you think Samantha will need in order to lead activity sessions with children?

3 How could Samantha encourage children to take part in her activity sessions?

Starting Point

* Why do you think people get involved in anti-social behaviour?
* What can be done to reduce anti-social behaviour?

Functional Skills

This activity will help to provide evidence of English reading, listening and speaking.

Personal, Learning and Thinking Skills

This activity will help to provide evidence of Self Manager and Independent Enquirer.

Over to you

Carry out research to find out:

* how participation in sport and active leisure benefits young people in your local area.
* if there is any anti-social behaviour happening in your local area and what is being done to try to combat it.

2.1 The benefits of participation for different groups

People of all ages and abilities benefit from participation in sport and active leisure. Most people are aware of the physical benefits of regular activity, such as improved health, fitness and body composition. There are also huge social benefits, which will be explored in this unit.

Benefits

Participation in sport and active leisure helps to reduce anti-social behaviour, including bullying, crime and drug misuse. Bullies usually lack self-esteem and try to gain confidence by picking on others. Participation in sport and active leisure helps to develop self-esteem and mental resilience, which makes people less likely to bully. Increased self-confidence also helps young adults to stand up to bullies and to resist peer pressure encouraging negative lifestyle choices. Boredom often results in anti-social behaviour such as petty crime and excessive alcohol consumption. Participating in a regular activity or joining a sports team gives young people something purposeful to do.

People who regularly participate in sport and active leisure often have a more developed sense of community spirit and take part in voluntary activities, such as running charity events or coaching children's sporting activities. Other valuable social skills can be learnt through sport and active leisure participation, including leadership, communication, cooperation and independence.

Participant groups

Whilst everybody benefits from participation in sport and active leisure, different people have different likes and needs when it comes to their choice of physical activity.

Different abilities

* **Beginners** – require lots of time to practise new skills and need lots of instruction and feedback. The activities should have a large 'fun' element.
* **Intermediate** – less skill instruction, more time spent practising in game or competition situations. Some fun elements but participants have now demonstrated their commitment.
* **Elite** – need specific feedback to improve their performance and tailor-made training programmes to enhance their fitness. They are focused on doing their best in their sport.

Gender

Females tend to enjoy class-based activities where they can socialise and there is a general preference for dance-related activities such as aerobics, and classes like Pilates and yoga. Males often prefer competition-related sports and active leisure activities such as football and golf.

Older people

Some older people prefer to take part in low-intensity activities where they can meet other people. Rambling or walking groups and bowls tend to be popular. Swimming and aqua aerobics classes are often chosen as these activities place little strain on joints – older people are more likely to suffer from painful **degenerative conditions** like **arthritis**.

Children and young people

Children's activities will usually be based on a game or imaginative play, which may incorporate obstacle courses set to a theme, such as travelling through a jungle. Activities incorporate some teaching of skills and techniques with fun elements to maintain interest.

Aqua aerobics is a popular choice for older people as it is sociable and does not place strain on the joints.

Obese people

Obese people are more suited to low-impact activities that don't put strain on the joints. Swimming is ideal, though obese people may feel self-conscious in a swimming costume.

People with health conditions

An exercise programme should be designed to ensure the health condition is being treated appropriately. These people need to do specific rehabilitation exercises that won't make the injury or health condition worse.

People from different cultures or religions

Your culture or religion may restrict the activities you take part in. Some sport and active leisure sessions take this into account, for example by running female-only exercise classes.

People with physical or learning disabilities

The type of physical or learning disability that a person has may impact upon the type of physical activity chosen. People in wheelchairs can take part in activities such as wheelchair basketball on regular courts, so no special facilities are required. People with learning disabilities will often require specially trained leaders to run activity sessions so that their needs are met.

People from different socioeconomic backgrounds

Some people may not be able to afford to participate in certain sport and active leisure activities. Certain providers take this into account and offer activities at reduced rates.

> ### JARGON BUSTER
> **Degenerative conditions**
> Conditions that get worse over time. They are related to ageing.
>
> **Arthritis** A group of conditions that damage joints, causing inflammation, swelling and pain.

> ### THINKING POINT
> What sport and active leisure activities can you think of that people can participate in for free or at very low cost?

> ### Just checking
> * Describe the social benefits of taking part in sport and active leisure.
> * Explain why different types of people require different types of activity session.

JARGON BUSTER

Laissez faire A French term that literally means 'let it be'.

The autocratic style of leadership is often used with groups of children.

Over to you

Describe situations where you have experienced autocratic, democratic and laissez faire styles of leadership. Do you think the types of leadership were appropriate for the situation? Explain your answer.

2.2 Leadership and motivation in sport and active leisure

The way a person chooses to lead a team or group of people affects how successful they are. A good leader can motivate, encourage and get the best out of a team and all the individuals in it. In this section different leadership styles and their impacts are explored to prepare you to lead a group.

Leadership styles

There are three main types of leadership style:

* autocratic
* democratic
* **laissez faire**

The autocratic style

The leader makes all decisions alone and imposes these decisions on the group. The group are expected to do exactly what they are told without question. This leadership style is often used with large groups, children and young people, or in situations where there may be potential hazards.

The democratic style

The leader involves the group in the decision-making process and asks for their opinions. The group are able to take responsibility for their actions, but the leader is still responsible for making overall decisions. This leadership style could be used by captains in local club teams.

The laissez faire style

This gives the group a lot of freedom and allows them to make most decisions for themselves. This method is used when a group of people are highly capable and motivated so don't need close supervision.

Impact of different leadership styles

Each leadership style has its strengths and weaknesses, as shown below.

Autocratic

Strengths:

* Good for teaching basic skills to beginners.
* Good for large groups.

Weaknesses:

* Participants unable to make suggestions – leader misses out on ideas that could improve group performance.
* Group is unable to carry out activities without their leader.

Democratic

Strengths:

* Good for improving communication between the leader and the group.
* Participants contribute to decision-making process.

Weaknesses:

* Can be time-consuming if lots of people want to share ideas.
* Should not be used if decisions need to be made quickly.

Laissez faire

Strengths:

* Helps a group take responsibility for their actions.
* Participants left to get on with activities on their own – can explore their skills and abilities without restriction.

Weaknesses:

* Group can suffer from lack of motivation.
* Participants can take longer to reach their goals.

Methods of motivation

When people are learning new skills they often go through periods when they feel like giving up. A good leader needs to encourage and motivate them so that they continue to practise and participate in the activity in order to reach their full potential. Good leadership can persuade people to increase their participation levels and help them achieve set goals. People need to be motivated to overcome perceived barriers to participation, such as thinking that they are not good enough or don't have the energy to participate. Some of the key methods for motivation used by leaders are shown in the diagram below.

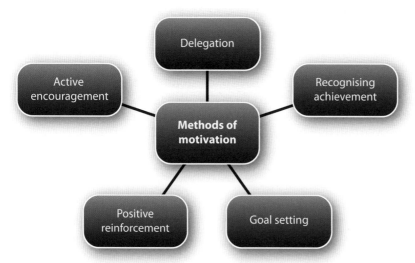

* **Active encouragement**: The leader supports an individual or group by praising good practice, for example, 'Great dribbling, you have controlled the ball really well.'

* **Delegation**: The leader gives people in the group some sort of responsibility, for example leading the warm-up or helping to demonstrate various skills and techniques. This helps to provide people with a sense of importance and develop confidence in their abilities.

* **Positive reinforcement**: The leader actively rewards people, providing praise or giving them a certificate to encourage them to repeat good behaviour and/or performance.

* **Recognising achievement**: When people, especially children, work hard they like to have their achievements recognised. A number of sport and active leisure schemes award badges and certificates when a participant has achieved a certain level of skill or ability.

* **Goal setting**: The leader and the group or individual decide on short- and long-term goals to help them progress. Goals need to be realistic and attainable so that they can be used as a motivational tool.

Over to you

* What sorts of motivation have you experienced?

* Which type of motivation did you respond best to and why?

* Which types of motivation do you think would work best in the following situations:
  - leading a group of young children aged between four and five in an obstacle course activity session
  - leading a group of older adults in a physical activity session
  - leading a club level group of 16-year-old female basketball players in a training session?

Just checking

* Can you think of three well-known people who each use one of the three different leadership styles?

* Describe which leadership style you would use with the following groups of people, and why you have selected that style:
  - a group of 20 children aged between five and six years
  - the school/college sports team that you play for.

* Why is it important that a leader knows how to motivate people?

Starting Point

* What sort of activity sessions have you been involved in?
* Which sessions went well and which did not run well?
* Why do you think some sessions you took part in did not run well?

Good communication is essential when working with other people.

2.3 Planning a sport and active leisure activity

For a sport and active leisure activity to be successful it must be planned thoroughly. In this section you will learn how to plan a sport and active leisure activity session that incorporates all the required components, and how to tailor these components to meet the needs of different groups of participants.

Collaboration with others

You will need to work with other people to decide what sort of activity you are going to plan. When working with other people you should try to share your ideas and listen to other people's thoughts. A person who listens well allows the other person to finish speaking and then asks questions to show that they have understood what has been said and to find out more. You should aim to have regular meetings to maintain effective communication, share ideas and agree decisions.

Every meeting should have an agenda – a list of items to be discussed. The agenda might look like this:

> Date of meeting
>
> 1 Decide on the type of participant group for the selected activity.
>
> 2 Decide which type of activity is best for the selected participant group.
>
> 3 Decide on the equipment to use with the selected participant group.
>
> 4 Define roles and responsibilities – what will each team member do?
>
> 5 Any other business? (This leaves room for anyone at the meeting to raise any relevant topic or issue that has not been covered already.)

Aims and goals

When you are in your group you will need to decide which type of participant group you are going to plan the activity session for. Different types of activities will appeal to different groups of participants. You will then need to determine the aims and goals of the activity – this will involve thinking about the requirements of the chosen participants and the methods that would appeal to them. For example, if the participant group is a group of children aged five and six, the main aims of the activity would be to ensure the children are active for the majority of the session and that they have fun. For a group of teenagers aged 14–15 playing basketball, the main aim may be for them to improve a skill such as a layup shot.

Functional Skills

This activity will help to provide evidence of English speaking and listening.

Personal, Learning and Thinking Skills

This activity will help to provide evidence of Creative Thinker and Team Worker.

Over to you

In small groups, decide on the aims and goals of an activity session for the following groups of participants:

* a group of females aged 30–40
* a mixed group of older people aged 50 plus
* a group of people who are obese
* a group of elite netball players.

Session plan

Every activity session should have a session plan containing information on when the session is happening and what equipment is required, and including a time schedule for carrying out the tasks. You can refer to it before and during a session.

Your session plan should look something like this:

Session plan				
Date:	Time:	Facilities:	Equipment:	Number of participants: Ability: Age:
Aims and goals of the session:			Leadership style:	
Time	Activity component	Activity	Teaching points	Equipment
10 mins	Warm-up			
40 mins	Main activity			
5 mins	Cool-down			
Evaluation of session				

Activity components

Each part of the activity session is split into different components. The warm-up component gets the body ready for the main activity and reduces the likelihood of injury. A warm-up consists of a mobiliser activity, where joints are taken through their range of movement, followed by the pulse raiser, which increases the heart rate to warm the body up. This is followed by a stretch, where the main muscles required for the activity are stretched.

The main activity takes up the majority of the activity session time. This could consist of one main activity, such as a circuit training session, or it can be broken down into a skills session followed by a game, for example 20 minutes spent practising a sports skill such as passing and 20 minutes spent playing a game and using the skill in the game situation.

The cool down helps the body recover from the activity session and consists of a **digressive activity** (to lower the pulse) and a stretch of all the main muscles used in the activity.

Functional Skills

This activity will help to provide evidence of English speaking and listening.

Personal, Learning and Thinking Skills

This activity will help to provide evidence of Creative Thinker, Team Worker and Effective Participant.

Over to you

Working in small groups, think about how you would plan an activity session for a participant group of your choice. Make a list of all the equipment you will need, the facilities that you would need access to and the roles and responsibilities of each member in your group.

Just checking

* Give an example of an agenda that you would use for a meeting to organise an activity session.
* Why do you think a session plan is important?
* Why do you think teaching points are important in a session plan?

Starting Point

* What sorts of sport and active leisure activities do you like to take part in?

* Are you able to take part in your sport and active leisure activities as often as you would like?

* Are there any sport and active leisure activities that you haven't tried but would like to have a go at? Why do you think you haven't tried them yet?

2.4 Activities to encourage participation in sport and active leisure

Different people like different things. Therefore, to encourage people to take part in sport and active leisure, you need to provide a range of different activities so they can choose to take part in the ones that are appealing and accessible to them.

There are lots of different ways of participating in sport and active leisure activities. Different methods to encourage people to take part in a more active lifestyle include:

* taster sessions
* drop-in sessions
* street games
* unusual venues
* formal or informal settings
* school visits

* sports days
* sports festivals
* fitness sessions
* tournaments
* outdoor expeditions
* activity days at summer camps.

Taster sessions, drop-in sessions, street games, school visits, unusual venues and formal or informal settings are covered in Unit 1.

Sports days

Sports days usually happen in schools. Children are selected to represent their school or their 'house' and compete against each other in a variety of sporting events.

Sports festivals

These quite large events often run over a weekend. They may include a number of sports being showcased, with experts providing demonstrations of their sport for people to watch. People are encouraged to try out new sports and get active.

Functional Skills

This activity will help to provide evidence of English reading.

Personal, Learning and Thinking Skills

This activity will help to provide evidence of Reflective Learner and Independent Enquirer.

Case Study: Florham Summer Sports Festival

Come to the Florham Summer Sports Festival.

See some of the world's top skaters perform a fantastic inline skate display, then have a go at our free taster session afterwards and get top tips from the experts. See the new sport parkour and watch athletes get from one point to the next using a variety of running, acrobatic and gymnastic movements. For the more traditional there will be county football and netball matches to watch, with free drop-in sessions for you to learn new skills. There will be a sponsored 5 k walk and a 10 k running race for people of all ages to enter, and a junior olympic event for children. A children's soft play area is available for little ones and a splash pool for kids to cool off. Bring your friends and your trainers for a fun-filled and active day!

1 What methods does this sports festival use to encourage participation in sport and active leisure?

2 What types of participant groups do you think this event will attract and why?

3 Carry out research to see if there are any sports festivals taking place near you and what they will offer.

Fitness sessions

These types of session are often in the form of an exercise class such as step aerobics, circuit training or Pilates. Participants attend these sessions to improve their fitness levels.

Participants in a fitness class.

Tournament

This is a competition in which competitors (either teams or individuals) play one another in various games. After each game, the losing competitor is either knocked straight out of the tournament or goes on to play another competitor in the same 'round', depending on the type of tournament. The competitor that wins the round overall will advance to play in the next round. These rounds continue until there are only two competitors remaining, who then play each other in the final. The winner of this final wins the entire tournament.

Outdoor expedition

Outdoor expeditions happen in the countryside and involve people undertaking a journey. The expedition could be a walking expedition or via another method of transport such as cycling or kayaking. People on an expedition need to carry everything they will need, such as a map, water, food and waterproof clothes.

Activity day at summer camp

Summer camps occur during the summer holidays and allow children to participate in group sports such as rounders or football. They may also introduce children to new sports such as rock climbing and abseiling.

Starting Point

* How do you find out about sport and active leisure activities near you?
* How do local sport and active leisure centres advertise the activities they offer?

JARGON BUSTER

Target participant group
The group an activity is aimed at because it is something that they may enjoy or see as beneficial. For example, a 'bums, legs and tums' class might be targeted at adult females aged between 30 and 40 years.

Media Methods of communication that reach and influence lots of people.

2.5 Use of media to promote sport and active leisure activities

There may be lots of sport and active leisure activities taking place that people would love to take part in, but if they don't know about them they can't participate. Advertising a sport and active leisure activity ensures the **target participant group** or groups are aware of what is going on and where it is happening. They can then make arrangements to attend the session.

There are different ways of advertising sport and active leisure activities, as shown in the diagram below.

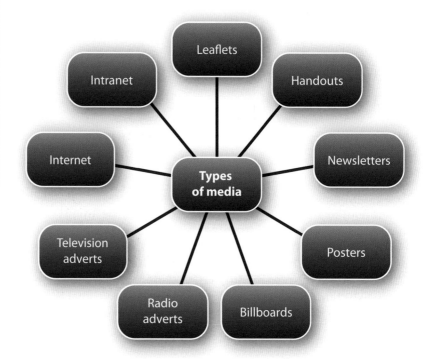

Personal, Learning and Thinking Skills

This activity will help to provide evidence of PLTS Creative Thinker and Independent Enquirer.

Over to you

Design an advert that could be used to advertise your planned activity session.

Explain where you would place this advert and why.

* **Leaflets**: Free documents containing detailed information about the activity, such as times and prices and who the activity is for. Leaflets can be kept and referred back to at a later date. Many leaflets are handed out on the street, posted into homes and made available for people to pick up from the centre hosting the activity.

* **Handouts**: Given out on the street or posted through people's letter boxes. They contain brief information about an event or activity with times, location and prices.

* **Newsletters**: Given to people who are members of a sport and active leisure club to update them with relevant information and let them know about any changes to the centre. They can also be used to make members aware of any upcoming events such as a new fitness class being introduced to the centre.

* **Posters**: Need to be eye-catching and contain images that people will be drawn to. Any writing needs to be kept to a minimum as people will usually only spend a few moments looking at a poster as they walk past it. Posters need to be placed in areas where the target participant group is likely to see them.

* **Billboards**: Large outdoor signs placed in public areas. You have to pay for the advertising space and for producing the advert. Advertising on a billboard follows the same principles as a poster campaign, except the billboard is larger and reaches a larger audience.

* **Radio adverts**: Allow people to hear about sport and active leisure activities whilst listening to their usual radio programme. An advert with a catchy jingle helps people remember it. Some radio stations have a free advertising slot for people to go into the studio and talk about their event.

* **Television adverts**: An expensive method of advertising; however, they reach a wide audience. Companies pay lots of money to have their adverts on during prime-time viewing hours and when popular programmes are showing so that they will reach an even wider audience. A television advert uses visual and aural communication.

* **Internet**: An effective and cheap method of advertising. Once a web page has been set up it can be updated regularly with new information to advertise events. However, it can take a while for people to find out about and start to regularly use a new website. Some companies buy advertising space on already successful websites.

* **Intranet**: An intranet allows people in the same organisation or club to access and share information. People outside the organisation can't access the intranet so this method of advertising ensures some privacy.

The type of media used can be tailored to an activity's target group. For example, younger people tend to use the internet more than people aged over 50. Therefore, if you want to advertise a Pilates class for the over-60s a leaflet or poster placed where older people tend to meet would be a better way of reaching the target group than using the internet.

Over to you

* What sorts of adverts are shown during football matches?
* What sorts of adverts are shown during gardening programmes?
* Why do you think there are differences?
* Describe and explain an advert that appeals to you and try to think about why you like it.

Functional Skills

This activity will help to provide evidence of English writing.

Personal, Learning and Thinking Skills

This activity will help to provide evidence of Independent Enquirer.

Just checking

Explain what would be the best method of advertising the following events and why:

* a new aqua aerobics class in a members-only gym
* a sports day at your school or college
* a sports festival
* a five-a-side football tournament
* a new sports drink
* a newly opened soft play area.

Starting Point

Have you been in a situation where your opinion was different from someone else's? How did you deal with it? Do you think you could have handled the situation better? If so, how?

2.6 Dealing with conflict in sport and active leisure activities

When you are working with other people there may be times when opinions differ. It is natural for people to disagree; however, there are ways of dealing with conflict that can resolve disagreements without any hard feelings.

Types of conflict

Conflict occurs because of differences between people. It occurs in various situations, but the main reasons for conflict are communication problems and personality clashes. There may be times when participants in a sport and active leisure activity are in conflict with you, the leader of the activity session, for example if they disagree with your decisions as a referee. This is an open clash of opinion. There may be other times when the participants would rather take part in other activities than the ones you have planned. As the leader you have to deal with these conflicts effectively and efficiently and maintain order within the group. There may also be times when a group of leaders have disagreements during the planning or delivery of the activity session. These conflicts need to be resolved so that you can continue to work well with the rest of the group with no bad feelings.

Personal, Learning and Thinking Skills

This activity will help to provide evidence of Reflective Learner.

Over to you

* What situations have you been in where participants have conflicted with the activity leader?
* How was the conflict resolved?
* Did you think it was handled appropriately? Explain your answer.

Why do you think it is a bad idea for footballers to become aggressive towards a referee?

Ways of resolving or avoiding conflict

Where conflict has arisen it should be recognised and dealt with swiftly. It should be possible to resolve a disagreement so that everyone involved feels that it has been dealt with fairly. However, if possible, it is best to avoid situations that may result in conflict in the first place. This can be done by using good communication skills. Communication problems arise through a number of factors:

* poor listening skills

* insufficient sharing of information

* lack of understanding or wrong interpretation of the information received.

To ensure you are communicating properly, check that both you and the group you are working with have understood what has been said in any discussion or instructions. If there is a conflict, empower the person you are in conflict with by listening to what they are saying. Repeat what you think they have said so that you are both clear. Ask questions to gain a better understanding of the conflict. And, when dealing with any conflict, always remember to:

* be respectful to everyone involved, as this shows that you value their opinions

* use a calm and even tone – raising your voice and getting angry makes the conflict worse

* be impartial, which means not taking sides with one person against another

* take a 'no blame' approach, which means that you acknowledge that there is a problem and try to find a way to respond that works for everyone

* keep any personal information gained from resolving the conflict confidential.

Personal, Learning and Thinking Skills

This activity will help to provide evidence of Reflective Learner and Independent Enquirer.

Over to you

What would you do in the following situations?

* You are taking part in a friendly sport and leisure activity with no officials, but someone keeps cheating.

* Two people in your team disagree on what sport and active leisure activity to offer.

* A member of your planning team decides that they want to be the leader and want to adopt an autocratic leadership style.

Just checking

* What are the main causes of conflict and how should these be dealt with?

* How would you ensure that you avoid conflict in planning sport and active leisure activities?

Starting Point

* Have you ever been injured whilst taking part in a sport or active leisure session?
* How did the injury occur?
* Could the injury have been prevented?

Over to you

Carry out research on the Children Act 2004 to find out what employers must do when recruiting and training members of staff who will be working with children. Why do you think these regulations are in place?

2.7 Managing risks in sport and active leisure

Taking part in any sport or active leisure activity involves some risk. People can get injured whilst participating in activity sessions through falls, tackles and collisions. You should be aware of any risks to participants and try to reduce or eliminate them.

Within sport and active leisure the main **legislation** that you need to know about is:

* The Health and Safety at Work Act 1994
* The Health and Safety (First Aid) Regulations (1981)
* The Children Act (2004)

The Health and Safety at Work Act (1994) ensures employers take reasonable steps to ensure the health, safety and welfare of their employees while at work. All staff within a sport and active leisure centre must be trained appropriately to ensure that health and safety are maintained.

The Health and Safety (First Aid) Regulations (1981) require organisations to have sufficient first aid facilities and equipment in place to treat injuries that occur on their premises. This means that the organisation needs to have accessible first aid boxes available and a first aid-trained member of staff on the premises during working hours.

The Children Act (2004) ensures the safety and welfare of children. It sets out rules and regulations for how a child should be treated. Anyone working with children must know these rules and regulations and adhere to them at all times.

Negligence

Negligence is failing to meet a standard of care. It may be that someone was careless or did not do everything necessary prior to or during an activity – for example, not carrying out a risk assessment prior to an activity session, which resulted in a participant being injured. The person found to be negligent could be prosecuted.

Duty of care

This means that a person must take all reasonable steps to protect themselves and other people. If a person's actions do not meet this standard of care, then they could be considered to be negligent and any damages claimed in a lawsuit. A higher duty of care is required when a person is supervising children. This means that the supervisor must be prepared for children to be less careful than adults would be in a similar situation.

Risk assessments

Risk assessments should be carried out prior to any activity. The purpose of a risk assessment is to identify hazards and their associated risks, and to reduce or eliminate them where possible.

A **hazard** is something with the potential to cause harm. For example:

* water in a swimming pool

* a wet sports hall floor

* glass on a sports pitch.

A **risk** is the chance of somebody being harmed by a hazard. Examples of risks include:

* drowning in a swimming pool

* slipping over on a wet floor and straining a muscle

* falling over onto some glass on a sports pitch and cutting your leg.

A risk is categorised by how likely it is and how severe the injury could be. The categories include:

Likelihood:

* Unlikely

* Quite likely

* Very likely

Severity:

* Low – minor injury

* Medium – injury requiring medical assistance

* High – major injury or fatality

Controlling risk

You can put controls in place to reduce the likelihood or severity of identified hazards and risks. These controls could involve using protective equipment, such as safety helmets in kayaking or pads in cricket, and safety equipment, such as ropes in rock climbing. Alternatively, you can plan to keep participants away from the identified hazards or prevent access to the hazard. You might even decide to choose a new, less risky activity.

Example of a risk assessment

Risk assessor's name:			Risk assessor's signature:		
Date:			Location of activity:		
Activity	**Participants**	**Hazard**	**Risk**	**Risk factor**	**Control measures**
Cricket	Children aged 6–7 years	Hard cricket ball	Injury from not catching the ball properly.	Likelihood – very likely. Severity – medium.	Replace hard cricket ball with tennis ball. Safety helmets to be worn.

Over to you

In the following list of sport and active leisure activities, identify the hazards and risks that participants may be exposed to:

* kayaking down some rapids

* rock climbing

* playing cricket.

Now assess the likelihood and severity of each risk that you have identified.

It is essential that the chemical levels in a swimming pool are checked regularly to ensure that the water is safe to swim in. If the water contained the wrong chemical mix, there is a risk that someone could fall ill.

Personal, Learning and Thinking Skills

This activity will help to provide evidence of Reflective Learner, Self Manager and Independent Enquirer.

Just checking

* Carry out a risk assessment for three sport and active leisure activities.

* What is the term used when a person doesn't carry out a risk assessment prior to an activity or doesn't supervise participants appropriately?

* What are the three main laws that a person working in the sport and active leisure industry needs to know?

* What does a higher duty of care mean?

Starting Point

* What are the different ways in which you could support a sport and active leisure activity?

* Have you ever supported this type of session? If so how?

2.8 Supporting the delivery of activities in sport and active leisure

Many people working in the sport and active leisure industry deliver or assist in the delivery of activity sessions. A number of characteristics need to be taken into consideration when a person is supporting the delivery of an activity session. The key characteristics are shown below.

Communication skills

Good communication skills are vital when working with people. You need to communicate with those supporting the delivery of the session and with the participants. Everyone needs to understand what you are communicating. There are different ways of doing this:

* verbal communication

* non-verbal communication

* demonstrations.

Verbal communication is speaking. Speak clearly and at the right volume so everyone can hear you. Face people you are speaking to so they can hear you and you can check that they are listening. Avoid saying too much and using technical terms that the group may not understand. You should communicate encouragement and positive reinforcement to participants so that they know when they are doing well. Also consider the **tone** of your voice – for example, if you are trying to encourage people to do well your tone should reflect that.

JARGON BUSTER

Tone The pitch, level and sound of your voice, which can be used to express how you are feeling.

Non-verbal communication is using other ways of communicating rather than speaking. In some sports halls or swimming pools it may be difficult for others to hear you, so non-verbal communication is essential. Examples of non-verbal communication include hand signals, gestures, facial expressions and demonstrations.

Over to you

Watch a sport or active leisure activity either live or on television. Observe the players and the coach and note the different methods of non-verbal communication used.

Sports coaches and managers often use hand signals and gestures to communicate.

Demonstrations allow participants to see the correct way in which a skill or technique should be performed. Demonstrations should be simple and performed correctly, so participants do not learn incorrect techniques.

Mentoring

This involves one person helping another, less experienced person to develop and achieve success. During the delivery of a sport and active leisure activity you may be expected to mentor participants to help them to achieve their goals – for example, this may be by providing a participant with teaching points and guidance to help them to complete a volleyball serve correctly.

Delegation

A good method of motivation is to ask a participant who has mastered a skill to demonstrate it to the rest of the group. Or a member of the group could be asked to lead the warm-up, the cool-down or even to run the main activity session. Assigning tasks to other people in this way is called delegation, which means allowing other people to take on some responsibility or carry out a task.

Organisation

Prior to any sport or active leisure activity, it is very important to be organised and make sure that you have everything that you need for the activity ready. For example, if you are organising a sporting activity, you will need to organise the equipment and set it up where required so that it is ready for participants. Check what equipment is available and that you have enough for the group. Check it is safe and working. When the participants have arrived they need to be organised into appropriate groups, such as according to ability, and the groups organised into game-play situations. At the end of the session all the equipment needs to be taken in and checked to ensure it is all in good working order.

Time management

Ensure you manage your time appropriately. Always plan to arrive well in advance of participants for an activity session. This gives you time to get the equipment ready and check the facilities to ensure that they are safe. Make sure that the activity session runs to time so you do not finish early or late.

Contingency plan

A contingency plan is a back-up – a plan to be used when unforeseen circumstances alter your intended course of action.. For example, you may plan to hold a rounders activity session outside. However, if the weather is bad and you can't run the activity outside, you need to have a contingency plan so you could still run an activity with the group, such as indoor volleyball.

Problem solving

During an activity session you may be faced with various problems, which you should try to deal with and resolve as they arise. For example, a piece of equipment may break and you would need to be able to either replace the piece of equipment or adapt the activity so that it can be continued without it.

Ensuring safety of participants

You must be aware of the health and safety of participants at all times – before, during and after the activity. Wherever possible, you should try to prevent accidents from happening in the first place. For example, if you spot that a participant's shoelaces have come undone, you should ask them to do them up before they continue with the activity, or if a drink gets spilt, the spill should be dealt with appropriately to stop participants slipping over if they step in it.

Over to you

If you were running an activity session in a school, what do you think would be the problems with the session finishing early or late?

Case study: Gareth and Susan's activity

Gareth and Susan are working together to deliver a ball skills activity to a group of 20 children aged eight and nine. Gareth arrives for the session at the same time as the children. Susan has tried to get all the equipment ready but has not been able to set up all the cones. The children mess about and become restless as Gareth and Susan finish setting up. Gareth tries to get the group organised for their warm-up but finds it hard to verbally communicate with the children as they are being noisy. When they come to the skills section, Susan has one child demonstrate with her how to pass the ball. During the practice session a child falls over and cuts her knee on a large stone on the rugby pitch. Gareth has a first aid kit and attends to her.

Half-way through the session it starts to rain hard and the children become very cold and wet. Gareth and Susan decide to finish the session early and wait in the changing rooms with the children for 20 minutes until the children's parents arrive to collect them.

1 Do you think that this was a successful activity session?
2 What were the problems at the start of the session? How could these have been resolved or avoided?
3 Do you think Gareth and Susan paid enough attention to the health and safety of the children?
4 Why did the session finish early? What could Gareth and Susan have done to prevent this?

Personal, Learning and Thinking Skills

This activity will help to provide evidence of Creative Thinker, Independent Enquirer and Reflective Learner.

Just checking

✴ Why are good communication skills required when supporting the delivery of a sport and active leisure activity?

✴ What are the different methods of communication? Give examples of when each can be used.

✴ What is a contingency plan?

Starting Point

* What activity sessions have you taken part in that went well?
* Why did you enjoy these sessions?
* Did the other participants enjoy the sessions?

2.9 Reviewing the effectiveness of encouraging participation in sport and active leisure

Once an activity session has been completed, you should review what has been done so you can consider what did and did not go well. This process of reviewing sessions allows you to improve your skills and any future activity sessions.

The assessment process

To discover the effectiveness of an activity session you need to carry out a review reflecting on how you thought the session went, and gain feedback from participants. To help you with your review, you should ensure you complete a review of the activity session that you helped to plan and lead, as well as assessing other activity sessions in which you are a participant, so that you understand what type of session works well for different people in different sectors of sport and active leisure. The assessment process requires an evaluation of the strengths and weaknesses of the activity session and a review of the leadership skills used in the session. Other factors to consider are:

* Was enough planning carried out prior to the event?

* How good was the organisation of the activity?

* How appropriate was the activity for the participants?

* Were there any health and safety concerns?

* Were the aims and objectives of the activity session met?

You need to carry out a **self-evaluation** exploring your own thoughts and feelings after the activity session, also taking into account the thoughts of the participants.

You will therefore need to gain participant feedback. To get feedback you could ask participants questions at the end of the session, such as:

* Did you enjoy the session?

* Which parts did you enjoy most and why?

* Which parts were you not so keen on and why?

You could also provide an anonymous questionnaire for participants to complete at the end of the session. This might allow them to provide more honest feedback.

Another method of assessing the activity session and your leadership skills would be to video the session. You can then review the tape and see how you communicated with the participants, how they responded to you and if they enjoyed themselves.

JARGON BUSTER

Self-evaluation Thinking about what you have done well and the areas that you need to improve.

Different sectors in sport and active leisure

Sport and active leisure covers the following sectors:

* sport and recreation
* health and fitness
* play work
* youth work
* the outdoors
* caravanning
* stewarding (spectator safety).

Each of these sectors is involved in some way in encouraging participation in sport and active leisure. Each has different types of participants. Activity sessions need to be tailored to meet their needs and interests so that they will continue to regularly take part.

Improvements

To help you explore the provision of sport and active leisure activities in your local area and ways in which this provision can be improved you can carry out research into the different types of activity sessions that are offered by each sector within the sport and active leisure industry. For example, you could look at class timetables or activity diaries that list the different types of activities offered and the age and ability levels that they are aimed at.

Personal, Learning and Thinking Skills

This activity will help to provide evidence of Independent Enquirer and Reflective Learner.

Over to you

List examples of activity sessions you think are appropriate for participants in the following sport and active leisure sectors:

* sport and recreation
* health and fitness
* play work
* youth work
* the outdoors
* caravanning.

Describe why you think each activity is appropriate for participants in the sector.

Functional Skills

This activity will help to provide evidence of English speaking and listening.

Personal, Learning and Thinking Skills

This activity will help to provide evidence of Independent Enquirer, Effective Participator, Self Manager and Reflective Learner.

Over to you

* Participate in or observe two activity sessions in two different sectors in the sport and active leisure industry.
* Once you have completed a session, ask other participants or parents of participants how they thought it went.
* Write a report explaining how the activity session could be improved. Cover planning, delivery skills, content, resources and health and safety in your report.

Just checking

* Why is it important to carry out a review of activity sessions once they are completed?
* Outline five different methods of giving feedback and explain how each could assist in writing a review of an activity session.

Case Study: Maria, Youth Worker at a summer activity sheme

Maria works in a sports centre and organises an activity scheme for children in the summer holidays. She has colleagues and volunteers who help with planning and leading the activities and holds regular meetings with them to ensure that they have carried out enough planning to make the scheme a success. She is aware that different types of leadership are important and has discussed this with her team, suggesting different ways of leading and encouraging the children. They have decided to give out certificates and medals at the end of each day to reward effort and achievement.

So far, Maria and her team have decided on obstacle courses, trampolining and some gym skills for the activity sessions for children aged between five and eight. For children aged between nine and 12 there will be some field and track athletics with rounders and tennis, and for those aged between 13 and 15 there will be football and trampolining activities. They have completed a full risk assessment for each activity. They have produced posters to advertise the event and put them up inside the sports centre.

1 What do you think Maria is doing well in the planning phase of this summer activity scheme?

2 Do you think the choices of activities are appropriate for each age group? Explain your answer.

3 Why do you think putting posters in the sports centre is a good way to advertise the summer activity scheme?

4 What other methods of advertising could Maria use to make people aware of this activity scheme?

5 Are sport and active leisure centres running similar holiday activity schemes in your area? If so, compare their scheme to this one and discuss their strengths and weaknesses.

For your project

This unit explores ways in which you can plan and assist in the delivery of an activity session. You examine what types of activities appeal to different groups of people and how you can try to cater to their likes and dislikes. You study methods of advertising an activity session and how to manage risks associated with activity sessions. You are aware from Unit 1 that the British public need to take part in more sport and active leisure activities, and now know of ways to encourage regular participation.

The following diagram gives some ideas for what you might decide to do your project on, based on the content of this unit.

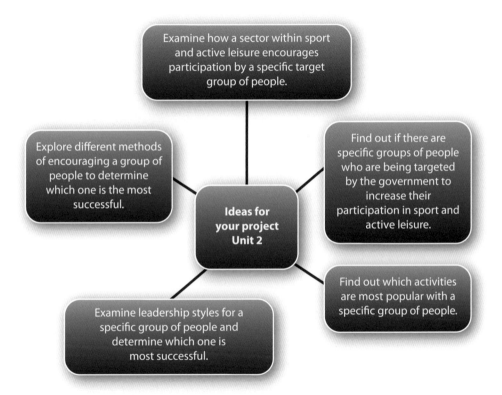

Examine how a sector within sport and active leisure encourages participation by a specific target group of people.

Explore different methods of encouraging a group of people to determine which one is the most successful.

Find out if there are specific groups of people who are being targeted by the government to increase their participation in sport and active leisure.

Ideas for your project Unit 2

Examine leadership styles for a specific group of people and determine which one is most successful.

Find out which activities are most popular with a specific group of people.

Possible project titles

* Is the autocratic method of leadership better for leading children's activities than the democratic leadership method?

* What are the best methods of advertising an activity session to a group of senior citizens?

* What is the best method to use to encourage participation in sport and active leisure in male teenagers aged 14-16?

* How can the health and fitness sector improve their activity timetable to cater for obese people?

Assessment guidance

This unit is assessed by one internally-set assignment. You will have a period of 12 hours to generate evidence for your assessment. In your assessment you will need to show that you know:

* the benefits of increased, regular participation in sport and active leisure for individuals and society

* the impact of using different leadership styles in delivering sport and active leisure activity sessions and the importance of motivating participants

* how to work and collaborate with other people to plan activities

* different methods that can be used to promote activities

* how to organise time and resources for an activity session

* how to resolve or avoid conflict with participants during a sport and active leisure activity

* how to identify what a hazard is, any associated risks with each hazard identified, and the likelihood of the risk happening

* about precautions that can be taken to reduce or eliminate the risks for a planned activity

* how to provide constructive support to others who are helping to deliver the activity session

* how to use appropriate communication skills so that the participants are able to understand you

* how to demonstrate or use others for effective demonstrations during the activity session

* how to assess the strengths and weaknesses of sport and active leisure activities in different sectors and how the activities could be improved.

Time management

* Although you have 12 hours to generate evidence for this assignment, this time frame does not include time spent researching the topic area or setting up equipment for your activity session.

* The internal assessment will be split into different tasks. You will be given set times to generate evidence for each task whilst being supervised by your tutor or employer.

* Your teacher may well give you ideas for resources to use to help you carry out research before you attempt the task. You should aim to make time to read this information and carry out research for the set task so that you have a good understanding of the subject area.

* Your teacher may give you practice assessments that are similar to the actual task. You should make time to complete these 'trial' assessments as these will help to prepare you for the 'real' task. Your teacher will be able to give you feedback on the areas that you have completed well and areas for improvement.

Useful links

Work experience within the sport and active leisure industry will enable you to talk to members of staff who have an understanding of different methods used to try and encourage participation in sport and active leisure. Members of staff may well lead activity sessions, so you will be able to ask them about different leadership styles and may be able to observe them leading a sport and active leisure activity. This will help provide you with ideas for when you are supporting the delivery of a sport and active leisure activity.

Some television programmes look at different aspects of participation in sport and active leisure. These may range from serious documentaries such as *Panorama* to reality TV programmes examining how well celebrities or members of the public can maintain an exercise programme.

There are lots of useful websites that will help you with your research for this unit. For details of how to access these sites see the **Hotlinks** section – **Introduction**, page xi.

How you will be assessed

For your Unit 2 assessment, you need to make sure that you can meet all of the assessment criteria for the six learning outcomes, as shown in the table below.

Learning outcome	Assessment criteria
LO1: Know the benefits of participation in sport and active leisure to individuals and society	**1** Identify the benefits to individuals and society of increased, regular participation in sport and active leisure.
LO2: Understand how leaders in sport and active leisure encourage participation	**1** Assess the likely impact of using different leadership styles on active participation. **2** Explain the importance of being motivational when encouraging active participation.
LO3: Be able to plan sport and active leisure participation activities	**1** Collaborate with others to plan activities. **2** Generate ideas for activities and media to promote them. **3** Organise time and resources for activities. **4** Propose practical ways of avoiding or resolving conflict with participants during activities.
LO4: Know how risks are managed in sport and active leisure	**1** Identify hazards, associated risks and the likelihood of the risks happening for planned activities. **2** Describe precautions to reduce or eliminate risks for planned activities.
LO5: Be able to use leadership skills to support the delivery of participation activities in sport and active leisure	**1** Provide constructive support to others in the delivery of group activities. **2** Use communication skills to meet the requirements of participants. **3** Demonstrate or use others to demonstrate components of activities.
LO6: Understand the effectiveness of sport and active leisure activities in encouraging participation	**1** Assess the strengths and weaknesses of sport and active leisure activities in different sectors. **2** Explain how sport and active leisure activities could be improved.

Introduction

Science and technology have a huge impact on sporting performances. Athletes can now run faster, jump higher and strike balls further than ever before. In this unit you will learn how science has helped to improve sporting skills and abilities. The first part of the unit explores the body systems and how knowledge of these systems has improved sports technology. You will then learn how to use physical tests to measure the performance of an individual, and be able to apply your knowledge of the human body to explain how the individual can try to improve their future performance.

What will you learn?

In this unit you will cover the following learning outcomes:

LO1: Know the basic principles of anatomy and physiology
LO2: Understand how principles of anatomy and physiology are applied in sport and active leisure
LO3: Know about the mechanics of movement
LO4: Understand how the mechanics of movement are applied in sport and active leisure
LO5: Understand the relationship between science, technology and sport and active leisure
LO6: Be able to use physical tests in sport and active leisure
LO7: Be able to review performance in sport and active leisure

The following table shows how these seven learning outcomes are covered by this unit.

Topic	Pages	Learning outcomes
3.1 The skeletal system	62–65	LO1
3.2 The muscular system	66–67	LO1
3.3 The cardiovascular system	68–69	LO1
3.4 The respiratory system	70–71	LO1
3.5 Applying the principles of **anatomy** and **physiology**	72–75	LO2
3.6 The mechanics of movement	76–81	LO3
3.7 Applying the **mechanics of movement**	82–85	LO4
3.8 The relationship between science, technology and sport and active leisure	86–89	LO5
3.9 Using physical tests	90–96	LO6
3.10 Reviewing performance	97	LO7

THINKING POINTS

* Why do you think it is important for people working in sport and active leisure to have some knowledge and understanding of the structure and function of the human body?

* How do you think people can improve their performance in sport and active leisure activities?

Functional Skills

Personal, Learning and Thinking Skills

This unit offers various opportunities to develop functional skills and personal, learning, and thinking skills. Where appropriate, different activities are signposted with the relevant skills that you can develop.

Diploma Daily

Super new space-age swimwear

At the International Swimming Games, the swimmers picking up the gold medals are all wearing custom-made 'NASA' swimsuits. The new space-age swimsuit has helped athletes smash swimming world records. The all-in-one body suit uses materials produced by NASA to help swimmers power through the water faster than ever before, and has helped take swimming up to a new level.

1 Do you think swimmers who wear this new swimsuit are cheating?

2 Why do you think sports clothing and equipment manufacturers spend so much money on helping athletes improve their performance?

3 What sorts of technology are you aware of that help sports players to improve their performance?

How you will be assessed

This unit will be assessed by one main assignment. You will need to carry out an appropriate fitness test and a test to measure movement on a sport or active leisure participant, so that you are able to draw conclusions about their performance. This information will then allow you to explain to the participant how they can improve their performance and provide them with ideas for new or improved sport or active leisure products or services. In your assessment you will need to provide the following information:

✳ A plan for carrying out a fitness test and a test to measure movement on a sport or active leisure participant. The plan will need to identify the test that you plan to use, the equipment required for the test and the time needed for the testing to be carried out.

✳ A completed observation record from your tutor or supervisor, as evidence of the process of you carrying out a fitness test and mechanics of movement test on a sport or active leisure participant.

✳ Evidence to show how the participant's performance in sport or active leisure could be improved.

✳ Ideas for new or improved sport or active leisure products or services.

Unit links

This unit links to Level 2, Unit 1: Positive lifestyle choices and sport and active leisure, in relation to how participation in sport and active leisure can have a beneficial effect on different body systems.

JARGON BUSTER

Anatomy To do with the structure of the body.

Physiology The physical and chemical processes involved in the functioning of the body.

Mechanics of movement The study of how a sports performer carries out different movements.

Case study: Anna's fitness

Anna is 15 years old and plays football for a club team. She hopes to play professionally one day. She has recently been told that she will need to increase her fitness levels to help improve her football performance. She knows that she needs to quicken her pace when sprinting to get the ball, and her overall stamina could also be improved.

1 What sorts of fitness tests could Anna take in order to test her current fitness levels?

2 Why do sports players take part in fitness tests?

Starting Point

* What is the function of your skeleton?
* What would you look like if you didn't have a skeleton?

Personal, Learning and Thinking Skills

This activity will help to provide evidence of Creative Thinker and Team Worker.

Over to you

In pairs, write each of the following names of bones onto sticky labels:

humerus, radius, ulna, femur, patella, tibia, fibula, vertebral column, sternum, cranium, ribs, clavicle, pelvis, scapula.

With one of your pair acting as the 'model', decide where each bone is located and stick it in the correct place. Close your textbook while you are deciding where to stick the labels. Now check your placements against the diagram of the skeleton (right). How many you have placed correctly?

3.1 The skeletal system

In this topic you will learn about the structure of the skeleton, including the main bones, the different classifications and types of joint, and the movements available at each. The function of the skeletal system will also be explored.

Major bones in the skeleton

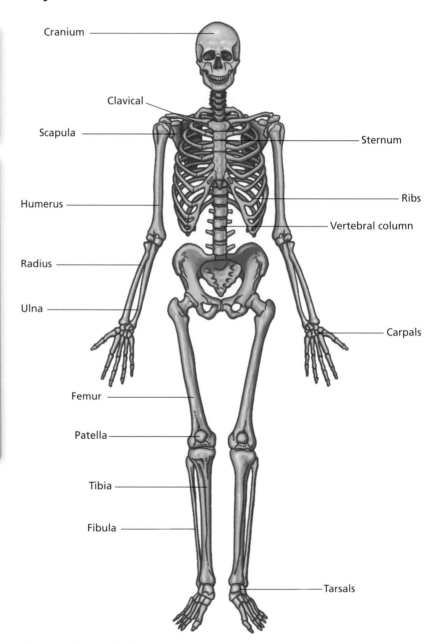

The major bones in the skeleton.

The diagram opposite shows the names and locations of the major bones in the skeleton that you need to know.

The vertebral column is made up of five different areas:

* cervical – neck to shoulders

* thoracic – chest area

* lumbar – lower back

* sacrum – pelvis

* coccyx – bottom of the vertebral column.

The vertebral column is in an S-shape. This provides the body with maximum support, which helps you to walk in an upright position.

Each bone in your skeleton can be placed into a different category based on shape. The table below describes each category and provides examples of where you can find them in your skeleton.

Lateral (side) Spinal Column

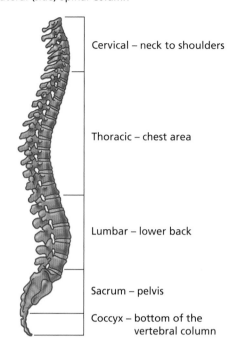

Cervical – neck to shoulders

Thoracic – chest area

Lumbar – lower back

Sacrum – pelvis

Coccyx – bottom of the vertebral column

The five sections of the vertebral column.

Type of bone	Description	Example
Long	These bones have a greater length than width.	Femur
Short	These bones are small and usually have a similar length and width.	Carpals
Flat	These bones have flat surfaces and provide protection for the body's internal organs.	Pelvis
Irregular	These bones have varying shapes.	Vertebrae
Sesamoid	This type of bone is found embedded in a tendon.	Patella (in a tendon)

Functions of the skeletal system

The skeleton has five main functions:

1 **Shape:** Your skeleton provides you with a frame within which body organs are placed and upon which muscles attach, and gives you your shape.

2 **Movement:** Muscles attach to the bones in the skeleton and pull on them to produce movement.

3 **Protection:** Bones are strong structures protecting your delicate internal organs, for example the vertebral column surrounds and protects your spinal cord.

4 **Blood production:** Some of the bones in your skeleton contain red bone marrow, which produces blood cells.

5 **Mineral storage:** Bones are strong and hard because of the minerals stored within them – mainly calcium and phosphorous. If your diet lacks minerals, your bones start to release their stores. This makes them weak and more likely to break.

Joints

There are three classifications of **joint**, based on the amount of movement that they allow.

1   **Fixed:** Where two bones have fused together and there is no movement. This type of joint can be found in the cranium.

2   **Slightly moveable:** Allow a little very limited movement. Found between the vertebrae in the vertebral column.

3   **Freely moveable** (also known as 'synovial joints'): Allow a wide range of movement. There are six types of freely moveable joint and their movements are determined by the shape of the joint.

The six types of freely movable joint

Freely moveable joint	Type of movements permitted	Example in the body
Hinge	Flexion and extension (bending and straightening)	Elbow, knee
Ball and socket	Abduction and adduction (moving away from and towards the body) Circumduction and rotation (performing a circular movement and turning inwards and outwards)	Shoulder, hip
Pivot	Rotation (as in shaking your head to indicate 'No')	Neck

Condyloid 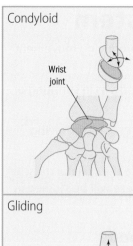	Abduction and adduction (moving away from and towards the body) Flexion and extension (bending and straightening)	Wrist 
Gliding 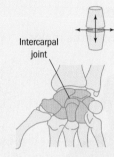	Limited sliding or gliding movements in all directions	Carpals 
Saddle 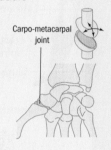	Abduction and adduction (moving away from and towards the body) Flexion and extension (bending and straightening)	Thumb 

Just checking

* What are the main functions of the skeleton?
* Describe the different types of bone.
* Explain the different types of joint.
* Give an example of how the joints shown in this table can be involved in sporting movements. One row has been completed for you.

Name of joint	Describe the type of movement	Sporting movement
Ball and socket	Performing a circular movement turning inwards and outwards – Circumduction	Overarm tennis serve
Hinge		
Saddle		
Condyloid		
Gliding		
Pivot		

3.2 The muscular system

The muscular system is mainly concerned with producing movement of two types:

* **external movement** where you move your body, as in sprinting or kicking a football
* **internal movement** such as your heart beating or food moving through your digestive system.

In sports, the main muscles that are examined are the skeletal muscles, which are used to produce body movements. These will be studied in more detail in this topic.

The major muscles in the human body

The diagram below shows the names and locations of the major muscles in the body that you need to know about.

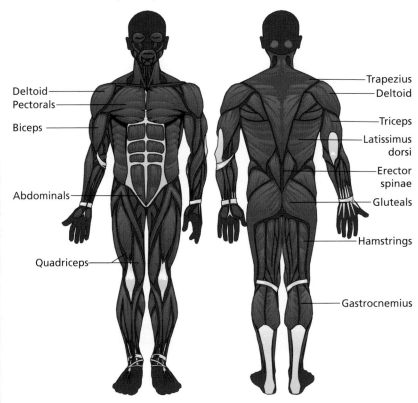

The major muscles in the human body.

Functions of the muscular system

There are two main functions of the muscular system: movement and posture.

Movement

Muscles produce movement as they are attached to the bones of your skeleton by **tendons**. They produce a pulling action to move the bone.

Muscles can only 'pull' on a bone; they cannot push it back to its original position. In order for your body to produce movements, muscles have to work in pairs, which are called **antagonistic muscle pairs**. As one muscle **contracts** the other relaxes. This means that one muscle pulls the bone in one direction and its partner pulls the bone back to its original position.

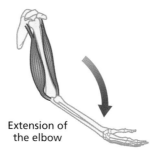

Flexion of the elbow

Extension of the elbow

The biceps and triceps muscles in your arms work as an antagonistic pair.

JARGON BUSTER

Tendon Attaches muscles to bones.

Antagonistic muscle pair Muscles that work in partnership to produce movement.

Contract When a muscle contracts it produces a force (and usually gets shorter) in order to give movement.

Over to you

Carry out each of the exercise movements shown below to help you understand and feel how muscles work in antagonistic muscle pairs. Now complete the table; one row has already been filled in.

Type of movement	Muscles in antagonistic pair that produces the movement	Partner muscle that relaxes
Bending your elbow	Biceps	Triceps
Straightening your elbow		
Bending your knee		
Straightening your knee		
Upwards phase of a sit up		
Upwards phase of a bench press		
Moving arms backwards for a chest stretch		

Functional Skills

This activity will help to provide evidence of English speaking and listening.

Personal, Learning and Thinking Skills

This activity will help to provide evidence of Team Worker, Creative Thinker and Self Manager.

Posture

You have probably heard the term 'posture' before in relation to whether a person has a good or a bad posture. Posture describes the way you stand and hold your body. Many people adopt a slouched body posture with shoulders forward, stomach relaxed and the upper back arched. Bad posture is not good for your appearance and can result in health complications, including back pain, migraines and an increased risk of a slipped disc.

A good posture is where the muscles in the shoulders are working to pull them back, the erector spinae muscles in the back are working to keep it straight and the head is looking forwards. The abdominal muscles are also used when standing and sitting to help support the spine and keep it straight. (See page 7 in Unit 1 for photos showing examples of good and bad posture.)

Just checking

* Think about a sporting movement of your choice and work out which muscles are being used to produce the movement.

* Explain why muscles have to work in antagonistic muscle pairs.

* What kind of exercises do you think a person could do in order to help to improve their posture? Explain your answer.

3.3 The respiratory system

Oxygen is essential for your body to stay alive. The respiratory system is responsible for getting oxygen into your body. In this section you will learn about the structure of the respiratory system and understand how it carries out this essential function.

Structure of the respiratory system

The respiratory system consists of airways that take air into your body, your lungs and the muscles that help you to breathe air in and out.

You take in food and air through your mouth but they need to go down different 'tubes' – food goes down your oesophagus to your stomach and air goes down your trachea to your lungs. To ensure food and air go down the correct tubes you have an epiglottis. This is made of **cartilage** and seals over the trachea (windpipe) when you are swallowing so that food does not go down it. You may well have experienced food 'going down the wrong way' – you will have had to cough to clear your airway.

Your trachea (or windpipe) has horseshoe-shaped pieces of cartilage to keep it open – you can feel these as bumps if you carefully run your fingers up and down your throat. The trachea then splits into two tubes called bronchi and these divide further into lots of smaller branches called bronchioles. The bronchioles lead to tiny air sacs called alveoli. The alveoli are surrounded by small blood vessels called capillaries.

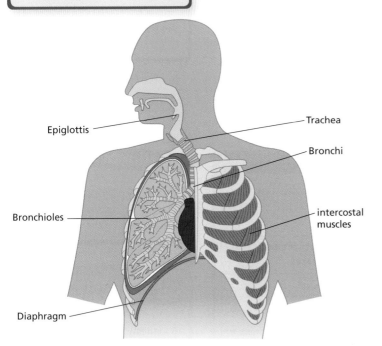

Epiglottis

Trachea

Bronchi

Bronchioles

intercostal muscles

Diaphragm

The respiratory system.

JARGON BUSTER

Cartilage Tough elastic tissue.

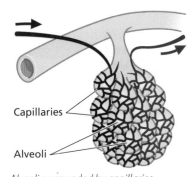

Capillaries

Alveoli

Alveoli surrounded by capillaries.

Functions of the respiratory system

Gaseous exchange and breathing are two key functions carried out by the respiratory system.

Gaseous exchange

A process called gaseous exchange takes place in the alveoli. Oxygen from the air you breathe in passes from the alveoli, through the capillaries and into your bloodstream. Your blood also transports carbon dioxide through the capillaries and into the alveoli to be breathed out. This process is called 'gaseous exchange' because oxygen and carbon dioxide are gases, and it is as if one is exchanged (or swapped) for the other.

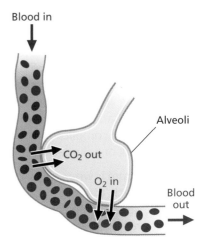

Blood in

Alveoli

CO_2 out

O_2 in

Blood out

This diagram shows oxygen entering the bloodstream and carbon dioxide leaving it.

Breathing

In order to breathe in and out you use two main types of muscles – the diaphragm and the intercostal muscles.

* **The diaphragm** is found underneath your lungs and is a large sheet of muscle. At rest it is slightly dome-shaped, but when you breathe in (inspiration) the diaphragm flattens and moves down.

* **Intercostal muscles** attach between the ribs. When you breathe in (expiration), they contract and push the ribs upwards and outwards. When you breathe out, the muscles relax and return the ribcage downwards and inwards.

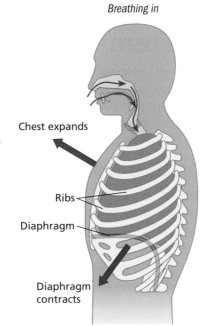

Breathing in

Chest expands

Ribs

Diaphragm

Diaphragm contracts

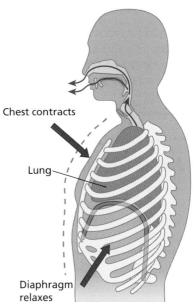

Breathing out

Chest contracts

Lung

Diaphragm relaxes

Inspiration (breathing in):

* diaphragm moves downwards
* intercostal muscles expand
* ribs move up and out
* increase in size of your chest cavity
* air is forced into the lungs

Expiration (breathing out) :

* diaphragm moves upwards
* intercostal muscles relax
* ribs move down and in
* decrease in size of your chest cavity
* air forced out of the lungs

Personal, Learning and Thinking Skills

This activity will help to provide evidence of Creative Thinker and Reflective Learner.

Over to you

Make your own model of the lungs. You will need two balloons, an empty drinks bottle, a hard straw, Blu-Tack®, Sellotape® and a pair of scissors.

1 Carefully cut off the bottom quarter of your drinks bottle.

2 Make a small hole through the lid of your bottle, insert the straw through the hole and secure with Blu-Tack®.

3 Place one of the balloons around the bottom part of the straw and secure with sellotape®.

4 Cut your second balloon in half and secure the wider half around the open bottom of the bottle. Secure with sellotape.

5 Pull down on the balloon around the bottom of the bottle and watch the balloon inside inflate; push up on the outer balloon and watch the balloon inside deflate.

Your model should look like this

Explain why the balloon inflates and deflates in this model and how it relates to your own lungs.

Pull down to see the balloon inside inflate; push up to see the balloon deflate

Did you know?

If you have ever eaten spare ribs or a rack of ribs then you were eating intercostal muscles!

Just checking

* In your body what performs the job of the outside balloon in the 'make your own lungs' model?
* What else in the structure of the respiratory system is used to help take air into the lungs?

Starting Point

The heart is always functioning and never takes any time to rest. What would happen if your heart stopped beating?

3.4 The cardiovascular system

The cardiovascular system carries out vital functions in your body, including taking blood loaded with nutrients and oxygen to all parts of the body and taking away waste products such as lactic acid and carbon dioxide. In this topic you will learn about the structure of the cardiovascular system and its various functions.

Structure of the cardiovascular system

The cardiovascular system consists of the heart and the blood vessels through which blood travels. Make a fist with your hand and then take a look at it. This is pretty much the same size as your heart. Your heart is a **hollow** organ, which means blood can travel through it.

JARGON BUSTER

Hollow Having a space or gap – for example, a straw is hollow as it has a gap for drinks to be sucked up through it.

The heart is divided into a left- and a right-hand side and consists of four hollow compartments called chambers. Each chamber has a name determined by the side of the body on which it is found and whether it is at the top or the bottom of the heart. The four chambers are:

* Left atrium – top
* Right atrium – top
* Left ventricle – bottom
* Right ventricle – bottom

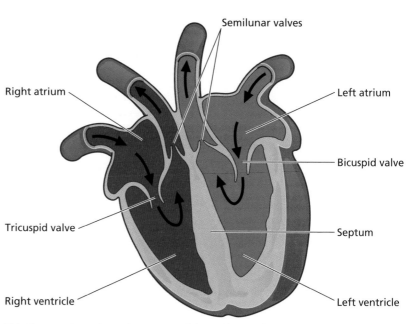

This diagram shows the main structure of the cardiovascular system.

Blood flows from the top chambers to the lower chambers through one-way valves, which stop blood flowing in the wrong direction. These valves are called the bicuspid and tricuspid valves. The bicuspid valve is found between the left atrium and left ventricle and the tricuspid valve is found between the right atrium and right ventricle.

As the heart contracts the ventricles squeeze blood out of it through semilunar valves. These are one-way valves that stop blood from flowing back into the heart.

TOP TIP

To help you remember which valve is placed where, remember that tricuspid has an **r** in the name and is found on the **r**ight-hand side of the heart.

Function of the cardiovascular system

The main functions of the cardiovascular system are:

✳ to transport oxygen and nutrients around the body

✳ to remove waste products, such as carbon dioxide.

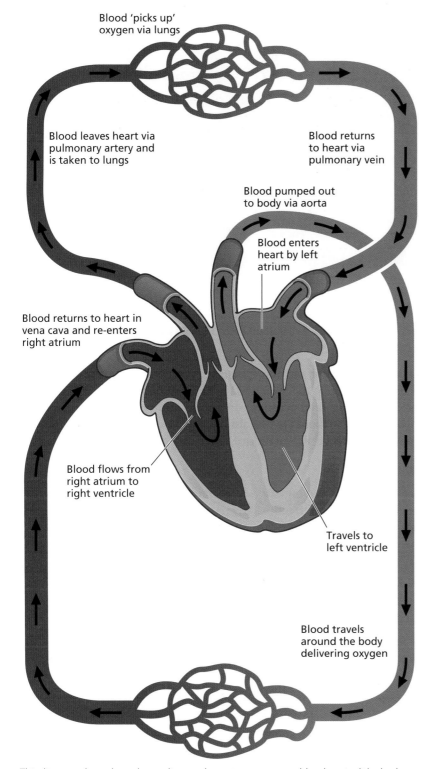

Blood 'picks up' oxygen via lungs

Blood leaves heart via pulmonary artery and is taken to lungs

Blood returns to heart via pulmonary vein

Blood pumped out to body via aorta

Blood enters heart by left atrium

Blood returns to heart in vena cava and re-enters right atrium

Blood flows from right atrium to right ventricle

Travels to left ventricle

Blood travels around the body delivering oxygen

This diagram shows how the cardiovascular system transports blood around the body and to the lungs.

Starting Point

* Why do some people get injured whilst taking part in sport or active leisure?
* How has technology improved safety in sport?

3.5 Applying the principles of anatomy and physiology

Knowing the structure and function of body systems has helped to improve understanding of many sports-related matters, including ways in which you can improve safety for sports participation and increase a person's fitness in order to advance their sporting performance.

Knowing more about body systems can help to make sport safer and prevent injuries like this.

Safe and effective participation in sport and active leisure

Taking part in sport and active leisure means that you place stresses on your body, such as lunging to hit a squash ball or making a rugby tackle. This stress and possible contact with other players can result in injury. However, there are precautions that you can take based upon a knowledge of anatomy to reduce the risk of injury.

Warm-up

Before taking part in any sport or exercise activity it is necessary to perform a warm-up to reduce the risk of getting injured. If the body is not warmed up it is more prone to injury – for example, when muscles are cold they are less **pliable** and more likely to tear when stretching.

The warm-up should incorporate movements that will be carried out in the main activity, to help the body prepare. A warm-up consists of a mobiliser activity, a pulse-raiser and a stretch to help prepare the body for exercise:

* **Mobiliser activity** – the first phase of a warm-up, where joints are taken through their range of movement. This increases the **lubricating fluid** (synovial fluid) in the joints and helps them to move more easily.

* **Pulse-raiser** – an activity designed to quicken the heart rate, which increases the rate of blood flow to the muscles and helps to warm them up.

* **Stretch** – the main muscles required for the activity ahead are stretched so that they are ready for the activity and are less likely to tear.

Cool-down

A cool-down after an activity helps the body recover and reduces the risk of injury. A cool-down consists of a pulse-lowerer and a stretch:

✱ **Pulse-lowerer** – gives a gradual decrease in your activity level, such as jogging at a slower pace down to a fast walk. It helps to remove any **lactic acid** produced in the activity, as lactic acid can cause muscle stiffness the next day. The pulse-lowerer is gradual so that the cardiovascular system can slowly return to normal. If you suddenly stopped exercising, there would be a sudden reduction in the rate of blood flow back to your heart. This could mean not enough blood getting to your brain and you could faint.

✱ **Stretch** – you should stretch the muscles involved in the activity session you have just finished to help them relax and get back their normal range of movement.

Fitness testing

Fitness tests are designed to work out how well your body systems are functioning. For example, flexibility tests measure the range of movement available at a joint – the more flexible you are naturally, the better suited you are to sports and activities that require flexibility, such as gymnastics or yoga. Also, if a fitness test shows that you have low levels of a particular area of fitness then training programmes can be designed to help you improve in this area.

Aerobic fitness tests

Aerobic fitness tests measure how well you take in and use oxygen. They examine the respiratory and cardiovascular systems. Oxygen is taken into the body, transported by the blood and used by the muscles, and aerobic fitness tests examine all three of these processes. Examples of aerobic fitness tests include:

✱ multi-stage fitness test (bleep test)

✱ Cooper 12-minute run

✱ Harvard step test

Strength tests

Strength tests measure the amount of force your muscles can produce. They examine the muscular system. Examples of strength tests include:

✱ 1 rep max

✱ hand grip dynamometer test

Flexibility tests

These tests measure the range of movement around your joints. They examine the muscular and skeletal systems. Examples of flexibility tests include:

✱ sit and reach

✱ calf stretch

✱ shoulder stretch

JARGON BUSTER

Lactic acid A chemical produced in the body when a person does anaerobic exercise (exercise without oxygen).

Personal, Learning and Thinking Skills

This activity will help to provide evidence of Creative Thinker and Independent Enquirer.

Over to you

Design a cool-down for a sport or active leisure activity of your choice.

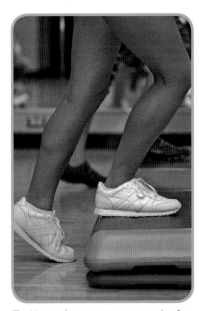

The Harvard step test is an example of an aerobic fitness test.

A good coach helps an athlete to improve technique, maximise performance and limit the risk of injury.

Muscular endurance tests

These tests measure how long a group of your muscles can continue to exercise. They examine the muscular and cardiovascular systems. The cardiovascular system delivers oxygen and nutrients to your muscles to keep them exercising. Examples of these tests include:

* 1 minute sit-up test

* 1 minute press-up test

Fitness testing will be explored in more detail in Topic 3.9 of this unit, where you will have the opportunity to carry out your own physical tests.

The coach

A coach plays a key role in improving an athlete's performance. Coaches need a good knowledge of the skills and techniques required for the sport, as well as the anatomy and physiology of the human body, to help maximise performance.

Improved coaching techniques

Injury can occur from incorrectly performing a sport or active leisure technique. Poor technique can cause immediate injuries, such as an incorrect starting position causing someone to overbalance and fracture a bone, or result in injuries over time, such as an incorrect grip on a racket causing someone to develop a strained shoulder.

A coach has a number of different methods available to assess a person's technique. Most of these will examine the mechanics of movement, which is explored further on in this unit. An athlete may be limited by the strength of some muscles or the speed at which they can move a body part. A knowledge of anatomy and physiology helps a coach to devise training sessions and programmes to help improve a sportsperson's performance and reduce their risk of injury.

Case study: Training for a marathon

Sean is 17 years old and is a cross country runner.
He has to run long distances in competition and in training in order to help to build up his aerobic fitness and muscular endurance. The furthest distance that he has run is a half marathon, which is 13 miles. However, he has now set his sights on running a full marathon. His coach will need to adapt his training programme so that his body will be ready to complete a full marathon distance. However, if the training programme is too intense, Sean will be at a greater risk of getting an overuse injury such as shin splints. The programme will have to include a gradual increase in training duration and intensity in order to help his body adapt and be able to complete the full marathon distance. The coach is also planning to carry out regular fitness tests so that they can determine how well the training programme is working.

1 What sorts of fitness tests do you think the coach will use and why?

2 How will Sean's body adapt to training?

Overtraining

Coaches know that if an athlete does not include sufficient rest periods in their training programme they will be at risk of overtraining – where an athlete does not give their body time to recover properly from training. Athletes who overtrain will not increase their fitness levels and may even find that their performance decreases. They are also more prone to overuse injuries such as shin splints or repetitive strain injuries. Most coaches will insist that athletes have at least one 'rest day' a week where no training is scheduled.

The development, design and testing of products and services

There are a huge range of products and services available that take into account the principles of anatomy and physiology to help improve sport and active leisure performance.

Equipment

Different types of equipment are available to help improve performance and safety for sport and active leisure participants. For example, there is now a huge range of shoes available for many different sports and active leisure pursuits. They are all designed to reduce the risk of injury and maximise performance for the chosen activity. For example:

* Running shoes are designed to reduce the risk of stress injuries to runners' bodies. Stress injuries to the skeletal system, such as shin splints and stress fractures, are caused by the continued strain from the impact of planting one foot in front of the other. Running shoes contain lots of cushioning to help absorb some of this impact.

* Outdoor walking shoes are designed to increase grip and reduce the risk of injury, such as a person slipping whilst out rambling. They are also made out of a range of materials to ensure they are suited to all of the different environments a walker will come across.

Sports clothing is designed for participation in specific sports. For example, waterproof clothing, using water resistant materials such as GORE-TEX®, is used in running and mountain walking.

Fitness training Equipment

Fitness training equipment helps to train and improve selected areas of fitness related to the different body systems. For example, you could run on a treadmill to improve cardiovascular, respiratory and muscular endurance fitness. New technology helps athletes train to their highest levels and ensures that training meets their requirements. The range of products and services available is huge and will be studied in more detail in Topic 3.8.

Design and testing

A product or service will be specifically designed to carry out a certain role and do a number of different things. For example, one of the things running shoes are designed to do is to cushion the feet from impact. To determine if a product or service fulfils the role that it has been produced for, practical tests will be carried out – for example, running shoes will be tested to see how well they cushion impact.

Functional Skills

This activity will help to provide evidence of ICT.

Personal, Learning and Thinking Skills

This activity will help to provide evidence of Independent Enquirer and Self Manager.

Over to you

Carry out research on sport and active leisure shoes for your particular area of interest. There are lots of useful websites that will help you with this – for details see the **Hotlinks** section – **Introduction**, page xi. Select three shoes that would be appropriate for your area of interest and explain why they meet your requirements.

Just checking

* Why is it necessary to warm up and cool down before and after an exercise or sports session?

* What is the purpose of fitness testing?

* How has knowledge of anatomy and physiology improved the range of products and services available for people who take part in sport and active leisure?

Starting Point

* Why do you think it is important to examine how athletes move?
* How do you think performance can be improved by changing the movement patterns of sport and active leisure participants?

JARGON BUSTER

Midline An imaginary line that splits your body into a left-hand and right-hand side.

3.6 The mechanics of movement

The mechanics of movement is the study of how a sports performer carries out different sporting movements. It is designed to improve sporting performance. You will learn the basics of the mechanics of movement, including the scientific terminology for different types of movement and the principles of mechanics.

Types of movement

The terms given in the following table are scientific words used to describe the different types of movement that occur at different joints in our body. Learning and using these words will help you to accurately describe exactly which movements a person is performing when you come to analyse the mechanics of sporting movements later on in this unit. All movements occur around a joint so always refer to the joint moving rather than the whole limb. For example, don't say that a person moved their arm, say how they moved their elbow and/or shoulder joint such as they flexed their elbow or abducted their shoulder.

Type of movement (term)	What this means	Example	
Flexion	Bending a joint	Flexing the elbow when you are holding a javelin	
Extension	Straightening a joint	Extending the knee when you are kicking a ball	
Adduction	Movement towards the **midline** of the body	Adducting your shoulders during a lat pull-down	
Abduction	Movement away from the midline of the body	Abducting your hips during the box splits	

Type of movement (term)	What this means	Example
Circumduction	Movement of the shoulder or hip in a circular manner	At your shoulder joint during an overarm tennis serve
Rotation	Movement of the joint inwards or outwards in a circular movement towards or away from the middle of the body	The shoulder joint is rotated inwards when holding the back part of a snooker cue

Principles of the mechanics of movement

The mechanics of movement refers to the study of movement and the factors that can affect it. In sport you study human movement, which is called 'biomechanics'. To get to grips with the basics of movement you need to understand the main principles of mechanics. They can then be applied to human movement.

Velocity

Velocity is the term given to the rate at which a person or thing moves from one place to another, and includes the distance between the start and finish points. The distance between the start and finish points is called displacement. Velocity is measured in metres per second; the shorthand version looks like this: ms^{-1}.

Acceleration

Acceleration is the term used to describe the increase in velocity over a period of time. Acceleration is important in running – competitors try to increase their speed to get to the finish line first. Deceleration is where velocity decreases over a period of time. Acceleration is measured in metres per second per second; the shorthand version looks like this: ms^{-2}.

Case study: Tina's triathlon

Tina regularly takes part in triathlons. A triathlon consists of swimming, cycling and running set distances. She is due to take part in an event with the following elements:

* Swimming course: 1.5 km in length, in a straight line between two buoys.
* Cycling course: six laps of a 5 km road circuit, with the start and finish line in the same position.
* Running course: one lap of a 10 km road circuit, with the start and finish separated by a 200 m straight.

1 What would Tina's displacement be for each of the three events?
2 What would her displacement be for the whole triathlon?

Functional Skills

This activity will help to provide evidence of Maths.

Personal, Learning and Thinking Skills

This activity will help to provide evidence of Independent Enquirer, Team Worker and Effective Participator

Over to you

* Watch a 100 m sprint. You can see examples on YouTube.
* Which athletes seem to accelerate as they get to the finish line and which athletes seem to decelerate?
* If possible, have a go at running 400 m around a running track. In which parts of the 400 m do you accelerate? In which parts do you decelerate?

Over to you

Give a sport or an active leisure example for each of the following ways that force can affect movement:

* changing the direction of a moving object
* making an object move
* stopping a moving object
* changing the shape of an object
* preventing something from moving.

You must use different examples from those listed in the text on the right.

Personal, Learning and Thinking Skills

This activity will help to provide evidence of Independent Enquirer and Reflective Learner.

Over to you

In the following situations, explain whether work has been carried out:

* lifting a barbell up above your head
* a complete bicep curl
* a complete sit-up
* a 100 m sprint on an athletics track
* a 400 m run on an athletics track.

Force

Force is a push or pull on an object or person and affects movement. Force can affect movement in a variety of different ways, including:

* changing the direction of a moving object, eg returning a volley in tennis
* making an object move, eg pushing a bobsleigh at the start of a race
* stopping a moving object, eg stopping a moving ball with a hockey stick
* changing the shape of an object, eg landing on the bed of a trampoline and changing its shape
* preventing something from moving, eg rugby players in a rugby scrum pushing against each other to prevent the other team from moving.

Force is measured in newtons (N) and can be external or internal. An internal force is generated from inside your body and comes from the contraction of muscles. External forces come from outside your body, such as a football being passed to you. Both the mass of an object or person and their acceleration affect the amount of force produced.

Work

Work is the term used to describe the amount of force produced by a person or object that causes displacement. In order for work to have been done, the object or person must have been displaced and moved from its original position. Work is measured in a unit called joules; the shorthand version looks like this: J.

Power

Power is required in events that use explosive actions, such as throwing, jumping and gymnastics, where a movement has to be carried out quickly. Power is a measure of how much energy can be used (or work done) in a certain period of time. Power is measured in watts; the shorthand looks like this: W.

Efficiency

Efficiency refers to how effectively the energy required for an activity or movement is used. An activity or movement should be carried out with as little energy as possible going to waste. An efficient runner will have a good technique that uses most of their energy in the actual running movement. They will use less energy and less oxygen to run at the same pace as a person who is a less efficient runner.

Levers

Your body contains lots of different levers. Three different parts of your body are used to create a lever:

1 bones

2 joints (also known as pivot points)

3 muscles.

A lever consists of a rigid structure (bone) that has a force acting upon it (muscle) to produce a turning movement around a fixed point (joint/pivot point). There must also be a load or some form of resistance that is placed on the rigid structure – this will be the weight of the body part being moved and anything that it is carrying, eg a hand weight. The technical term for the fixed point that a lever turns around is the fulcrum.

There are three classifications of lever found in your body. They are known as first-, second- and third-class levers.

First-class lever

A first-class lever looks very similar to a seesaw. The fulcrum is in the middle of the effort and the load.

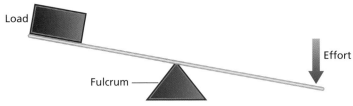

A first-class lever.

This type of lever is used in your head and neck when you nod – your skull/vertebra joint is the fulcrum, the weight of your head is the load and your neck muscles provide the effort.

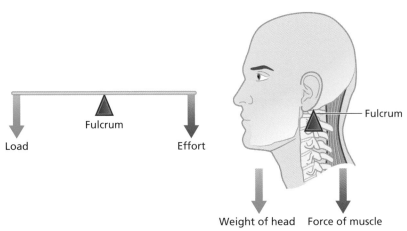

Nodding your head: a first-class lever.

Second-class lever

A second-class lever has the fulcrum at one end, the load in the middle and the effort at the other end.

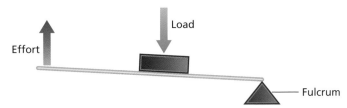

A second-class lever.

This type of lever is used in your lower leg when you stand on tiptoe – the ball of your foot acts as the fulcrum, the weight of your body is the load and the effort comes from the contraction of the calf muscle.

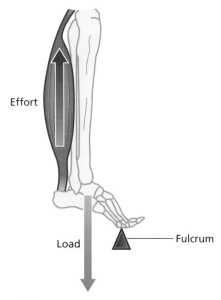

Standing on tiptoe: a second-class lever.

Third-class lever

A third-class lever has the fulcrum at one end, the effort in the middle and the load at the other end.

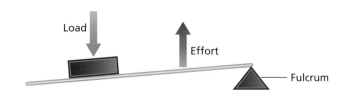

A third-class lever.

This type of lever is used to perform a bicep curl – the fulcrum is the elbow joint, the effort comes from the biceps contracting and the resistance is the weight of the forearm, plus any weight being held.

TOP TIP

An easy way to remember the order of the levers is to use the term '**FLE**' to indicate which part of the lever is found in the middle:

* in a first-class lever the **F**ulcrum is in the middle

* in a second-class lever the **L**oad is in the middle

* in a third-class lever the **E**ffort is in the middle

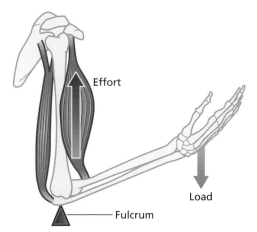

Performing a bicep curl: a third-class lever.

Moment

Moment is also known as **torque** and describes the turning effect of a force upon an object. For example, in a biceps curl the biceps pulls the forearm upwards, which produces a rotating movement around the elbow joint. The force applied by the biceps is called the moment.

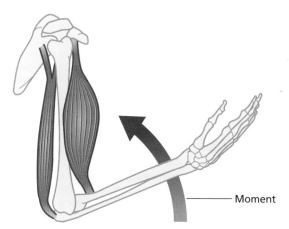

Moment

Moment applied by the biceps during a biceps curl.

Moment is measured in units called newton metres – the force is measured in newtons and the length in metres. The shorthand version of newton metres is Nm.

The direction of the moment must also be included. If it is being applied in a clockwise direction it is referred to as a positive moment; if it is in an anticlockwise direction it is called a negative moment.

Starting Point

Why do you need to take measurements to determine how well a person is performing in a particular sport?

3.7 Applying the mechanics of movement

Now you have an understanding of the basics of mechanics, these principles can be applied to sport and active leisure. In this topic you will learn how to take measurements in mechanics and find out how knowledge of mechanics can improve a sports performer's technique and overall sporting performance.

Key equations with worked examples

To help you to understand the mechanics of movement, the following definitions and worked examples should be studied in the order in which they appear – they build upon each other. Where possible, try to work through the 'Over to you' sections as you go along, as they will help you to understand the mechanics of movement more fully.

Velocity

To measure the velocity of a person or object you need to be able to measure the displacement from their starting point to their finish point and the time it took them to cover the distance between the two.

The equation for velocity looks like this:

velocity (ms⁻¹) = displacement (m)/time (s)

velocity (ms^{-1}) = displacement (m)/time (s)

Usain Bolt ran the world record 100 m sprint in 9.58 seconds at the 2009 World Championships; the calculation below shows you how to work out his average velocity for this race.

velocity = 100 m/9.58 s

velocity = 10.44 ms⁻¹

Over to you

If you have access to a running track and a stopwatch, try out this next activity.

* Working in pairs or small groups, time how long it takes you to run 100 m.
* Now use the equation for velocity given above to work out your velocity over this 100 m sprint.
* Remember to write your result in ms⁻¹.

Usain Bolt set a new world record in the 100 m sprint at the 2009 World Championships in Berlin. His average velocity was 10.44 ms⁻¹.

Acceleration

To measure a person or object's acceleration, you need to be able to measure the change in velocity of this person or object over a period of time.

The equation for acceleration looks like this:

acceleration (ms^{-2}) = change in velocity (ms^{-1})/time (s)

To work out the change in velocity you need to measure the velocity at the starting point, the velocity at the finishing point and the time taken between these two points. For example, if you wanted to measure Usain Bolt's acceleration in the first 10 m of his world record 100 m sprint, you need to perform the following calculations.

The time for Bolt to reach 10 m was 1.85 seconds, and his velocity at 10 m was measured at 10.8 ms^{-1}

starting point velocity = 0 (in the starting blocks)

velocity at 10 m = 10.8 ms^{-1}

change in velocity = finishing velocity – starting velocity = 10.8 – 0 = 10.8 ms^{-1}

acceleration = change in velocity / time = 10.8/1.85

acceleration = 5.84 ms^{-2}

Force

In order to measure force you need to know the mass of the object or person and their acceleration.

The equation for force looks like this:

force = mass × acceleration

Mass is measured in kg; you can work out a person or an object's mass by using a set of weighing scales. Acceleration can be worked out using the equation given above. Therefore, to work out the force produced by Usain Bolt in the first 10 m of his 100 m sprint you will need his mass, which is approximately 95 kg, and his acceleration, which you worked out to be 5.84 ms^{-2}. You now need to perform the following calculation:

force = 95 × 5.84

force = 554.8 N

Functional Skills

This activity will help to provide evidence of Maths.

Over to you

From the velocity information gained in the last 'Over to you' section, work out your acceleration over the 100 m sprint using the equation for acceleration given above.

Functional Skills

This activity will help to provide evidence of Maths.

Personal, Learning and Thinking Skills

This activity will help to provide evidence of Independent Enquirer and Reflective Learner.

Over to you

Using a set of weighing scales, find out your mass in kg. Use the acceleration results from the previous 'Over to you' section and the equation for force given above to work out the amount of force you produce over the 100 m sprint.

Work

To find out the amount of work a person has carried out, you need to know the amount of force that they used and the distance between their starting and finishing points (displacement).

The equation for work looks like this:

work = force × displacement

Therefore, the amount of work Usain Bolt produced in the first 10 m of his 100 m world record sprint would be:

work = 554.8 × 10

work = 5548 J

Power

To work out the amount of power a person or object has produced, you need to know how much work they have performed and the length of time it took them to perform this work.

The equation for power looks like this:

power = work/time

This is how you would work out the power produced by Usain Bolt in the first 10 m of his 100 m world record sprint:

power = 5548/1.85

power = 2999 W

Moment

The equation for measuring the moment of a force looks like this:

Moment = force × length of the 'resistance arm'

Therefore, if a tennis player hits an overarm serve with a force of 80 N and has a resistance arm length of 2 m (length of tennis racket and arm), the moment can be worked out by:

moment = 80 N × 2 m

moment = 160 Nm

Levers

Levers are used in sport all the time. Your bones and muscles act as levers to produce movements, but the equipment you use also helps to increase the amount of force that can be produced. For example, a golf club increases the force produced when you strike a golf ball.

A long lever produces a small range of movement but requires little strength. A short lever produces a large range of movement but requires a lot of strength. This difference in lever length related to its function can be explained using the following information:

* The distance between the fulcrum and the effort is called the effort arm.
* The distance between the fulcrum and the load is called the load arm.

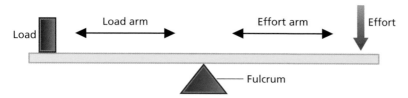

A lever showing the load arm and effort arm.

* Changing the distance from the fulcrum to the load changes the amount of force that can be produced by the lever.

* If the load is a long way from the fulcrum, more effort needs to be applied to the lever to produce movement, but a greater range of movement is produced.

A longer distance between the load arm and the fulcrum means that more effort is required to move the load but the load can travel further.

A shorter distance between the load arm and the fulcrum means that less effort is required to move the load but the load does not travel very far.

For athletes this means that the longer the limb, the longer the load arm so the more strength is required to move it, but the greater the distance of the movement. The fact that a shorter load arm requires less strength to move it helps to explain why elite power lifters tend to be below average height – they have shorter limbs and are therefore able to lift heavier weights.

Over to you

Use a light-weight dumbbell for this activity.

* Lift the dumbbell using a bicep curl – here your elbow acts as the fulcrum.

* Repeat the activity but this time keep your arm straight so that your shoulder acts as the fulcrum.

* Which method of lifting the weight requires less effort? Explain why you think it requires less effort.

* Which method produces the most movement? Explain why you think it produces the most movement.

Just checking

Select a sport or active leisure activity of your choice and then answer the following questions:

* Does a person need to have a high velocity or a high acceleration during any part of your chosen activity? If so when?

* Does your activity require a lot of work? Explain your answer.

* Does your activity require a lot of power? Explain your answer.

* Is moment a force that is used in your activity? If so how is it used?

* Do you use levers in your activity? If so, explain how they work and what they do.

Starting Point

* How has science and technology affected your sport or active leisure activity?

* What pieces of new technology do you use and benefit from?

3.8 The relationship between science, technology and sport and active leisure

Knowledge of anatomy, physiology and the mechanics of movement, and how each of these things affects an athlete's performance, can help to improve technique. This knowledge has led to huge improvements in the design of equipment, clothing, playing surfaces, fitness testing, training methods and services for sport and active leisure participants.

Improvements to existing products

Most sports equipment and products that you are familiar with will have changed and been improved over time thanks to advances in science and technology. Tennis rackets are just one example.

Tennis rackets

The game of tennis has changed a lot over the years, partly due to advances in science and technology. Tennis players are hitting the ball harder and faster than ever before.

The design of a racket should allow a player to give their best performance, for example by allowing them to serve the ball as fast as possible. Racket design must consider the length of time a player can compete to reduce the risk of overuse injuries.

Did you know?

The 2009 Wimbledon men's final lasted four hours and 15 minutes and went to 30 games in the fifth set before Roger Federer finally won. Federer's fastest first serve speed was 143 mph.

The design of Roger Federer's racket helped him to serve at high speed in the 2009 Wimbledon men's singles final.

The labelled photograph below shows how the key features of rackets have changed over time to try to improve performance.

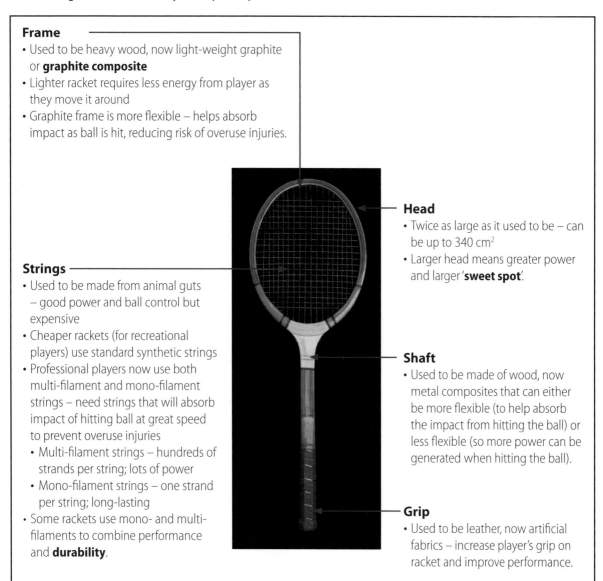

Frame
- Used to be heavy wood, now light-weight graphite or **graphite composite**
- Lighter racket requires less energy from player as they move it around
- Graphite frame is more flexible – helps absorb impact as ball is hit, reducing risk of overuse injuries.

Head
- Twice as large as it used to be – can be up to 340 cm^2
- Larger head means greater power and larger '**sweet spot**'.

Strings
- Used to be made from animal guts – good power and ball control but expensive
- Cheaper rackets (for recreational players) use standard synthetic strings
- Professional players now use both multi-filament and mono-filament strings – need strings that will absorb impact of hitting ball at great speed to prevent overuse injuries
  - Multi-filament strings – hundreds of strands per string; lots of power
  - Mono-filament strings – one strand per string; long-lasting
- Some rackets use mono- and multi-filaments to combine performance and **durability**.

Shaft
- Used to be made of wood, now metal composites that can either be more flexible (to help absorb the impact from hitting the ball) or less flexible (so more power can be generated when hitting the ball).

Grip
- Used to be leather, now artificial fabrics – increase player's grip on racket and improve performance.

As you can see, tennis rackets have changed a lot since these old wooden styles were used.

Over to you

❋ What equipment do you use in your selected sport or active leisure activity?

❋ How has the equipment changed and developed through the use of science and technology?

JARGON BUSTER

Graphite composite Material made from graphite mixed with other materials, like titanium and Kevlar.

Sweet spot The best place on the racket head to hit the ball.

Durability The ability to last and resist wear

New products

Most new products that are produced thanks to advances in technology enhance athletic and sports performance and are well received by the competitors, the sport's national governing bodies and the spectators. However, some new products have proved to be quite controversial, such as new developments in swimsuit technology.

Swimsuit technology

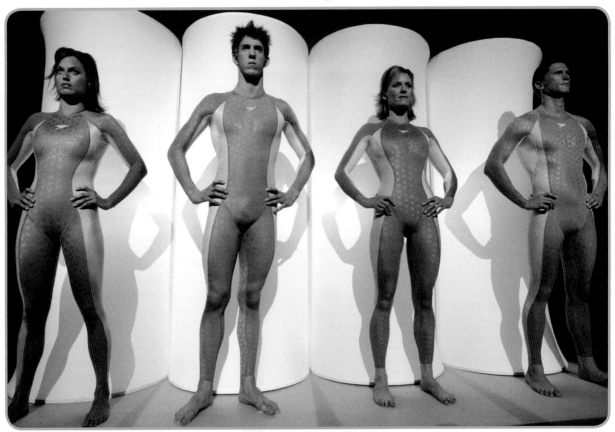

Michael Phelps and other US swimmers wearing Speedo Fastskins®.

Recently, swimsuit technology appears to have had a significant effect on elite swimmers' performance. New full body suits (with or without arms) such as the Speedo Fastskin® have a range of features that reduce drag and allow swimmers to increase their speed. In a sport where success is measured in hundredths of a second, the small advantages of swimsuit design can make a big difference to performance. Since these suits have been used in competition, over 130 new swimming world records have been set. In July 2009, FINA (Fédération Internationale De Natation–the world governing body for swimming) issued a new rule to prevent the use of this new swimming technology in competition, as they believe that those wearing the suits have an unfair advantage.

Services

A large range of services are available to sportspeople to help them improve their performance and recover from injury. Each of these services has benefited from science and technology, which has allowed the professionals providing the service to develop a better understanding of the human body and what can be done to help individuals to perform at their best.

* **Exercise physiologists** examine how well a person's body systems are functioning to determine if training is producing the right fitness benefits. They will carry out tests in a sports science lab and out in the field. A range of scientific equipment has been developed for their use, including gas analysers to test **VO$_2$ max**, **blood lactate** analysers and body composition testing equipment.

* **Fitness trainers** have access to lots of different training devices to improve targeted areas of fitness. To train for speed, they might use bungee cable trainers, chute trainers or power sleds.

* **Sports therapists** help to prepare a sportsperson for activity and help their body to recover afterwards. For injured sportspeople they use a range of scientific techniques and equipment to help speed up the recovery process.

* **Sports nutritionists** ensure that a sportsperson is eating the correct foods to give them as much energy as possible for their activity. Food can have a significant effect on performance. Technology has helped to produce sports drinks such as **glycogen-loading** and **creatine drinks**, which help to improve performance in certain sports.

* **Biomechanists** study a sportsperson's technique and help them to improve it. Science and technology has played a key role in developing the equipment that is used by biomechanists to help them with their analysis.

Over to you

Do you know how a fitness trainer would use bungee cable trainers, chute trainers and power sleds to improve certain areas of a client's fitness? Do some research to see if you can find out.

JARGON BUSTER

VO$_2$ max This is a measure of a person's aerobic fitness and is the maximum amount of oxygen that a person can take in and use.

Blood lactate Lactic acid is produced by the muscles when they are exercising without any oxygen. Lactic acid is converted into lactate as it enters the bloodstream. The amount of lactic acid produced by the body is estimated from the amount of lactate in a person's blood.

Glycogen-loading sports drinks Drinks containing high levels of carbohydrates in the form of sugars.

Creatine sports drinks Creatine is a legal substance that is believed to help increase muscle strength and speed and to help muscles recover more quickly after exercise.

Just checking

* How has science and technology affected the development of sport and active leisure equipment?
* How has science and technology affected the services available to people taking part in sport and active leisure?
* Do you think the effects of science and technology on sport and active leisure have helped to improve your performance or your overall experience of a selected sport or active leisure activity? Explain your answer.

Starting Point

Why do you think fitness tests are used in sport and active leisure?

3.9 Using physical tests

To work out whether an athlete has improved their performance in a particular sport or an area of their physical fitness, it is necessary to perform tests. Usually, you would take two sets of tests, one before a new coaching technique, training programme or piece of equipment is used and one after. You will learn about a range of tests available for measuring different components of fitness and the mechanics of movement in order for you to select and use the ones most appropriate for your assessment.

Fitness tests

These measure different components of fitness – first identify the component you wish to measure, then select a suitable test to take this measurement. For each fitness test example the equipment required is listed followed by the protocol, which is the procedure you must follow to make sure that the test is carried out properly. Make sure that you carefully record and check the measurements that you take from each test that you carry out.

A full warm up should be carried out before any fitness test is used.

Aerobic fitness tests

These tests assess how well you take in and use oxygen. Tests can be maximal or non maximal. In a maximal test the participant is encouraged to exercise to exhaustion, whereas in a non-maximal test the participant does not have to exercise to exhaustion.

TOP TIP

A test should always be reliable. This means that if you were to carry out the test again you would get similar or exactly the same results.

VO_2 max test

This person is undergoing a VO_2 max test.

This test uses specialist sport and exercise science equipment and must be supervised by a qualified person. It is the most valid and reliable test for measuring aerobic fitness and is a maximal aerobic fitness test.

Equipment
* Gas analyser
* Treadmill/cycle ergometer/ ergometer that is specific to the participant's sport
* Stopwatch

Protocol
* The participant exercises on the treadmill or ergometer and expired air is collected.
* The treadmill incline or the exercise intensity is increased at various stages.
* The participant exercises to exhaustion.
* Expired air is analysed and a VO_2 max is determined.
* Results of the estimated VO_2 max are compared to tables of norms.

The multistage fitness test

This is a maximal test, which means that the participant is expected to exercise until they are exhausted. The results of the test provide you with an estimated VO₂ max, which is the measure of your aerobic fitness level.

Equipment
* Pre-recorded CD or tape
* Flat area with distance of 20 m marked out

Protocol
* Start the tape or CD – the participant will start to run or jog when the first bleep sounds.
* Complete the 20 m run before the second bleep sounds.
* When the second bleep sounds they turn around and run back.
* This continues and the time between the bleeps gets shorter so the participant has to run faster.
* If the participant fails to get to the other end before the bleep on three consecutive occasions then they are out.
* Record the point at which the participant dropped out.
* Use the table provided in the multistage fitness test pack to work out the participant's predicted VO₂ max ml.kg⁻¹.min⁻¹ You will need to know the level and the shuttle number in order for you to do this.

Other tests to measure a person's aerobic fitness include:

* the 12-minute Cooper run

* the Rockport walk test.

Flexibility

These tests measure the range of movement permitted at different joints. The participant should carry out a thorough warm-up prior to testing.

Harvard step test

This is a non-maximal test.

Equipment
* A 45 cm high step
* A heart rate monitor
* Stopwatch
* Metronome

Protocol
* The participant steps up and down on the step for five minutes in total.
* They must step up once every two seconds – use the metronome to set this rate.
* One minute after finishing, record the participant's heart rate.
* Two minutes after finishing, record the participant's heart rate.
* Three minutes after finishing, record the participant's heart rate.
* Work out the score using the following equation:

Score = (100 × test duration in seconds) divided by 2 × (total heartbeats in the test periods)

Compare these results to the table of normative data below.

Score	Male	Female
Poor	below 55	below 50
Below average	55–64	50–60
Average	65–79	61–75
Above average	80–90	76–86
Excellent	over 90	over 86

Sit and reach

This test measures the flexibility of the muscles in the hamstrings and the lower back.

Equipment
Sit and reach box

Protocol
* The participant removes shoes.
* Legs are out straight ahead and feet are placed flat against the box.
* The participant slowly leans forward and reaches as far forward as possible, holding the stretch for two seconds.
* The furthest distance that the participants fingers reach to is recorded from the sit and reach box in cm.
* Compare the result to the table of norms for 16- to 19-year-olds shown here to assess the flexibility of the participant (all values are in cm).

Score	Male	Female
Poor	below 4	below 4
Below average	4–6	4–6
Average	7–10	7–11
Above average	11–14	12–15
Excellent	over 14	over 15

Other tests to measure flexibility include the calf muscle flexibility test, the shoulder flexibility test, the trunk rotation test and the groin flexibility test.

This woman is testing her upper body strength.

Over to you

Investigate other methods of recording a person's strength such as the hand grip dynamometer and the 7-stage abdominal strength test.

Strength tests

These tests measure the strength of selected muscle groups.

1 rep max (1RM) test

This test can be carried out on a range of different muscle groups.

Equipment
Resistance equipment to test required muscle group, eg chest press to test the pectorals

Protocol
* Using a light weight, the participant performs the test exercise for around 10 reps to warm the muscle group up appropriately.
* They rest for one minute.
* They lift a resistance that can be lifted for 3–5 reps.
* They rest for two minutes.
* They lift a resistance that can be lifted for 3–5 reps.
* They rest for two to three minutes.
* They lift a resistance that can be lifted for one repetition.
* If successful, they rest for two to four minutes.
* Add a little more weight and they complete one repetition.
* Weight is gradually added until the participant is unable to complete the lift.
* The 1 rep max is the last weight that could be completed successfully.

There are no norm tables for 1RM tests; they are used to help to monitor progress and strength gains and help determine training programmes for an individual.

Muscular endurance

These tests measure how long a specific muscle group or groups can continue to exercise before fatiguing or during a set amount of time.

1 minute press-up test

This test measures the muscular endurance of the upper body.

Equipment
* Mat
* Stopwatch

Protocol
* The participant starts in a press-up position with their hands and toes touching the floor, their body and legs in a straight line, feet slightly apart, elbows extended and hands shoulder width apart.
* Start the stopwatch and instruct the participant to start.
* Keeping the back straight, the participant flexes their elbows so that the body is lowered and there is a 90-degree angle at the elbows.
* Elbows extend to return the body back to the starting position.
* The participant repeats this action for as many times as possible in one minute.

Females may use the box press-up technique, where their knees are in contact with the floor. There are no norm tables for this test as it is used to help to monitor progress and muscular endurance gains.

NCF abdominal curl conditioning test

This test measures the muscular endurance of the abdominal muscles. It uses timed beeps that increase in speed as the test progresses.

Equipment
* NCF pre-recorded tape/CD
* Tape/CD player

Protocol
* The participant lies on the floor with their fingers on their temples, knees bent and feet flat on the floor.
* Start the tape. The participant remains in the lying position for the first bleep, then completes a full sit up so that their elbows touch their knees in time for the second bleep.
* The participant returns to the start position in time for the next bleep.
* Repeat the process for as many sit ups as possible in time with the recorded bleeps.
* The number of stages completed will determine the rating for the participant's abdominal muscular endurance.

The table below shows ratings for male and females based on the total number of sit-ups completed in the test.

	Stages							
	1	**2**	**3**	**4**	**5**	**6**	**7**	**8**
Total number of sit-ups completed by this stage	20	42	64	89	116	146	180	217
Rating for reaching this stage – Males	Poor	Poor	Fair	Fair	Good	Good	Excellent	Excellent
Rating for reaching this stage – Females	Poor	Fair	Fair	Good	Good	Very good	Excellent	Excellent

Other muscular endurance tests are available, including the pull up test and the wall sit test.

Body composition

Body composition tests help to determine the amounts of fat and muscle in your body. For some sport and leisure activities athletes perform better with a lot of muscle and very little body fat, such as in sprinting. In other sports a body composition with a lot of body fat is desirable, for example sumo wrestling. Most people monitor body composition so that they can detect increases in muscle size and/or decreases in body fat so that they can calculate if training and diet programmes are producing the intended results.

Skin fold assessment

This test is performed using skin fold callipers. The skin folds can be taken at different sites – the protocol shown below measures the skin folds at four places on the body and this is known as the Durnin and Wormsley method.

Equipment
* Skin fold callipers * Measuring tape

Protocol
* All measurements should be taken on the left-hand side of the participant's body.
* Mark the sites that you plan to measure:
  – Triceps – a vertical pinch halfway between the shoulder and elbow on the back of the arm.
  – Biceps – a vertical pinch 1 cm above the site for the triceps on the front of the arm.
  – Subscapular – taken at a 45-degree angle, 2 cm below the lowest point of the shoulder blade.
  – Suprailiac – taken just above the hip bone in a direct line from below the front of the shoulder.
* Take a pinch of the skin 1 cm above the marked site.
* Make sure your participant is comfortable. If the pinch is hurting then you probably have some muscle in your pinch.
* Place the callipers halfway between the top and bottom of the skin fold. Wait 1–2 seconds and then record the reading on the callipers.
* Repeat the process and record a second reading.
* Take an average reading of both scores.
* Add up the total averages for all four measurements.
* Calculate body fat percentage using the tables shown below.

Males aged 16–29 years:

Total of averages for all 4 measurements (mm)	**Percentage of body fat**	**Total** of averages for all 4 measurements (mm)	**Percentage of body fat**
20	8.1	80	24.8
22	9.2	85	25.6
24	10.2	90	26.3
26	11.2	95	27.0
28	12.1	100	27.6
30	12.9	110	28.8
35	14.7	120	29.9
40	16.3	130	31.0
45	17.7	140	31.9
50	19.0	150	32.8
55	20.2	160	33.6
60	21.2	170	34.4
65	22.2	180	35.2
70	23.2	190	35.9
75	24.0	200	36.5

Rating:

Percentage of body fat	**Rating**
under 7%	very little fat
7–12.9%	slim
13–17.9%	average
18–28%	high fat
over 28%	obese

Females aged 16–29 years:

Total of averages for all 4 measurements (mm)	Percentage of body fat	Total of averages for all 4 measurements (mm)	Percentage of body fat
14	9.4	75	32.2
16	11.1	80	33.1
18	12.7	85	34.0
20	14.1	90	34.8
22	15.4	95	35.6
24	16.5	100	36.3
26	17.6	110	37.7
28	18.6	120	39.0
30	19.5	130	40.2
35	21.6	140	41.3
40	23.4	150	42.3
45	25.0	160	43.2
50	26.5	170	44.6
55	27.8	180	45.0
60	29.1	190	45.8
65	30.2	200	46.6
70	31.2		

Rating:

Percentage of body fat	Rating
under 13%	very little fat
12–20.9%	slim
21–25.9%	average
26–32%	high fat
over 32%	obese

Bioelectric impedance

This test measures the amount of body fat by measuring the resistance to a very small electrical current passed through the body tissues. There is more resistance to this electrical current in fatty tissues, so people with more body fat show a higher resistance to the current.

Equipment
Bioelectric impedance analyser

Protocol
* Ensure that the participant is fully hydrated.
* Attach the electrodes to the specified areas on the subject – this is usually on the wrist and ankle but will vary depending upon the make and models that you are using.
* Record the reading provided.
* This reading gives you an indication of the percentage of body fat for that participant and the results can be compared to the information on male/female body composition given on page 4 in Unit 1.

Hydro-densitometry or underwater weighing is another technique used to measure body composition but few centres have access to the equipment needed for this test. The results from this type of testing are usually more accurate than other methods of testing.

Mechanics of movement tests

The following tests explore ways in which you can measure the mechanics of a person's movement. The tests included in this section are for power and velocity only; however, you can refer back to Topic 3.6 for ideas on further mechanics of motion tests.

Margaria Kalamen Power Test

This test measures the power produced by the participant's legs.

Equipment
* Stopwatch
* Timing gates or mats if available
* Tape measure
* Flight of 12 steps (each step around 17.5 cm high)
* Weighing scales

Protocol
* Weigh the subject and record their mass in kg.
* The subject is given a few practice runs up the steps to warm up.
* The subject stands 6 m from the first step.
* Using the timing gates/mats or a stopwatch, record the start time.
* The subject must run up the steps taking three steps at a time.
* When they get to the top, use the timing gates, mat or stopwatch to warm up record the end time in seconds.
* Repeat the test twice more with at least three minutes' recovery time between each test.
* Work out their power using the following equation (9.8 refers to the force of gravity acting): power (W) = (mass × displacement × 9.8) / time. Displacement will be the vertical displacement in metres from the starting position to the top of the flight of steps.

Velocity test

This test measures the velocity of a runner or swimmer.

Equipment
* Stopwatch or timing gates
* Running track or swimming pool

Protocol
* Mark out a 100 m straight line distance on the running track or a 25 m lane in a swimming pool.
* Using a stopwatch or timing gates, record when the subject starts running or swimming.
* Record the time the subject takes to complete the required distance.
* Work out their velocity using the following equation:
velocity = displacement / time

Just checking

* Which components of fitness are important for your selected sport?
* Which fitness tests would measure these components of fitness?
* Why does a test need to be reliable?
* What does it mean when we say that a test has to be valid?
* Why do we measure the mechanics of motion to help to improve a sports person's performance?

3.10 Reviewing performance in sport and active leisure

Once an athlete or sports performer has carried out physical tests, the results of the tests need to be examined and conclusions drawn. This information can then help to determine ways in which the participant can improve their performance, eg through the use of new products or services.

Analysing the results

Once you have carried out tests on an athlete or sports performer, it is necessary to work out what the results of these tests mean. The first port of call is to compare the fitness test results to either:

* **Tables of norms**: This allows you to compare your subject's results to the rest of the population and work out if they are strong in this area of fitness (getting results in the elite category) or if they need to improve in this area (getting results in the average or below average category).

* **The pre-test results**: This would be done if you had given your athlete some sort of training aid or new diet to help improve their performance. If the results taken after completing the training or eating the new diet are better than the pre-test results, it shows that the training or diet is having the desired effect.

Ask the subject for feedback too, including such questions as:

* How did you feel?

* What do you think your strengths are?

* What do you think are your areas for improvement?

New products or services

The information gained from your subject and from analysing test results will help to provide you with ideas for new products or services that could improve your subject's performance. Factors to consider include:

* Do they need to improve a component of fitness? If so what technology is available (or could be improved upon) to help them improve their fitness?

* Is their body type and composition appropriate for the sport? For example, do they have too much body fat and not enough muscle?

* Are they using the best technique for their sport and leisure activity? What technology is available (or could be improved upon) to help your participant improve their technique?

* Are they using the best equipment for their sport? For example, if they are a runner are they using a running shoe that is suitable for their needs?

Starting Point

* How do you think you could review your performance in a selected sport or leisure activity?

* What sorts of tests could you take part in?

* How would you assess the results of the tests?

Over to you

* Which physical tests did your subject do well in?

* What are their areas for improvement?

* What sort of new technology or services could you suggest to help improve your subject's performance?

Just checking

* What types of new technology could you use to help you improve your performance in a selected sport or leisure activity?

* Do you think it is fair to use technology to improve a person's sporting performance? Explain your answer.

Jonathon is a rugby player and plays right wing. He has to have good cardiovascular fitness, strength and muscular endurance. He has been trying to increase his velocity and acceleration over short distances to help him to score tries.

Jonathon has taken part in a strength and speed training programme and has incorporated plyometrics into his programme to help increase his explosive power. He is quite tall at 6 foot 6 inches, which means he has long arms and long legs. He is aware that having long levers can help him to run quickly, but he has to build up his muscle strength in order to move his limbs quickly enough.

1 How do Jonathon's heart and lungs provide oxygen and energy to his muscles to help him participate in rugby games?

2 What sort of technology would you use in Jonathon's training programme to help increase his speed?

3 How would you test to see if Jonathon is improving his acceleration and velocity over short distances?

4 Explain why having long levers could:

   a help him to sprint quickly

   b slow him down in sprinting.

For your project

This unit explores how science and technology are used to help improve performance in a sport or active leisure activity. From studying this unit you will have a good understanding of different fitness tests and methods used to test the mechanics of movement, which will help you to make comparisons of a person's performance before and after using performance-enhancing technology or equipment.

The following diagram gives some ideas for what you might decide to do your project on, based on the content of this unit.

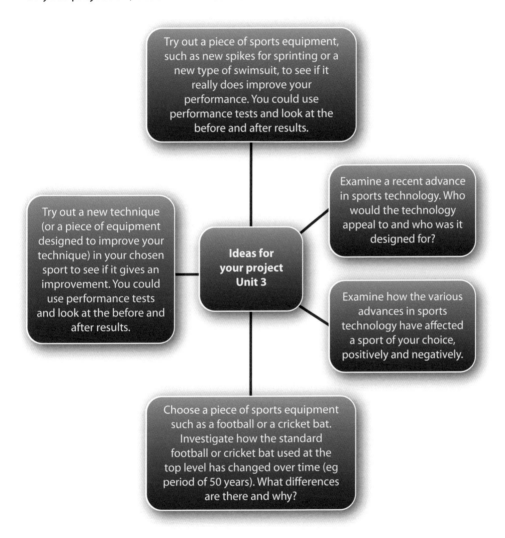

Try out a piece of sports equipment, such as new spikes for sprinting or a new type of swimsuit, to see if it really does improve your performance. You could use performance tests and look at the before and after results.

Try out a new technique (or a piece of equipment designed to improve your technique) in your chosen sport to see if it gives an improvement. You could use performance tests and look at the before and after results.

Ideas for your project Unit 3

Examine a recent advance in sports technology. Who would the technology appeal to and who was it designed for?

Examine how the various advances in sports technology have affected a sport of your choice, positively and negatively.

Choose a piece of sports equipment such as a football or a cricket bat. Investigate how the standard football or cricket bat used at the top level has changed over time (eg period of 50 years). What differences are there and why?

Possible project titles

* How do different sizes of golf club affect the distance a golf ball can be hit?
* How does strength training affect a person's power?
* How does using speed chutes increase a person's velocity?
* How have modern tennis rackets affected the overarm tennis serve?
* How has new technology affected long distance cycle racing?

Assessment guidance

This unit is assessed by one internally-set assignment. You will have a period of 16 hours to generate evidence for your assessment. In your assessment you will need to show that you:

* know how to accurately describe the structure and functions of the main body systems, including the skeletal system, muscular system, cardiovascular system and respiratory system

* know how to explain the core elements of improving performance in sport and active leisure using knowledge of anatomy and physiology

* know how to describe the use of levers in sport and active leisure equipment and in the human body

* are able to provide an explanation of how knowledge of anatomy and physiology is applied in sport and active leisure

* are able to provide an explanation of how technological innovation is used to improve products and services in sport and active leisure

* can identify new ideas for products or services in sport or active leisure

* are able to identify fitness tests to be carried out, including the required equipment and the timing of test activities

* are able to record and check test measurements with accuracy

* are able to perform calculations using test findings with accuracy

* are able to draw conclusions about the participant performance in sport and active leisure based upon the test data that you have found.

Time management

* Although you have 16 hours to generate evidence for this assignment, this does not include time spent researching the topic area or setting up equipment.

* The internal assessment will be split into different tasks. You will be given set times to generate evidence for that task whilst being supervised by your tutor or employer.

* You will be expected to identify and carry out physical tests in sport and active leisure as part of your assessment. It is a good idea to try and carry out mock tests first, where you can practise the protocols and recording the information, so that you are fully prepared for your assessment task.

* Your tutor may well give you ideas for resources to use to help you carry out research before you attempt some of the tasks. You should aim to make time to read this information and carry out research for the set task so that you have a good understanding of the subject area.

* Your tutor may give you formative assessments that are similar to the actual task. You should make time to complete these 'trial' assessments as these will help to prepare you for the 'real' task. Your tutor will be able to give you feedback on the areas that you have completed well and areas for improvement.

Useful links

Work experience within the sport and active leisure industry will enable you to learn about new technology that is being used to help assess and improve participants' performance. Talking to members of staff and observing them at work will help you to understand how the technology can be applied in the industry. Observing instructors or coaches delivering activity sessions will help you understand how knowledge of anatomy and physiology is used to prepare the body for exercise, return the body back to pre-exercise conditions and improve coaching techniques.

Look out for television programmes such as sports science and sports technology documentaries, which are often shown on Sky channels. Sports coverage will also often demonstrate some analysis of participants' performance, such as match analyses at half time in football games.

There are lots of useful websites that will help you with your research for this unit. For details of how to access these sites see the **Hotlinks** section – **Introduction**, page xi.

How you will be assessed

For your Unit 3 assessment, you need to make sure that you can meet all of the assessment criteria for the seven learning outcomes, as shown in the table below.

Learning outcome	Assessment criteria
LO1: Know the basic principles of anatomy and physiology	**1** Describe the structure and functions of the main body systems.
LO2: Understand how principles of anatomy and physiology are applied in sport and active leisure	**1** Explain how to improve performance in sport and active leisure using knowledge of anatomy and physiology.
LO3: Know about the mechanics of movement	**1** Describe the use of levers in sport or active leisure equipment and in the human body.
LO4: Understand how the mechanics of movement are applied in sport and active leisure	**1** Explain how to improve performance in sport and active leisure using analysis of the mechanics of movement.
LO5: Understand the relationship between science, technology and sport and active leisure	**1** Explain how knowledge of anatomy, physiology and mechanics is applied in sport and active leisure. **2** Explain how technological innovation is used to improve products and services. **3** Identify new ideas for products or services in sport or active leisure.
LO6: Be able to use physical tests in sport and active leisure	**1** Identify tests to be carried out, required resources and timing of test activities. **2** Record and check test measurements. **3** Perform calculations on test findings.
LO7: Be able to review performance in sport and active leisure	**1** Draw conclusions about performance of participants in sport and active leisure.

Introduction

Working in the sport and active leisure industry can be a very fulfilling and varied experience. To find a suitable job in this industry you need to discover where these jobs are advertised and carry out some research. You will also need to be able to assess your own skills to help you determine if certain job roles will suit you. As well as teaching you to do these things, this unit will explore the skills required to prepare for a job interview. You will also explore how national and local government policy initiatives affect the sport and active leisure facilities and employment opportunities available within your local area.

What will you learn?

In this unit you will cover the following learning outcomes:

LO1: Be able to carry out research into employment opportunities in the UK sport and active leisure industry

LO2: Know the structure of the UK sport and active leisure industry

LO3: Understand the impact of government policy on the sport and active leisure industry

LO4: Understand how personal attributes relate to job roles

LO5: Be able to communicate personal suitability for jobs in sport and active leisure and related industries

The following table shows how these five learning outcomes are covered by this unit.

Topic	Pages	Learning outcomes
4.1 Researching employment opportunities in the UK sport and active leisure industry	104–105	LO1
4.2 Structure of the sport and active leisure industry	106–107	LO2
4.3 Job roles in sport and active leisure	108–111	LO2
4.4 Skills and attributes required for jobs in sport and active leisure	112–115	LO2
4.5 Government policy initiatives	116–119	LO3
4.6 Responses of sport and active leisure organisations	120–121	LO3
4.7 Assessing your own personal attributes	122–123	LO4
4.8 Reviewing your personal attributes for suitable job roles	124–125	LO4
4.9 Preparing for a job interview	126–129	LO5

THINKING POINTS

* Name some different types of sport and active leisure employers in your local area.
* What sort of careers in the sport and active leisure industry are you interested in pursuing?

Functional Skills

Personal, Learning and Thinking Skills

This unit offers various opportunities to develop functional skills and personal, learning and thinking skills. Where appropriate, different activities are signposted with the relevant personal, learning and thinking skills that you can develop.

Diploma Daily

No nerves 'interviews'!

Candidates no longer have to worry about the 'dreaded interview' to get the job of their dreams! A new interview-free recruitment process has just been introduced in the sport and active leisure industry. Candidates submit their CV and then take part in tests to check out their skills and abilities and determine their suitability for job opportunities. These tests have been specifically designed for a variety of roles and help businesses to recruit the right person.

1 Do you think having a recruitment process with no interview is a good idea?

2 Why do you think interviews are usually used as part of the job recruitment process?

3 What are the benefits of interviews?

4 What are the drawbacks of interviews?

Unit links

This unit links closely to Level 2, Unit 5: Businesses in the sport and active leisure industry and Unit 7: Access for all in sport and active leisure.

Case study: A job for George

George has just completed his GCSEs at school and is looking for full-time work. George is 16 years old and lives near a large caravan park. During the summer his local area is full of tourists who provide extra custom for shops, restaurants and sport and active leisure providers. The caravan park has its own swimming pool, bowling alley, tennis courts and squash courts. His local football team have just been promoted to the second division in the football league so the local community are also expecting to have increased custom from visitors during the autumn and winter.

1 What are the benefits for George of living near this caravan park?

2 What sort of job opportunities might be available for George in his local area?

3 What are the potential problems with job opportunities for George?

How you will be assessed

For this unit you need to be able to carry out research to find out about the structure of and provision for the sport and active leisure industry, and the different types of employment opportunities within it. You will need to present evidence of the following in your assignment:

✳ A review of the impact of government policy initiatives on the national or local sport and active leisure industry. This should include suggestions on how sport and active leisure provision can be improved, taking into account government and industry priorities.

✳ A signed learner observation record form, completed by your tutor, careers adviser or employer. This will show that you have asked industry representatives, a careers adviser or your tutor questions related to job roles and opportunities in sport and active leisure.

✳ A review of your personal skills and abilities relating to possible job roles within the sport and active leisure industry.

✳ A description of the skills and attributes required for two sport and active leisure jobs, with an assessment of your suitability for the roles.

✳ A signed individual learner observation record form from your tutor, employer or careers adviser that comments on your performance in an interview for a chosen sport or active leisure job.

✳ Evidence of research that you have carried out into employment opportunities in the sport and active leisure industry and related industries, including your interview notes and a list of research sources signed by your tutor.

Starting Point

* Where would you look to find out about jobs in your local area?
* Do you know of any magazines, newspapers or websites with information about job opportunities?

Personal, Learning and Thinking Skills

This activity will help to provide evidence of Independent Enquirer and Reflective Learner.

Over to you

* Can you think of different ways of carrying out primary research?
* What are the benefits of primary research?
* What types of secondary research have you used to help you research topic areas in sport and active leisure?
* What are the benefits of secondary research?

4.1 Researching employment opportunities in the UK sport and active leisure industry

There are lots of different types of jobs available in the sport and active leisure industry, but you need to know where to find the one that is right for you. One of the most important factors in looking for a job is knowing where to look. Most sectors have specific magazines, journals and websites where they advertise jobs. This section will explore a range of research techniques that you can use to help you find your perfect job.

Research techniques

There are two main methods of carrying out research:

* primary
* secondary.

Primary research is where you find out information for yourself. Examples of primary research include questionnaires, interviews and observations. In each of these examples you carry out the research yourself and get information directly from other people or from observations of people or situations.

Secondary research is where you examine the results of research carried out by other people, for example by reading information in textbooks, surveys or reports. For each of these examples another person has carried out the direct observations and then written about what they have observed.

A library is a good place for conducting secondary research.

Asking questions

An excellent primary research method is to ask people questions. To ensure that the answers to your questions are useful, you need to carefully consider what sort of questions you will ask and make sure that they are appropriate for the people questioned. For example, there is no point asking a gym instructor about the job role of a pool lifeguard.

There is a wide range of people that you can question and seek advice from, including:

* your careers adviser
* your tutor
* people from the sport and active leisure industry who come to your centre to deliver talks
* people in their place of work in the sport and active leisure industry
* friends and relatives working in sport and active leisure.

The questions you could ask your careers adviser or tutor would be related to general information about different careers and types of jobs available in sport and active leisure, perhaps including basic descriptions of each job role. For people who are working in the industry you can ask very specific questions about their particular job, such as the hours they work, what the job involves, and what they like and dislike. This will help to provide you with a more complete understanding of that particular job.

Other research sources

Secondary research sources provide a huge array of information on lots of different job roles. For example, there are many different websites that contain specific information for people working in different sport and active leisure sectors.

Other sources of secondary research include:

* newspapers (including local, regional and national newspapers)
* trade publications such as *Leisure Management, Leisure Opportunities, All Sport and Leisure Monthly, Health and Fitness, Journal of the Institute of Leisure and Amenity Management* (ILAM)
* promotional material from specific sport and active leisure industries.

Just checking

* Explain how you could carry out primary research to find out about employment opportunities in a job of your choice.
* Name five specific secondary sources of information that you could use to help you find out about employment opportunities.

Functional Skills

This activity will help to provide evidence of English writing.

Personal, Learning and Thinking Skills

This activity will help to provide evidence of Independent Enquirer, Creative Thinker and Reflective Learner.

Over to you

* Write down four questions that you think would be appropriate to ask your tutor or careers adviser in order to explore potential job roles in sport and active leisure.
* Think of a job role that you are interested in and then write down four questions that you think would be useful to ask a person who is working in that job role.

Hotlink

Can you find any websites that might help you learn about interesting employment opportunities in the sport and leisure industry? There are some useful examples given in the **Hotlinks** section – **Introduction**, page xi.

Functional Skills

This activity will help to provide evidence of ICT.

Personal, Learning and Thinking Skills

This activity will help to provide evidence of Independent Enquirer and Reflective Learner.

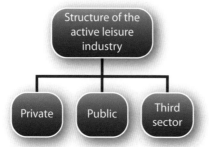

Starting Point

* Have you been to a sport and active leisure centre that has very advanced technology and/or luxurious facilities?

* What are the facilities like in your usual sport and active leisure centre?

4.2 Structure of the sport and active leisure industry

There are three main sectors within the sport and active leisure industry – public, private and third sector (which is also known as the voluntary sector). Each sector differs in the types of facilities and activities it provides; each of these sectors will be explored in this topic.

```
Structure of the
active leisure
industry
    │
  ┌─┼─┐
Private  Public  Third
                 sector
```

Private sector

The main aim of the private sector is to make money. It includes professional clubs such as Premier League football clubs, as well as private sport and active leisure facilities. Individuals or companies invest money into the club or facility in order to make a profit. Many private sector facilities use brand names, such as Virgin Active, Cannons, Acorn Adventure and Montessori. Branches of these can be found all over the UK. Others are named after the businessperson who founded them, such as David Lloyd or Bannatyne's. Private facilities are often quite luxurious compared to public or third sector facilities – for example, in private sports centres they often provide soaps, shampoo and towels in the changing areas and have the latest equipment. However, the cost to use these facilities is higher than the other sectors and their use is usually restricted to members.

Private sector facilities tend to be well-equipped and luxurious.

Public sector

Public sector sport and active leisure facilities are funded with money collected from the public through direct and indirect taxes. National Lottery funds sometimes contribute too. This money helps to fund sport and leisure centres, outdoor pursuit centres and school facilities. The aim of the public sector is to ensure that there is provision for the local community to participate in sport and active leisure and so the cost of using these facilities is kept to a minimum.

Third sector

The third sector is also known as the voluntary sector, as most people involved in this sector carry out the work as volunteers and do not receive any payment. The third sector does not make a profit. It runs sport and active leisure events to enable people to participate in competitive sport and improve their performance. Examples include amateur sports clubs such as cricket and netball teams. Players usually pay a subscription that covers the costs of hiring the facilities, equipment and so on. Some funding for the third sector can also come from sponsorship, National Lottery grants or through the local authority.

Differences in provision

Different locations in the UK have differing proportions of sport and active leisure provision from each sector. In richer areas where people have more **disposable income** there tends to be a higher proportion of private sector providers, as the people living in these areas can afford the higher costs. In more deprived areas there is usually a higher proportion of sport and active leisure provision from the public sector, as most people living there cannot afford private sector facilities. The needs and interests of specific populations will determine how successful the third sector provision is in an area. For example, Rugby League is very popular in the north of England, while Rugby Union tends to be more popular in the south.

Urban and **rural** areas also tend to differ in their provision. Rural areas have better access to outdoor activities such as walking and mountain biking, whereas urban areas have more health clubs and leisure centres.

Personal, Learning and Thinking Skills

This activity will help to provide evidence of Independent Enquirer.

Over to you

Visit a private, public and third sector sport and active leisure facility in turn and, for each, make a note of:

* the prices for participation
* the types of equipment available
* the range of activities available.

JARGON BUSTER

Disposable income Money available to spend on non-essential goods and activities.

Urban An area that is built up such as a town or city.

Rural An area in the countryside.

Just checking

* How would you describe your local area? Is it affluent or deprived? Urban or rural?
* What do you think are the most popular sports and active leisure activities in your local area? How has this affected the third sector provision?
* Carry out research to find out which sectors provide the various sport and active leisure facilities and events in your local area.

Starting Point

How many different job roles can you think of within the sport and active leisure industry?

4.3 Job roles in sport and active leisure

This topic explores some of the different jobs available in the sport and active leisure industry and how they vary between locations. There are a huge range of jobs available in the sport and active leisure industry, with each sector differing a little in the range of the job roles that are available within them. Different jobs are also available in different places.

Different areas within the sport and active leisure industry

The sport and active leisure industry includes the following areas:

* sport and recreation
* health and fitness
* the outdoors
* play work
* caravanning
* youth work
* stewarding.

Possible job roles for the first four areas are shown in the following diagrams.

Sport and recreation

Jobs in sport and recreation are based within all three sectors – public, private and the third sector.

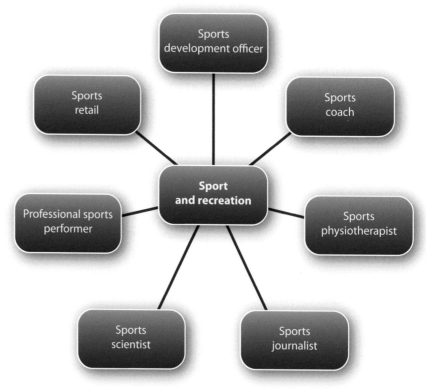

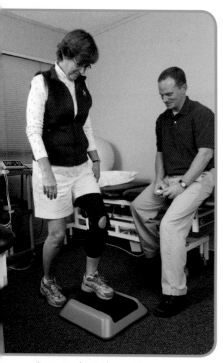

A sports physiotherapist

Health and fitness

Jobs in health and fitness are based mainly within the public and private sectors.

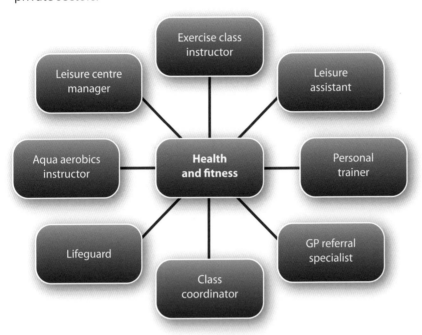

- Exercise class instructor
- Leisure centre manager
- Leisure assistant
- Aqua aerobics instructor
- **Health and fitness**
- Personal trainer
- Lifeguard
- Class coordinator
- GP referral specialist

A personal trainer

The outdoors

Jobs in the outdoors are based within all three sectors – public, private and the third sector.

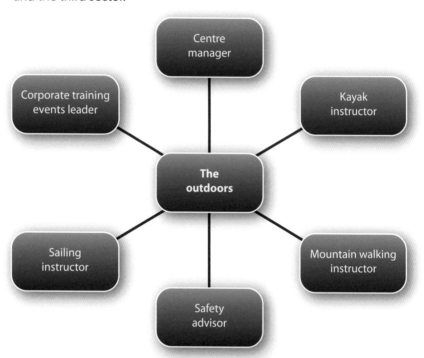

Over to you

What sort of sport and active leisure job opportunities would be available to you in your local area? Explain your answer.

A kayak instructor

Play work

Jobs in play work are based within all three sectors, but most commonly in the public and private sectors.

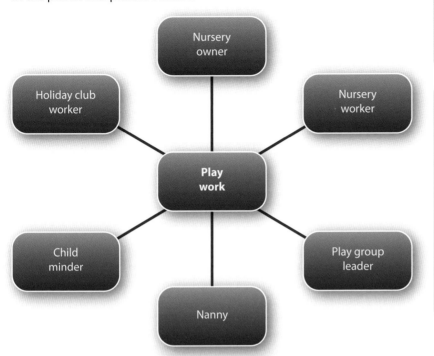

Over to you

For jobs in each of these four areas (sport and recreation, health and fitness, the outdoors, and play work), list and explain which types of jobs you think would be available in the:

* public sector
* private sector
* third sector (remember, you are unlikely to find much for health and fitness here).

A child minder

The opportunities available in each of these different types of job in sport and active leisure will differ between localities. For example, in rural places such as the Lake District there are many jobs in the 'outdoors' area, as the local environment with its mountains and lakes offers lots of opportunities to take part in outdoor and adventurous activities.

Just checking

Carry out research to find out why the number of job opportunities in the sport and active leisure industry has increased over the last 10 years.

4.4 Skills and attributes required for jobs in sport and active leisure

As the sport and active leisure industry is so large and diverse, the skills and attributes required for the different jobs within it do vary. However, you will find that a number of skills acquired in one role can be transferred to other jobs within the industry, such as leadership, time management and communication skills. This section examines the types of employment available in sport and active leisure and the skills and attributes required for a selection of jobs in the industry.

Types of employment

Shift work

At the moment you probably have a set routine where you go to school or college and return home at about the same time each day. This type of routine may suit you, working the same hours every day with no variation. However, some jobs in the sport and active leisure industry require you to carry out 'shift work'. This means that your working hours might vary depending on your shift and this may involve working unsociable hours. Shifts often consist of either an early morning to mid-afternoon working period, or an afternoon until late evening shift. For example, leisure centres with a pool often have staff in from around 6am to clean and get the centre ready for customers, and may then stay open until after 10pm to provide facilities for people in the evenings. Play workers may have to start very early to care for children whose parents leave to go to work early in the morning. Shift workers may also have to work for one or both days at the weekend and have their days off during the week.

Full- or part-time work

The total number of hours you work can vary. If you work in your job full time then you will probably be working five days a week for around 40 hours in total. However, there are often part-time roles available in many jobs in sport and active leisure. A part-time job means that you are working fewer hours than full-time workers. For example, you may work an occasional evening after finishing school or college and on one or two days at the weekend. Some people may choose to work part-time hours as they have other commitments such as looking after children.

Seasonal employment

Seasonal employment is where the demand for certain job roles increases at different times of the year. For example, at Christmas time there is a greater demand for people to work in the sports retail industry as there are more people shopping at this time of year. During the summer holidays there is a greater demand for workers in the areas of play work, sport and recreation and the outdoors at children's activity camps, as children are not at school and have free time to take part in activities or need to be looked after whilst their parents are working. Seasonal work is temporary and usually lasts for just the period of a few weeks or months while the demand is high.

Volunteering

Volunteering is unpaid and often takes place at weekends and in the evenings after people have finished their day at work or at school or college.

Casual work

Casual work is usually temporary, such as working in a leisure centre during the summer holidays to help supervise a children's summer activity scheme. It doesn't usually offer much in the way of career progression or benefits. A lot of seasonal work in the sport and active leisure industry could also be classed as casual work.

Qualifications

For many jobs in the sport and active leisure industry you need specific qualifications before you can be considered for the role. You may also need work experience in the role that you are applying for, eg as part of the practical work needed to gain the required qualification, or to show the employer that you are committed to the job and have a good understanding of what it actually involves. The job descriptions below examine the qualifications, skills and attributes required for a person working in a job role from each of the four main sectors in sport and active leisure.

Sport and recreation – Sports Development Officer

As a Sports Development Officer Vicki must be a good communicator.

Job role: The aim of this job is to help ensure that people of all ages and levels of ability in your local area have the opportunity to take part in sport and develop their skills. A sports development officer may need to focus on promoting one particular sport, such as tennis, or may promote participation in a variety of different sports and activities.

Skills and qualifications: Most sports development officers will have a sports-related degree or BTEC Higher qualification for this job. The skills required include an enthusiasm for sports and coaching, excellent communication skills, the ability to work alone or as a member of a team, good leadership and organisational skills and the ability to be flexible and adapt to different situations.

Case study: Vicki, Sports Development Officer

Vicki is a sports development officer in outer London.
Her main role is to encourage participation in sport and active leisure for targeted groups of people in the area, such as women and older adults. The best part of her job is that she gets to meet lots of new people and she is passionate about helping people to incorporate physical activity into their everyday lives. The part that she doesn't enjoy is having to travel around London, which can be especially difficult in the rush hour.

As a Leisure Centre Manager Julie must be able to lead and manage others.

Health and fitness – Leisure Centre Manager

Job role: Leisure centres vary in size. Some just consist of a small sports hall whereas others may have a wide range of facilities including competition and leisure swimming pools, athletics tracks, playing fields and restaurants. The leisure centre manager is responsible for the overall running of the leisure centre. Part of the role involves encouraging people in the local community to use the centre's facilities and ensuring that they have a safe and enjoyable experience. A centre manager will help to recruit staff and will manage and motivate them. They will also have to organise the programmes of activities that the centre runs, establish systems and procedures for the operational side of running the centre, prepare and manage budgets, monitor sales and centre usage, ensure the health and safety of staff and customers and deal with any customer complaints or incidents.

Skills and qualifications: Leisure centre managers may have worked their way up through the different jobs in the centre after having entered the industry with GCSEs or a vocational qualification such as a BTEC in Sport or a Diploma in Sport and Active Leisure. Alternatively leisure centre managers may enter the industry at a senior level with a higher-level qualification such as a degree in Sports and Leisure Management. The skills required for this role include confidence, excellent leadership skills, assertiveness, good communication skills, good time management, self-motivation, presence and professionalism.

The outdoors – Mountain Leader

Job role: A mountain leader may be based at an outdoor pursuits centre leading mountain walks, or work with different groups of people in various locations, such as training a Venture Scouting group in the expedition part of the Duke of Edinburgh Award.

Skills and qualifications: A mountain leader will need to have a lot of experience of walking and navigating in the outdoors. They will need to attend a mountain leader instructor course, gain further walking experience and pass a mountain leader assessment in order to qualify as a mountain leader. The skills required for this job role include excellent navigational skills, high levels of personal fitness, a first aid qualification, good communication skills and excellent health and safety knowledge.

Case study: Julie, Leisure Centre Manager

Julie is a leisure centre manager and works for a well-known health and fitness chain. Her job requires her to meet regularly with other staff at her leisure centre to monitor progress in their specified areas, such as sales or class timetables. The best parts of the job are the fact she works with a great team of people and is able to use her initiative to promote new ideas and carry out research into new technology and equipment that can be bought for her centre. The worst part of her job is when she has to discipline staff, which thankfully doesn't happen very often!

As a mountain leader Mike must use his walking and navigational skills.

Case study: Mike, Mountain Leader

Mike is a mountain leader based in an outdoor pursuits centre in the Lake District. He works with children from the age of 12 up to adults of all ages. His main role is to lead groups of walkers on suitable walks that are appropriate to their ability levels and fitness. He has to ensure that they all have the correct kit, check the weather forecast and then lead the group on the walk. His favourite part of the job is when he leads a group on an expedition where they cover long distances and camp out at night. The worst part of his job is when he is unable to complete a walk because the weather conditions become unsafe.

Play work – Nursery Assistant

Job role: This role requires involvement in all aspects of caring for children, which includes a child's emotional, intellectual, social and physical development. A nursery assistant will be involved in planning and preparing children's activities, liaising with parents, recording observations of children's development for their records, managing children's behaviour, maintaining the cleanliness of the playrooms and equipment, supervising meals and feeding children.

Skills and qualifications: To work as a nursery assistant it is necessary to have or be working towards childcare-related qualifications. A person working in this role needs to enjoy working with children, work well as a member of a team and be patient, energetic and enthusiastic. A nursery assistant must be caring, friendly and understanding and need good communication and time management skills.

As a nursery assistant Jeanette must be patient and enthusiastic.

Case study: Jeanette, Nursery Assistant

Jeanette is a nursery assistant at a private village nursery. Her main roles are planning and taking part in activities for the children and monitoring their progress to feed back to their parents and add to their records. Her favourite part of the job is getting to know the children and building up good relationships with them. Her least favourite thing about the job is the amount of paperwork that needs to be completed in order to monitor the children's development.

Just checking

Select one of the jobs from the four examples given in this topic and then carry out research to find out:

✳ the hours of work

✳ the salary range

✳ where a person could work in this job role in your local area.

Functional Skills

This Hotlink activity will help to provide evidence of ICT.

Personal, Learning and Thinking Skills

This Hotlink activity will help to provide evidence of Independent Enquirer and Reflective Learner.

Hotlink

Go to the SkillsActiveCareers website to research case studies of different job roles in the sport and active leisure industry. For details of how to access this website see the **Hotlinks** section – **Introduction**, page xi.

Starting Point

What government policy initiatives are you aware of that aim to promote participation in sport and active leisure?

JARGON BUSTER

Policy initiatives This phrase is used to cover a wide range of things that the government does to help it achieve its aims, such as new laws being passed, new schemes, new targets, or new rules on funding.

4.5 Government policy initiatives

You have now examined jobs in the sport and active leisure industry and considered the skills that are needed. However, in looking at these roles you must understand how national government **policy initiatives** can change the nature of the job market.

Diploma Daily

Government Initiative to Get Everyone Active

A new government policy initiative has set a target to increase the activity levels of the British population. In 2003 24.4% of the population were classed as regularly active. The government's target is to increase this to 70% of the population by 2020. This initiative will have a significant effect on the nature of the jobs and opportunities that exist within the sport and active leisure industry.

Government policy initiatives relating to sport

A range of government policies relating to sport and active leisure exist, including:

* education initiatives
* health initiatives
* social and community initiatives
* sports Lottery funding
* major games
* equal opportunities
* local provision.

Each one will be discussed in further detail in this topic.

Education initiatives

Within the national government, the Department for Culture, Media and Sport (DCMS) is responsible for sport and the Department for Children, Schools and Families (DCSF) is responsible for schools. These two departments work closely together on initiatives involving school sport. An example of one such initiative is the PE and Sport Strategy for Young People (PESSYP). This initiative has recognised the growing importance of PE in schools and has led the way in increasing the percentage of children doing at least two hours per week of high-quality PE – from 25% in 2002 to 90% in 2008. This initiative has recently been updated and it is now aiming to encourage young people under 16 to take part in five hours of sport and PE per week – by 2013 it is hoped that 60% of young people will be meeting this target. These five hours can be made up of PE and sports classes, school sport and sport in the community.

Another development was the creation of School Sport Partnerships (SSPs), designed to improve sports opportunities for 5–16-year-olds. A person called a Partnership Development Manager (often based in a sports college) works with around eight local secondary schools that each have a member of staff designated as a School Sports Coordinator. These in turn work with nearby primary schools who each nominate a Primary Link Teacher. All these staff are allocated time to perform these roles. This policy has introduced changes to the way people work and created new opportunities for those working in school sport.

Sometimes sport is affected by broader government policies. For example, the Specialist Schools Programme has enabled secondary schools to specialise in one of 10 subject areas such as science, arts, engineering and music. Sport is one of these 10 specialisms and there are now over 400 specialist sports colleges.

Health initiatives

The Register of Exercise Professionals have identified that there is now a huge demand for qualified exercise referral instructors. To understand why this situation came to exist in the job market you need to look again at the government policies behind this. With rising concerns about the consequences of an unhealthy population there has been a growing focus on the role that sport and active leisure can play in tackling this problem. As a result there has been a rise in the number of **GP referrals** to leisure centres or health clubs. The GP referral scheme means that people can be referred by their doctor to exercise programmes to help improve their health.

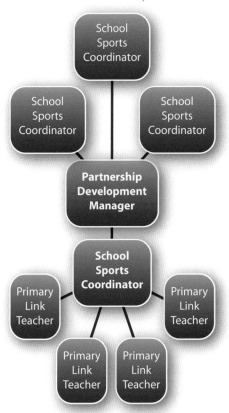

School Sports Partnerships – an example of a government policy and how it has affected jobs in sport and PE.

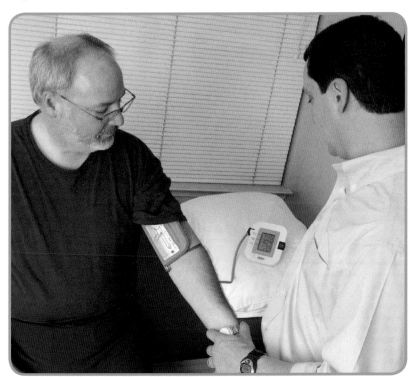

More and more people are involved in GP referral schemes which aim to improve their fitness levels and overall health.

Personal, Learning and Thinking Skills

This activity will help to provide evidence of Reflective Learner.

Over to you

If you were a School Sports Coordinator in your area, what changes would you make to the activities that take place? Give reasons why.

JARGON BUSTER

GP referral Being referred by a doctor to a leisure centre or health club to begin a specialised exercise programme.

Hotlink

If you are interested a career in exercise referral, check out the Register of Exercise Professionals website and look at the Level 3 and Level 4 qualifications. For details of how to access this website see the **Hotlinks** section – **Introduction**, page xi. The same site also has information on personal training and fitness instructing.

Hotlink

If you are interested in active youth work, check out the National Youth Agency website to see what qualifications are available. For details of how to access this website see the **Hotlinks** section – **Introduction**, page xi

When people who have been referred by a GP to a leisure centre or health club arrive in the centre, it is important that they are met and supervised by properly-trained staff. This has not only introduced a new type of job opportunity (as specialist staff are needed to look after these people) but also the development of training courses to meet this demand. Due to the importance of this work, only those with higher qualifications recognised by the Register of Exercise Professionals can carry out 'Exercise Referral' roles. Increasingly, this is allowing a growing opportunity for fitness professionals to obtain additional qualifications and to specialise in the populations they work with, such as stroke victims or the elderly.

Social and community initiatives

The government see their involvement in sport as a good way to bring communities together and reduce anti-social behaviour. For example, the government's Play Strategy, launched in 2008, aims to see supervised or unsupervised play areas in every residential area, and by 2020 the objective is that 'all children and young people will be able to access world-class play and recreation spaces near where they live, within communities that are child-friendly' (Play Shaper website). Furthermore, from 2006 local authorities have had a responsibility to provide access for young people to sufficient positive leisure-time activities.

Sports Lottery funding

The advent of sports Lottery funding in 1994 was one of the most significant developments in community sport. Profits from the National Lottery have helped to provide funding that has allowed local authorities, schools, clubs and other organisations to build and upgrade their facilities. Many people now work in these facilities as coaches, youth workers, fitness instructors, managers and leisure attendants.

Major games

The UK government has developed a policy to support attempts to bring major games and events to the UK. These include the London 2012 Olympics, the 2014 Glasgow Commonwealth Games, the 2015 Rugby World Cup and the bid for the 2018 FIFA World Cup. These games raise the profile of the sport and active leisure industry and create new jobs and opportunities for people to volunteer. The UK government has become increasingly active in promoting sporting excellence and, in 2002, launched the English Institute of Sport (EIS). The EIS provides access for sports professionals such as sports nutritionists, sports psychologists and sports physiologists to help them to prepare for and compete in major events.

Celebrations as London wins the bid to host the 2012 Olympic Games

Equal opportunities

One of the most important factors in sports development policy over recent years has been the idea of inclusivity (including everybody). This means that organisations such as Sport England have promoted an ongoing series of programmes to increase participation amongst all sections of society, including disabled people, women and girls, the elderly, young people and people from ethnic minorities. For example, in many local authorities women now instruct women-only exercise classes.

Local provision

Despite all of these government policies, the sporting opportunities that you can enjoy in your local area will depend on your local authority's policies. Some local authorities are more committed to sport and active leisure than others, and some are better at delivering high-quality services. The policies of your local council can affect sport and leisure organisations (and job opportunities) in many ways. For example:

* Numbers and locations of facilities: This can include how many leisure centres, parks, youth clubs and playgrounds are in your area.

* Pricing: Local clubs that use council facilities, such as football clubs hiring playing fields will be affected by the fees they have to pay.

* Grants policy: Some clubs rely on the financial help they receive. A change to the local policy on funding clubs could have a big effect on these organisations. It could also affect coaches doing 'sessional work' at these clubs as a cut may mean their fees can no longer be paid.

* Opening hours: Are the facilities near you open at times that make them accessible?

* Fair access: Do policies give everyone a fair chance to use facilities?

Sport and active leisure organisations

The government policies that you have looked at can affect all types of organisations involved in sport. Some examples are:

* Private sector: Under the Taylor Report, which followed the Hillsborough disaster, professional football clubs are required to provide effective stewarding. This means that qualifications have developed, such as NVQs in Spectator Safety, and large numbers of stewards are employed at football grounds on match days.

* Public sector: Public sector organisations such as local authorities can apply for National Lottery funding to improve facilities.

* Third sector: Many different policies can affect the third sector, for example many local authorities insist that coaches must be insured before they can hire out facilities for activities like martial arts.

* Sports media: The government has policies covering the broadcasting of major events that means events such as the FA Cup Final must remain available on free-to-air television, while secondary coverage must be available for events like the Ryder Cup. Events not on the list can be bid for by satellite and cable TV companies.

* Commercial sponsors: Government policies can affect sponsorship activities, such as the ban on tobacco sponsorship of sports events that came into effect in 2003.

Personal, Learning and Thinking Skills

This activity will help to provide evidence of Independent Enquirer and Reflective Learner.

Over to you

* Do you think it is better for a council to invest in a single large sports facility, such as a multi-use leisure centre, or to divide the money between lots of smaller centres nearer where people live?

* Find out if any facilities or clubs in your local area have had to respond to changes in local policies like those mentioned above.

Just checking

* Is your school or college offering two or more hours of sport and PE a week?

* In what ways is your school or college trying to address the new government initiative for five hours of PE and sport provision a week?

* Do leisure centres or health clubs in your local area offer a GP referral scheme?

* How do local communities benefit from social and community initiatives?

* Why do you think sport and active leisure providers should encourage equal opportunities for participation?

Starting Point

How have organisations in your local area undergone changes as a result of government policy initiatives?

JARGON BUSTER

Best value Councils have to get as much for their money as they can in order to improve their service.

Personal, Learning and Thinking Skills

This activity will help to provide evidence of Reflective Learner.

Over to you

You are managing a leisure centre that is fully booked, apart from a new vacancy in your only sports hall on Thursday evenings. You know that you could fill the sports hall with fitness classes every Thursday and hundreds of people would take part but, on the other hand, a local volleyball team for very talented youngsters with Olympic aspirations need extra training time in order to fulfil their potential.

* What would you do?
* In your opinion, which decision would be more in line with government priorities? Give reasons to justify your answer.

4.6 Responses of sport and active leisure organisations

Government policies can have a significant effect upon an organisation. They can result in changes in staff roles and responsibilities and job opportunities. This topic will explore the responses of organisations to government policies.

Government and sport and active leisure industry priorities

You can see where government policies have had a significant effect on organisations by looking at what has happened in local authority leisure centres. In the past, all the staff in local authority leisure centres were council staff. However, now, under the '**Best Value**' legislation, all councils must attempt to get the best value for the money they spend. This means that some councils employ management companies to manage the leisure centres for them. As a result the staff employed at these leisure centres do not work for the council but for the company managing the centre; often, many of these staff can be part-time or casual employees.

Conflicting priorities

Having good intentions is great, but when resources are limited hard choices have to be made. For example, in an indoor tennis centre you want to encourage more people to play tennis, but on the other hand junior county tennis players need lots of practice time if they are to improve. Finding the right balance is not easy. Similarly, should popular swimming pool time be given over to a water polo club who need to train for competition, or to the general public for recreational swimming?

Providing new facilities

One of the key weapons in the drive to increase participation is to provide new facilities. This is not easy. Many areas of the country still don't have adequate facilities and many of the facilities that do exist are now ageing and in need of updating. While finding the money to build a new leisure centre may be a challenge, this is not the end of the story. Often, local authority leisure centres do not make enough money to cover their costs, so the council needs to find funds each year to keep them open and to staff new and existing facilities.

Do you think this facility is adequate?

Improving sport and active leisure provision

Your assignment for this unit needs to include suggestions on how sport and active leisure provision can be improved, taking into account government and industry priorities. There are several things that you can think about when suggesting potential changes to improve sport and active leisure provision in your area. The following should give you some ideas:

* Suggest new facilities that are needed in your neighbourhood. This could be a new open play space, an adventure playground, or new floodlit play areas. Try to find a suitable site and think about what is needed most in your area.

* Suggest changes to what goes on in your current centres. You may feel that the local leisure centre doesn't offer enough coaching in a certain sport or enough of a certain type of fitness class.

* Suggest changes to the sport and active leisure policies of your local council. You may feel that the pricing policy is unfair, that the opening times need to be extended or that the company managing your local centre on behalf of the council is not doing a good enough job.

When coming up with your ideas, think about:

* How your ideas fit in with the government priorities mentioned earlier, such as:

  – helping children have five hours of sport per week

  – improving the nation's health by reducing levels of obesity and heart disease

  – providing safe local play space in all areas by 2020

  – improving the chances of winning medals at major events

  – raising participation rates (target of 70% active by 2020).

  Does your idea help to deliver any of these priorities in your neighbourhood?

* Are there any conflicting priorities involved in your suggestion? For example, are you going to use up money that could be used elsewhere or are you taking up space that could be used for another purpose?

* How would your ideas affect local job opportunities in sport and active leisure?

Just checking

* Suggest how 'best value' could be applied in your local area.
* What new facilities do you think could be brought into your local area to try to increase participation in sport and active leisure?

Starting Point

How could you assess your own suitability for a job role of your choice?

4.7 Assessing your own personal attributes

Some jobs in the sport and active leisure industry may sound perfect for you. However, before you can think about applying for them you should ensure that you have all the required personal attributes so that you are in with a chance of getting the job. In this section you will learn how to assess your own personal attributes to help you determine which job roles could be suitable for you.

Personal attributes

Your personal attributes include:

* skills
* achievements
* experience
* knowledge
* qualifications
* interests.

Over the years you have probably collected a wide range of personal attributes without really thinking about it. To help a potential employer determine if you are suitable for a job, you need to select the relevant personal attributes to discuss with them. Now is a good time to think about and make notes of all of your personal attributes so that you have a clear picture of all that you have done, which may well help you on your way to getting your perfect job in the sport and active leisure industry. To help clarify each personal attribute, some ideas and suggestions have been listed below.

Skills

These are all the things that you have learnt to do over time. You need to provide examples of how you have demonstrated each of these skills:

* Time management skills – examples include getting to school/college on time, and completing and handing in coursework on time.

* Communication skills – examples include giving presentations and working with other people.

* Leadership skills – examples include being a sports captain, leading sports or children's activities, or leading a team of people to organise an event.

* Teamwork skills – examples include collaborating with others when planning an event or being a member of a sports team.

Achievements

These are all the awards that you have received, goals that you have achieved and positions that you hold. Examples of achievements include:

* captain of a sports team

* Duke of Edinburgh Award

* prefect

* County Champion at a sporting event.

Over to you

* What sorts of activities or courses could you do in order to improve your skills, achievements and experience to help you when you come to apply for a job in the sport and active leisure industry?

Experience

Experience includes the time that you have spent observing or working in the sport and active leisure industry or on other related work experience. It can include experience you have had in order to improve your own personal skills in a selected activity. Examples include:

* part-time work in the sport and active leisure industry
* voluntary sports coaching
* voluntary work at a Rainbows or Beavers group with young children
* assisting in leading a walking expedition.

Knowledge

This includes information that you have learnt through school or from hobbies and other pastimes. For example:

* English, maths or science knowledge
* in-depth knowledge of a particular sport or activity
* ICT knowledge – Microsoft Windows, Microsoft Excel, PowerPoint etc.

Qualifications

These include any academic or vocational qualifications that you have gained. You may have gained some additional qualifications whilst working on your main qualification at school or college. Examples include:

* National Pool Lifeguard Award
* First Aid at Work qualification
* Health and Safety at Work qualification
* BTEC First Certificate in Sport
* Functional Maths
* CYQ Level 2 Fitness Instructor

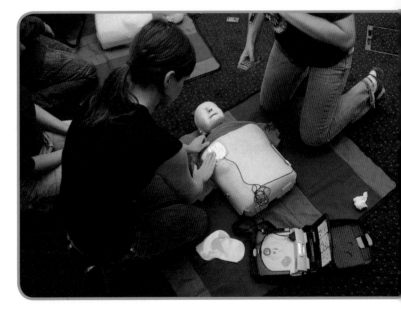

Your personal attributes might include things like First Aid qualifications.

Interests

Interests include the things that you like to do in your free time. You should try and include some that are relevant to the sport and active leisure industry, but they don't have to be directly related. Examples include:

* rock climbing
* going to the cinema
* computer gaming
* playing the piano
* ice skating
* ballroom dancing.

Just checking

Make a list of your own personal attributes. Use the following headings to structure your list:

* skills
* achievements
* experience
* knowledge
* qualifications
* interests.

Starting Point

Which people could you go to in order to gain useful feedback about your personal attributes?

4.8 Reviewing your personal attributes for suitable job roles

To help you to fully understand your personal attributes and how they may be suitable for different job roles, it is a good idea to get feedback from other people and spend time reflecting on what you enjoy and what interests you the most.

Methods of reviewing personal attributes

Some people can be hesitant about giving themselves praise and recognising their true abilities. Others may think they have excellent skills in some areas, but in reality they may not be quite as good as they thought. Getting feedback from other people is a good way of finding out how others view you, and this can give you some real perspective on your true skills and abilities.

In order for feedback to be useful, you should aim to get it from more than one person. Friends, tutors, coaches, parents and/or people who have supervised you at work or on work experience will all be able to give different perspectives on your personal attributes. You could ask each person for feedback about your:

Asking other people for feedback can be a good way of reviewing your attributes.

* communication skills
* leadership skills
* teamwork skills
* time management skills.

Wherever possible, try to ask them for examples so that you can understand exactly what they mean. You may find that different people see different sides of you. For example, a parent may say that your time management skills need to be improved as you are often late home from social events or cannot get up in the morning, whereas a work supervisor may say that you have excellent time management skills as you always arrive at work on time.

Written reports, such as end-of-year reports from your school or college, will also help to provide information for your review. If you have been on a work experience placement you may have a written report from your supervisor that you can use. Certificates that you have been awarded over the years can help you to remember any achievements that you have gained, and it is a good idea to keep these in a safe place so that they can be used as evidence for prospective employers. Once you have gathered all the information, carry out a full review of your personal attributes, including your strengths and areas for improvement.

Once you have identified your areas for improvement, try to set targets to help you carry out these improvements. For example, to help you improve your time management skills, one of your targets could be to get out of bed 10 minutes early every day for a week.

Personal, Learning and Thinking Skills

This activity will help to provide evidence of Independent Enquirer, Self Manager and Reflective Learner.

Over to you

* Carry out a review of your personal attributes using feedback from a variety of different people, written reports and any certificates that you may have.
* Set yourself realistic targets to help you with your identified areas for improvement.

Suitability for job roles

Now that you have carried out a thorough review of your personal attributes you can assess your suitability for any job roles that you are interested in. You will need to find out the following information about the job role:

* qualifications required

* skills required

* nature of duties required in the job role.

You will need to give examples of how your skills, achievements, experience, knowledge and qualifications match up to each of your selected job roles and identify how you plan to address any areas for improvement.

Case study: Shaznee's dream job

Shaznee is 17 years old and wants to become a football coach for children aged 5–16. The job role of a football coach is to develop football skills, tactics, techniques, teamwork and understanding of the game in groups of children. Most training sessions will take place at weekends or after school. She knows that the skills required for this job include:

* a good knowledge of and interest in football

* good communication skills

* an ability to motivate and encourage children

* good time management skills

* good leadership skills.

She will also need an FA coaching qualification for this job role. After carrying out a review of her personal attributes she has assessed her suitability for this job role:

* She has played football for her school team and now plays for her county, so she has a very good knowledge of and interest in football.

* She has carried out some work experience assisting her local club's football coach. The coach has provided a written report stating that she has excellent communication skills, both with the children she worked with and with the coach.

* The report also states that she had trouble with time management skills and often arrived only just on time or a few minutes late to the training sessions.

* Her school report and work experience report prove that she was always on time for lessons and training sessions and always handed coursework in on time, which demonstrates her good time management skills.

* Her leadership skills were demonstrated when she organised a successful five-a-side football tournament to help to raise money for a charity event.

Shaznee has a Level 1 FA coaching award and is planning to go on a Level 2 coaching course once she has completed enough football coaching hours from her voluntary coaching to qualify.

Just checking

* Having read the case study, how well do you think Shaznee has related her personal attributes, skills and qualifications to the job role that she is interested in?

* Why do you think it is a good idea to identify any areas for improvement and decide how to address them in a review?

Starting Point

* Have you ever had an interview before? If so, how did it go?

* What do you think are the most important factors in an interview?

4.9 Preparing for a job interview

For virtually all jobs you are expected to meet with your prospective employer and answer a series of questions during the application process. This helps them to find out about you and determine if you are suitable for the job that they have to offer. This process is called an interview. To help you to do well, it is a good idea to spend some time preparing yourself for the interview.

What to do before the interview

The job role and the company

Before your interview find out as much as possible about the job role. This will help you to explain why you have applied for the job and demonstrate your full understanding of what the job involves. Make sure you know the following information about the job role:

* pay

* working conditions

* promotion opportunities

* how your personal interests relate to the job role.

You can do this by looking up information on the internet or, even better, visit the organisation to get a real feel for the place. You should have been given a job description so make sure you have read it thoroughly. If you visit the organisation, try and ask a member of staff who is working in the job role that you are interested in for more information.

Dress

Decide on what you are going to wear before the interview so that you have the appropriate clothing ready. If you are not sure exactly what to wear, choose clean, smart, dark-coloured clothes such as a suit or smart trousers/skirt and a shirt/blouse. Ensure that you have clean hair and that is it styled appropriately.

Questions

Spend some time thinking about the questions that you may be asked. For example:

* What do you know about this job?

* What do you like about this job?

* How are you qualified for this job?

* What could you bring to this job role?

* How well do you work as a member of a team?

* What are your strengths?

* What are your weaknesses?

Work out how you are going to answer each of these questions and provide examples where possible to show how you have used appropriate skills effectively and successfully. Once you have worked out suitable answers, practise saying the answers out loud either with another person or in front of a mirror. If you are able to practise with another person they can give you feedback about what you did well and where you could improve. By watching yourself in front of a mirror you can study your body language whilst answering the questions, which is another very important method of communicating during an interview. Think about questions that you can ask the interviewer at the end of the interview too, as this shows the interviewer that you are interested and want to know more about the company or job role.

On the day of the interview

Arrival

Aim to arrive at your interview location at least 10 minutes before the interview so you have time to compose yourself and will be on time. When you're introduced to your interviewer, greet them with a firm handshake.

Body language

Many people form a first impression about someone based on their body language alone. It is therefore very important to use the right body language to convey the right message. Ensure that you are using body language that portrays self-confidence, enthusiasm and interest in the job role.

Over to you

Look at the two photos shown on the right. If you were the person giving the interview, how would you describe each candidate based upon their body language?

Speaking

Throughout the interview, make sure you speak at a volume that is loud enough for the interviewer to hear. If you are too quiet it gives the impression that you are lacking in self-confidence and the interviewer may not be able to hear what you are saying. Vary the pitch of your voice so that you do not speak in a monotone, as this gives the impression that you are bored and lack enthusiasm.

Eye contact

Try to maintain eye contact with your interviewer as this shows that you are interested in what they have to say. However, don't stare at them as this can sometimes look threatening.

Posture

Sit up with your back straight as this communicates enthusiasm and confidence. A slouched posture gives the impression that you are not interested or lack confidence in yourself.

Listening

When the interviewer is talking, nod your head and smile to show that you are actively listening and interested in what they have to say.

Answering questions

Answer the questions the interviewer asks you in detail, using appropriate examples of previous experience or current skills. Use persuasive arguments to show how your personal attributes make you suitable for the job role, giving examples of how your knowledge or experience matches the job requirements. Explain how any skills or knowledge that you do not have can be acquired in the future. Emphasise favourable things about yourself and what you have done, and make sure you explain any negative facts. For example, if your school report stated that you had poor time management skills, try to explain how you have addressed this issue so that it will not be a problem in the future.

You may be faced with some questions that you have not prepared for. Take a little time (but not too much) to think about the answer you want to give. If you do not understand the question, ask the interviewer to repeat it. If you are still uncertain about what the interviewer is asking, you can answer by saying 'Do you mean…?', which helps to show that you have understood some of what they have said but need further explanation. Alternatively, you could ask them to explain their question in more detail.

Maintaining eye contact with your interviewer can help you make a good impression.

Case study: Raj's interview

Raj has an interview at a well-known health and fitness centre for the job role of a gym instructor. The following shows how the interview went.

Interviewer: Hello Raj, my name is Andrew.

Raj: Hiya Andy, nice to meet you.

They shake hands.

Interviewer: So tell me why you are interested in this job?

Raj: (*sitting upright and smiling*) Ummmmm, well, I like working out in the gym, I train almost every day and this job will give me free access to all of your fantastic facilities. I also have a Level 2 CYQ gym instructor award so I do have a good understanding of the job role requirements.

Interviewer: Our instructors work together as a team to ensure the smooth running of the gym. How would you describe your teamwork skills?

Raj: I'm captain of my school football team so I'm good at motivating others and working with a team. I have also achieved all of my personal learning and thinking skills for Team Work, which shows that I've proved I work well as a member of a team.

Interviewer: What do you think about the hours of the job role?

Raj: As long as I don't have to start too early, I'll be okay!

Interviewer: You do realise that the job requires shift work, which entails some early mornings and late nights, and a day at the weekend?

Raj: I don't mind that as long as I don't have to work Friday or Saturday nights. I go out with my mates on those nights.

Interviewer: What do you think you could bring to the role?

Raj: (*Fidgeting and twiddling his thumbs*) Ummm, I am very enthusiastic about getting fit and can help to motivate people to get the best out of their training session. I also had good feedback from my tutor on the gym instructor course, which stated that I was a patient instructor and was able to provide clear instructions to clients.

Interviewer: Thank you Raj. Do you have any questions for me?

Raj: Yes, how much will I get paid for this job?

Interviewer: Did you receive the information on the job role we sent out?

Raj: Yes, but I can't remember what the pay rate was.

Interviewer: The starting salary is £16,000.

Raj: Okay, that would be alright to start.

Interviewer: Thank you Raj, we will be in touch.

1 What parts of the interview did Raj do well in?

2 What parts of the interview did Raj not do so well in?

3 How could Raj have improved his answers to the interview questions?

Functional Skills

This activity will help to provide evidence of English reading and writing.

Personal, Learning and Thinking Skills

This activity will help to provide evidence of Independent Enquirer and Reflective Learner.

Just checking

* Why is preparation important before an interview? Suggest what might go wrong if you did not prepare properly.

* Explain how you would prepare for an interview.

Paul is 16 years old and is looking for some casual work during the summer holidays. He has eight weeks off and is hoping to earn enough money to pay for driving lessons when he turns 17. After the holidays he will return to his school sixth form to study for a BTEC National in Sport, so it would be a bonus if he could find work in the area of sport and active leisure.

Paul has always been a strong swimmer and swims at least twice a week. He also recently completed and passed his pool lifeguard qualification at his local public swimming pool. He is happy to work shifts and his parents have agreed that they will pick him up from work if he has to stay late. Paul has good access to town via public transport in the daytime and also has a bike that he could use to cycle to work if it is not too far away. There are a number of private sector facilities quite close to where Paul lives and ideally he would like to work in this sector as he has heard that the pay rates are usually better than in the public sector. He is also keen to receive benefits such as free membership.

Paul has some experience of working with children from his Junior Sport Leadership Award, which he completed in school. Whilst he found it quite good fun, he is not sure if he wants to work with children every day for eight weeks.

1 What resources could Paul use to help him look for work?

2 What sorts of jobs do you think would be appropriate for Paul? Explain your answer.

3 Do you think it will be helpful to Paul's job search that he is happy to work shifts? Explain your answer.

4 What sorts of personal skills and attributes would Paul need to work as a lifeguard?

5 How would you advise Paul to prepare himself for an interview?

For your project

In this unit you have explored research techniques for finding out about job opportunities in the sport and active leisure industry. You have also covered the structure of the sport and active leisure industry, which includes three sectors: public, private and voluntary (also known as the third sector). You should be aware of how each sector differs from the others in terms of provision and organisation.

Every job role requires specific skills and attributes and you have learnt how to examine your own skills and attributes to help you determine which sorts of job you are more suited to. You have also had the opportunity to learn to prepare and practise for a job interview, which will help you with any job interviews you may have in the future.

This unit has also explored various government initiatives and the impact these have had upon the sport and active leisure industry.

The following diagram gives some ideas for what you might decide to do your project on, based on the content of this unit.

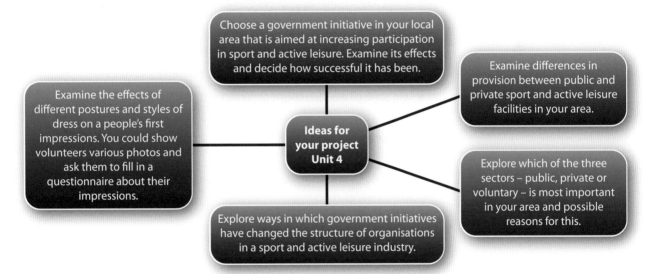

Choose a government initiative in your local area that is aimed at increasing participation in sport and active leisure. Examine its effects and decide how successful it has been.

Examine differences in provision between public and private sport and active leisure facilities in your area.

Examine the effects of different postures and styles of dress on a people's first impressions. You could show volunteers various photos and ask them to fill in a questionnaire about their impressions.

Ideas for your project Unit 4

Explore which of the three sectors – public, private or voluntary – is most important in your area and possible reasons for this.

Explore ways in which government initiatives have changed the structure of organisations in a sport and active leisure industry.

Possible project titles

✳ How are local education initiatives being addressed by a particular school/college in my area?

✳ How is a local school/college trying to achieve the five hours a week provision of PE and sport recommended by the government?

✳ How are the different sectors of health and fitness represented in my local area and why?

✳ How can a person working in play work go from being a nursery assistant to a nursery manager?

✳ How can body language affect the outcome of an interview?

✳ How has National Lottery money helped to fund a project or projects in my local area?

✳ How do community initiatives decrease anti-social behaviour?

Assessment guidance

This unit is assessed by one internally-set assignment. You will have a period of 16 hours to generate evidence for your assessment. In your assessment you will need to show that you:

* are able to carry out research into employment opportunities in the UK sport and active leisure industry

* know the structure of the UK sport and active leisure industry at either a local or national level

* know the job roles and career opportunities in the sport and active leisure industry

* know the skills and personal attributes required for sport and active leisure jobs

* understand the impact of government policy initiatives on the sport and active leisure industry

* understand how sport and active leisure organisations respond to local policy initiatives

* understand how local provision can be improved based upon government and sport and active leisure industry priorities

* understand how personal attributes relate to job roles

* are able to ask questions to explore potential job roles

* are able to respond to questions in order to communicate your personal suitability for job roles within the sport and active leisure industry

* are able to use communication skills to project your personal image.

Time management

* Although you have 16 hours to generate evidence for this assignment, this time frame does not include time spent researching the topic area.

* The internal assessment will be split into different tasks. You will be given set times to generate evidence for each task whilst being supervised by your tutor or employer.

* You will be expected to complete an interview as part of your assignment, so it is a good idea to spend time rehearsing possible answers to interview questions whilst observing your own body language to check you are communicating the appropriate messages. Try rehearsing your answers in a mock interview with a friend or parent/guardian.

* Your tutor may well give you ideas for resources to use to help you carry out research before you attempt some of the tasks. You should aim to make time to read this information and carry out research for the set task so that you have a good understanding of the subject area.

✳ Your tutor may give you formative assessments that are similar to the actual task. You should make time to complete these 'trial' assessments as these will help to prepare you for the real task. Your tutor will be able to give you feedback on the areas that you have completed well and any areas for improvement.

Useful links

Work experience within the sport and active leisure industry will give you the opportunity to talk to members of staff and find out more about their job roles. This will help you to determine if you have the appropriate skills and personal attributes needed for these particular job roles.

Look out for any stories in local news programmes and local newspapers that may provide information on initiatives to increase participation in sport and active leisure in your area.

There are lots of useful websites that will help you with your research for this unit. For details of how to access these sites see the hotlinks section – Introduction, page x.

How you will be assessed

For your Unit 4 assessment, you need to make sure that you can meet all of the assessment criteria for the five learning outcomes, as shown in the table below.

Learning outcome	Assessment criteria
LO1: Be able to carry out research into employment opportunities in the UK sport and active leisure industry	1 Carry out research to investigate employment opportunities. 2 Ask questions to explore potential job roles.
LO2: Know the structure of the UK sport and active leisure industry	1 Describe the structure of the national or local sport and active leisure industry. 2 Describe the different job roles and career opportunities available from sport and active leisure sectors. 3 Describe the skills and attributes required for jobs.
LO3: Understand the impact of government policy on the sport and active leisure industry	1 Examine the effects of government policy initiatives on the local or national sport and active leisure industry. 2 Explain how sport and active leisure organisations respond to local policy initiatives. 3 Suggest potential changes to improve sport and active leisure provision, taking into account government and industry priorities.
LO4: Understand how personal attributes relate to job roles	1 Review personal attributes to inform job aspirations. 2 Assess personal suitability for job roles.
LO5: Be able to communicate personal suitability for jobs in sport and active leisure and related industries	1 Present cases justifying personal suitability for job roles. 2 Give responses that provide answers to questions. 3 Use communication skills to project personal image.

Introduction

There are many different businesses in the sport and active leisure industry. Anyone working in the sport and active leisure industry needs to understand and apply some basic principles of business to help their organisation to run effectively and efficiently. In this unit you will learn about business and management skills that will help you in your future career in the sport and active leisure industry. You will identify simple business problems and learn how to develop and present solutions to these problems. One day you may run your own sport and active leisure business!

What will you learn?

In this unit you will cover the following learning outcomes:

LO1: Know about successful business models used in the sport and active leisure industry

LO2: Know how different types of businesses interrelate in the sport and active leisure industry

LO3: Understand the impact of volunteers on the effectiveness, profitability and success of sport and active leisure businesses

LO4: Know the management skills that contribute to successful sport and active leisure businesses

LO5: Be able to develop solutions to business problems

The following table shows how these five learning outcomes are covered by this unit.

Topic	Pages	Learning outcomes
5.1 Business models in the sport and active leisure industry	136–139	LO1
5.2 Successful business models	140–141	LO1
5.3 Interrelated businesses in the sport and active leisure industry	142–143	LO2
5.4 The impact of volunteers on sport and active leisure businesses	144–145	LO3
5.5 Management skills in sport and active leisure	146–147	LO4
5.6 Business problems	148–149	LO5
5.7 Implementing best practice	150–151	LO5
5.8 Developing solutions	152–153	LO5
5.9 Presentation skills	154–155	LO5

THINKING POINTS

* Name three successful businesses in the sport and active leisure industry.
* Why do you think each business has been successful?
* What types of sport and active leisure business are there in your local area?

Functional Skills

Personal, Learning and Thinking Skills

This unit offers various opportunities to develop functional skills and personal, learning and thinking skills. Where appropriate, different activities are signposted with the relevant personal, learning and thinking skills that you can develop.

Diploma Daily

Obesity Businesses Make Big Fat Profit

Business is booming for sport and active leisure providers who are targeting the 'larger market'. Government initiatives and funding to promote physical activity for obese people have really paid off. Fitness classes and new gym equipment specifically designed for obese adults and children are bringing in customers galore. Never has there been a better time to be a fitness professional, a healthy food and drink franchise or a centre manager; there's more work available than you could imagine!

1 How do market trends such as this example increase business opportunities?

2 What do you think the employment opportunities in sport and active leisure are really like today?

How you will be assessed

This unit is internally assessed. For this unit you will need to be able to carry out research and present evidence to demonstrate that you are able to develop and present solutions to identified business problems in a sport and active leisure business. You will need to present the following evidence in your assignment:

✱ An assessment of how best practice can be implemented in a sport and active leisure business.

✱ A signed learner observation record form, completed by your tutor or employer, commenting on your presentation of solutions to the business problems of a sport and active leisure business.

Unit links

This unit links closely to Level 2, Unit 4: Working in the local sport or active leisure industry and Unit 7: Access for all in sport and active leisure.

Case study: Rob goes freelance

Rob is 18 years old and has just completed a personal trainer qualification. He works full time in a health and fitness centre as a gym instructor but would also like to make some more money by working freelance as a personal trainer in his spare time. He knows some health clubs allow staff to carry out personal training sessions in the gym where they work as gym instructors and thinks this could be a good idea. However, he is unsure of the prices that he should charge per hour for this service. He hasn't had any experience of marketing so he is concerned that he will not be able to get any clients. He knows of one other personal trainer in his local area, who is female and 45 years of age.

1 What could Rob do in order to help work out how much he should charge per hour for personal training?

2 How could Rob advertise his personal training service?

3 How could Rob combine his work in the gym and his personal training service?

5.1 Business models in the sport and active leisure industry

There are different business models in the sport and active leisure industry. The main differences between the different types are related to the number of people who own the business and how much of the business they own. The different types of business model in the sport and active leisure industry are explored in this topic.

Types of business model

The main types of business model used in sport and active leisure are shown in the diagram below:

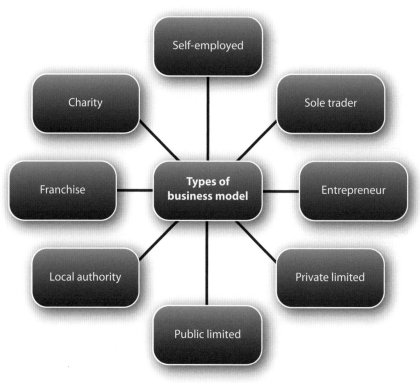

Self-employed

A self-employed person works for themselves and is responsible for seeking out job opportunities. They determine their own hours of work. However, a self-employed person does not receive benefits such as a pension, paid leave or sick pay. In the sport and active leisure industry there are many self-employed workers. Examples include freelance aerobics instructors, personal trainers, tennis coaches, child minders and outdoor pursuits instructors.

Sole trader

A sole trader business model has one person in charge of the business who makes all the decisions on how the business operates. That person is able to keep all the profits made by the business. However, they are personally liable for any debts, which may mean that they would have to sell their house and other personal possessions to pay off these debts.

Personal, Learning and Thinking Skills

This activity will help to provide evidence of Independent Enquirer and Reflective Learner.

Over to you

* What do you think are the benefits and drawbacks of being a sole trader business?
* What examples of sole traders do you know of in the sport and active leisure industry?

Entrepreneur

An entrepreneur is a person who has started their own business, often an innovative or risky one, and has worked hard to build and grow the business to the extent that they may now have a number of people working for them.

Richard Branson is a well-known entrepreneur.

Private limited company

A limited company is one that has been registered on a government list called 'Companies House' and has limited risk. Limited risk means that if the company were to go bankrupt or have any debts, the money to pay these debts comes out of the company bank account and not from the company employees' personal bank finances. A limited company is owned by a number of people who hold 'shares' of that company. Each person with shares in the company is called a shareholder. The profits of a private limited company are divided between the shareholders, with the people who own lots of shares receiving a greater percentage of the profits compared to those who own a smaller number of shares. This money paid out to shareholders is called dividends. In a private limited company only certain individuals are able to buy shares. For example, family-based businesses may be private limited companies so that only family members are given access to buy shares. In the sport and active leisure industry there are large-scale private limited companies such as Manchester United Football Club.

Over to you

* Why do you think companies choose to become limited companies?

* Take a look in the newspaper or on the internet to see the stocks and shares values of various public limited companies.

* Which sport and active leisure public limited companies are doing well?

* Which sport and active leisure public limited companies are not doing so well?

Public limited company

A public limited company is similar to a private limited company; however, anyone can buy the shares. These shares can be bought and sold on the stock market and all shareholders receive dividends.

Case study: Craig's company

Craig is a self-employed freelance personal trainer.
He has been building up his client base for the last five years and is now considering starting up his own company. There are a number of public and private health and fitness centres in his town so he has access to lots of fitness equipment and facilities. There is also a large park, which he uses to train clients when the weather is good.

Craig knows some recently-qualified personal trainers in his local area who have expressed an interest in working with him as they have very few clients of their own at the moment. He is thinking about hiring two of these personal trainers, who he would employ on a casual basis, to help him to build up his client base even further. He would also need to employ someone to handle the administration, take bookings and deal with the accounts. He is quite happy to take on most of the marketing himself as he studied this when he was at college.

1 Craig was a self-employed freelance personal trainer; however, when he sets up his own company he will be paying staff to work for him. What sort of company model do you think would be best for Craig's business plan?

2 Explain why you have chosen this structure for Craig's company. Include in your answer:

   a the benefits of this structure

   b the drawbacks

   c any other structures that could be appropriate.

3 Do you think it would be a good idea for Craig to employ the other personal trainers on a part-time basis? Explain your answer.

4 If Craig's business plan works well, how could he expand his business in the future?

Local authorities

A local authority receives money from the national government and from taxes paid by people living in the local area (council tax). The local authorities will then use this money to pay private companies such as running children's play schemes or to help fund public leisure centres who are running the government's free swimming programme.

Franchises

A franchise is when an individual buys into a successful business model. The person or company sets up in a different location but uses the same business name and provides the same services or sells the same products as the original successful business. The **franchisee** has to buy a licence to use the name, products and services of the business and run the business in line with an agreement drawn up between the **franchisor** and the franchisee. The franchisee may need to pay ongoing fees to the original business or give them a percentage of their profits. In return the franchisee gets support in setting up and running the business. Examples of franchises in the sport and active leisure industry include Fit Kid and Tumble Tots.

Charity

The aim of a charity is to raise money for a specific cause or support other people. Some people who work for charities do so voluntarily; however, there may also be paid managers and workers. An example of a charity in sport and active leisure is the Youth Sport Trust – the money that they make is used to improve the quality and quantity of physical education and sport for young people.

JARGON BUSTER

Franchisee An individual who buys the rights to use a company's name and successful business model for their own business.

Franchisor A successful business that other businesses can buy into.

Over to you

* What other franchises are you aware of in the sport and active leisure industry?
* Why do you think people use franchises?
* What are the benefits of a franchise for a franchisee?
* What are the drawbacks of a franchise for a franchisee?

Personal, Learning and Thinking Skills

This activity will help to provide evidence of Independent Enquirer and Reflective Learner.

Just checking

What do you think are the benefits and drawbacks of being:
* a sole trader
* self-employed
* a limited company
* a franchisee

Give examples of public limited and private limited companies in the sport and active leisure industry and try to explain why you think each is public or private.

Starting Point

Why do you think businesses need to make a profit to be successful?

Personal, Learning and Thinking Skills

This activity will help to provide evidence of Independent Enquirer and Reflective Learner.

5.2 Successful business models

In order for a business to be classed as successful, it will usually need to be making a profit. However, there are various other methods of helping to determine if a business is successful and each of these will be explored in this topic.

Success indicators

A range of factors determine if a business is successful. These include:

* **Income:** the amount of money that the business brings in. Some of this income then needs to be used to pay employees, taxes and so on. These payments are called the 'outgoings'.

* **Profitability:** Profit is the money left over once all the outgoings have been paid. If the money coming in is greater than the money going out, the business will make a profit. Making a profit is important for any private company and is a key success indicator for this sector. However, there are many sport and active leisure centres in the public sector where making a profit is not a key success indicator.

* **Pricing strategies:** A business needs to price its goods or services high enough to make a profit. However, they also need to ensure that they are not pricing their goods or services so high that customers can't afford them. They need to ensure that the pricing is competitive, which means the prices are the same as or less than those of similar providers in their area.

Sales are one method used by sport and active leisure retailers to keep prices competitive and attract custom.

Personal, Learning and Thinking Skills

This activity will help to provide evidence of Independent Enquirer, Self Manager and Reflective Learner.

Over to you

* Compare the pricing for two sport and active leisure centres with similar provision in your local area.
* What are the similarities and differences in pricing? Can you explain these similarities and differences?

* **Staff size:** In many cases, successful businesses will expand by taking on more staff to cope with the greater demand for the product or service.

* **Market penetration:** This refers to how available or accessible a service or product is. For example, with sports shoes, certain brands such as Nike® and Reebok® have a high market penetration as they are very accessible and can be bought in most high street sports retailers.

* **Target market's disposable income:** The target markets are the types of people who will buy or use a product or service. Their disposable income is the money that they have left after paying for all their living essentials. If the target market's disposable income is reduced or increased then it affects the amount of money they have to spend on a product or service.

* **Sustainability of market:** This refers to whether the demand or customers for a particular product or service will always exist.

* **Customer or supporter base:** This refers to whether a provider has a good foundation of customers or supporters who can help ensure that their product or service is sustainable.

* **Competition:** Virtually all businesses have some sort of competition. For example, you will rarely find just one childcare provider or one gym in a large community. A business may try to make themselves different from their competition by having a **unique selling point**.

* **Demand and trends:** Sport and active leisure businesses are often affected by changes in the market's demands due to new trends. New exercise classes like spinning and boot camp are regularly emerging. A sports business must assess whether there will be a demand for a new class then buy equipment and ensure that they have the right instructors. If the business fails to keep up with trends, they may lose customers to other businesses who are responding to them.

* **Customer satisfaction:** All businesses need customers to buy their products and/or use their services, so it is important that customers are satisfied. A happy customer will keep coming back. When customers are satisfied they tell others, which brings in new custom.

* **Employee satisfaction:** When employees are satisfied they usually do their jobs well, which helps keep customers happy. If staff are not satisfied they may not perform as well and are more likely to take time off or leave. Having a high staff turnover costs businesses money in recruiting and training and can affect customer satisfaction. For example, if there was a high staff turnover in a nursery, the children might become unsettled. Employee satisfaction is influenced by a range of factors including being treated fairly, being paid enough, job satisfaction and receiving benefits such as paid leave and pensions.

* **Effectiveness and reliability:** A sport and active leisure product or service should be effective and reliable to ensure customer satisfaction. It should do the job that it is supposed to do and continue to do so for an appropriate length of time.

* **Contribution of volunteers to profitability:** Paying employees costs an organisation money, which affects their profit margins. If people are prepared to offer their work voluntarily then this will reduce outgoings and therefore increases the profit for a business.

JARGON BUSTER

Unique selling point
Something that a business offers its customers that is exclusive to that business.

Personal, Learning and Thinking Skills

This activity will help to provide evidence of Independent Enquirer and Reflective Learner.

Over to you

* Name a range of different trends you are aware of in sport and active leisure in your local area.
* How have sport and active leisure centres provided for these new trends?

Just checking

Select a sport and active leisure provider or service in your local area. Carry out research to find out which success indicators it meets, including:

* staff size
* market penetration
* customer or supporter base
* reliability
* income
* customer satisfaction
* employee satisfaction.

Starting Point

What examples of interrelated businesses do you know of in your local area?

5.3 Interrelated businesses in the sport and active leisure industry

Different business models have been explored earlier on in this unit. In the sport and active leisure industry, you will often find that many different types of business work together to help provide specific services and products to meet customers' needs. In this topic, examples of interrelated businesses in sport and active leisure will be explored.

Interrelated companies are ones that have a close relationship with each other. It can be a relationship where one company couldn't exist without the other (eg a freelance tennis coach who teaches at a tennis club) or one where both companies could exist without the other but get mutual benefits from having a close working relationship (eg Nike® and Manchester United).

Exercise class instructors are often self-employed.

Self-employed in different sectors and national chains

People who are self-employed will usually carry out work with different sport and active leisure providers. For example, in the fitness industry a personal trainer or aerobics instructor may work for several different providers, providing instruction in public leisure centres, private health clubs, private limited national chains of health clubs and a franchise.

National governing bodies and volunteers

Most sports and active leisure activities will have a national governing body that represents that sport. For example, the British Canoe Union is the governing body for canoeing and kayaking, and the Rugby Football Union is the national governing body for rugby union. Many national governing bodies (NGBs) have volunteers working for them. People who are passionate about sport are prepared to give up their time to help improve participation in and awareness of their sport. Many NGBs have an income that relies on membership fees, which are usually kept as low as possible to help promote participation.

Personal, Learning and Thinking Skills

The activity below will help to provide evidence of Independent Enquirer.

Over to you

Carry out research by looking at appropriate websites or talking with someone who is self-employed and works in the sport and active leisure industry, such as an aerobics instructor or personal trainer. Find out about the different types of businesses models that they work with.

Functional Skills

The activity below will help to provide evidence of ICT.

Personal, Learning and Thinking Skills

The activity below will help to provide evidence of Independent Enquirer and Reflective Learner.

Over to you

* Visit the national governing body website of a sport that you are interested in.
* How does the national governing body make money?
* In what ways can people offer to volunteer to help the national governing body?

Therefore, NGBs tend not to make a lot of money. By not paying volunteers, it reduces the outgoings of an NGB so that any profits can be used to promote and encourage participation.

Sports therapists and sports clubs

A sports therapist may be self-employed and hold sports therapy clinics in different sports clubs. Some professional sports clubs employ a full-time sports therapist so there is always a qualified person to deal with injuries, provide rehabilitation for players, prepare them for competitions and help them recover afterwards. Some sports therapists may offer their services voluntarily for local sports clubs in which they have an interest, which otherwise may not be able to afford this service.

Large corporate companies and franchises

Large sport and active leisure companies often provide a wide range of services for their customers. By providing a greater range of products and services, the company becomes more attractive to customers and is helped to maintain and attract new customers. To help increase the services and products a company can offer its customers it may buy into a franchise such as beauty salon. Using the name and business model of a successful beauty salon franchise means customers will be more likely to use the new salon as the franchise has already established customer confidence.

Sponsorship of sports events by businesses

Many large businesses will pay money to sponsor sporting events to help advertise and sell their product or service. By sponsoring a sports event, the business is trying to associate itself with success and excitement. The sports event will gain from this sponsorship money in a variety of different ways, such as by being able to offer competition money to competitors to help to attract elite participants. Businesses compete with each other to gain exclusive rights to sponsor certain sports events such as the British Grand Prix or football World Cup. Individual players are also sponsored to advertise a particular product or service. Therefore, both the sport and individual players can make a significant income from sponsorship.

Captains of England women's and England men's cricket teams promoting a new sponsorship deal.

Over to you

* How do sport and active leisure providers in your local area use franchises to provide additional services such as:
  – a beauty salon
  – crèche facilities
  – food or drinks.
* Why do businesses spend a lot of money advertising their products or services?
* What are the benefits of sponsoring successful sports performers?
* What are the potential problems associated with sponsoring individual sports performers?

Just checking

* How do providers in your local area demonstrate the interrelationship between the sport and active leisure industry and other businesses?
* Are there any other industries that you can think of that provide services for sport and active leisure businesses?

Starting Point

* What sport or active leisure provider or service would you like to volunteer for?
* What sort of services do you think you could help out with?

5.4 The impact of volunteers on sport and active leisure businesses

According to Sport England around 2 million adults volunteer at least one hour a week to support the provision of sport in the community. A volunteer is someone who gives their time and expertise for free for a specific cause. In sport, people usually volunteer because they are passionate about a sport. In this topic you will examine the impact of volunteers on the effectiveness, profitability and success of sport and active leisure businesses.

Volunteers

If a business uses volunteers to help provide a service it can gain substantial benefits. However, there are also risks associated with using volunteers that businesses should be aware of, some of which are explored in this section.

Reasons why people volunteer

Businesses need to understand why people volunteer if they want to encourage them to do so. Examples of reasons why people volunteer include:

* Learning new skills – eg learning first aid skills with St John Ambulance.
* Using existing skills – eg providing a sports therapy service to a local rugby team.
* Addressing a specific problem in the community – eg trying to reduce anti-social behaviour.
* Gaining coaching qualifications – to qualify for a range of coaching awards you must have spent a certain amount of time coaching a particular sport.
* Feeling useful – people may have time on their hands that they want to put to good use.
* Experience – looks good on a CV.
* Making new friends – volunteering is a good way of meeting like-minded people.
* Wanting to improve access to a specific sport – if you are passionate about a sport you will want to promote it so that more people will participate.

If these needs are not met by volunteering then the volunteer will either move to another organisation or into a different activity. Therefore, it makes sense for a business to find out what motivates its volunteers and to monitor how well their needs are being fulfilled.

Impacts of Volunteers

Profitability

As a volunteer does not get paid for their time, a business reduces its outgoings by using them. This can help to increase the profit a business makes and make it more successful.

Effectiveness

Volunteers need to be trained so they can carry out their role effectively and efficiently. A business needs to manage and train their volunteers so they feel like they are providing an effective service and enjoy what they are doing. If a volunteer is unhappy with what they are asked to do they can leave the organisation! Tasks that are set for volunteers should not be set in stone and should be adapted to suit the needs of individuals. The roles of volunteers may need to be updated regularly to maintain their interest.

Reliability

Paid employees have to work in order to pay for their everyday living expenses. This means they are committed to going to work even on days when they do not feel like it. However, a volunteer only provides their service because they choose to do so. To encourage volunteers to provide a reliable service, the work that they do should be recognised. At the very least, businesses should show their appreciation verbally by saying 'Thank you', or they could use some sort of reward scheme. To increase the reliability of volunteers, they should be made to feel important within the organisation by involving them wherever possible in decision making. Volunteers could also be encouraged to use their voluntary experience to work towards a specific qualification such as an NVQ or coaching qualification. This gives them a goal that they will need to fulfil a certain amount of volunteer time to attain.

National governing bodies

Many sports' national governing bodies (NGBs) are 'not-for-profit' organisations, which means that the business is not set up to make a profit. Therefore, most of the people working for NGBs are volunteers. Volunteers play an essential role in the administration and success of a national governing body and without them many would no longer be functioning.

Hotlink

If you are aged between 11 and 19, find out how you can volunteer in sport – go to the Youth Sport Trust website. For details of how to access this website see the **Hotlinks** section – **Introduction**, page xi.

Did you know?

The following events depend upon volunteers in order for them to take place: the London Marathon, the British Rally Championship, the Tour of Britain, Formula One Grand Prix, the Grand National and the FA cup.

The London Marathon couldn't happen without volunteers.

Over to you

* Carry out research to find out how volunteers in one NGB help it to improve its effectiveness.

Just checking

Organisations that rely on volunteers can sign up to try and attain an award called 'Investing in Volunteers', which recognises an organisation's commitment to volunteering.

* How do you think this award could help a business to attract volunteers?

* Carry out research to find out about 'volunteers' week'. When is it and how does it help to promote volunteering?

Starting Point

* Do you know any successful sport and active leisure managers?
* What sorts of skills do they have that make them successful?

5.5 Management skills in sport and active leisure

A manager in a sport and active leisure business requires a range of skills in order to help the business succeed. Most relate to working with other people such as members of staff and customers. This topic will help you to explore management skills that you may require in your future career in the sport and active leisure industry.

Communication skills

Effective communication is essential in business. The range of communication skills that a good manager will possess fall into two categories: verbal and non-verbal.

Verbal communication skills: What we say and how we say it. A manager should clearly explain what they want a staff member to do and how they want it done. Managers should have regular one-to-one and team meetings with staff to maintain effective communication.

Non-verbal communication skills: Includes body language, written communication and listening. Using posture, expressions and gestures to communicate is termed 'body language'. This shows others how we feel and how confident we are, so a manager should convey the right message in their body language. Your body language should reflect the verbal message you are communicating – if you are praising staff, it will seem more sincere if you smile!

A manager must be a good listener so that they can find out exactly how their staff are feeling and provide support or more responsibility as needed to keep them motivated.

Organisational ability

A manager needs to be organised in a number of different areas, including managing their time, prioritising tasks, and putting systems in place to ensure that they keep up to date with what staff are doing and whether they are meeting their targets. For example, the manager could have regular meeting times with other members of staff, and more regular meetings with senior staff.

Leadership

Leadership skills require a manager to influence their staff to work together to achieve the organisation's goals and targets. A good leader will ensure that each member of the team understands their role and will motivate them to achieve their set targets. They will often try to include their staff in setting the goals and targets in the first place, which helps staff to feel part of the decision-making process and so motivates them to do their best to achieve their goals.

Team building

When members of staff work well together as a team they are generally much more productive. A good manager will encourage team building so that their staff work effectively together, which also helps improve employee job satisfaction.

Forming effective teams: The key to forming an effective team is recruiting the right people. They should have the correct qualifications for the job and a personality that will suit the team. Staff need to be trained so that they are effective in their job and work well within the team. Many managers also put time aside for team-building activities, where staff work together on tasks that are unrelated to their jobs, such building a raft or playing team sports.

Motivating and leading staff

Staff need to be motivated so that they will do their job well and enjoy it. A good manager needs to be aware of ways to encourage their staff, such as praising good practice, or setting targets and rewarding members of staff when they achieve them.

Staff development

Mentoring: A mentor helps another, less experienced person to achieve something. The mentor provides them with help and support, often one-on-one and in confidence.

Coaching: The process a manager uses to help staff arrive at correct conclusions by questioning and guiding them through the thinking process.

Managing staff

Delegation: This is when a manager gives a member of staff a particular role/task. For successful delegation, the manager must give the right task to the right person at the right time. With regular feedback on progress and open lines of communication, they can give support if required. Once the task is completed, success should be rewarded or poor performance dealt with appropriately . Delegation promotes team building and allows a manager to spread their workload and be more productive.

Staff behaviour: A manager must ensure that staff know what is expected of them and have been trained to behave in the right way. They must discipline staff who behave inappropriately.

Decision making: Staff will look to the manager to make decisions on what they need to be doing and when, as well as staff training requirements etc.

Customer care: The manager must ensure that staff have been trained to deal with customers appropriately, including how to greet customers, how to deal with conflict or complaints etc.

Awareness of equality and diversity issues: A manager should ensure that they treat all members of staff equally and fairly. Employment legislation enforces this. Managers need to be aware of this legislation and demonstrate that they are abiding by it. Examples of relevant legislation include: Equal Treatment Directive 1975; Equal Pay Directive 1975; EU Employment Directive 2000; and EU Race Directive 1976 (amended 2003).

Over to you

* What sorts of team-building activities could a leader arrange?
* Explain why you have selected each type of event.

Mentoring and coaching are important parts of the staff development process.

Just checking

* Name a person in sport and active leisure who you think is a good manager.
* Consider this person's management skills. What are their strengths?
* Do they have any skills that could be improved?
* How does this manager encourage team work?

Starting Point

What problems might a business in the sport and active leisure industry face?

JARGON BUSTER

Profit The difference between income and expenditure (costs) where income is greater than expenditure.

Costs Money that the business spends on its activities.

Income The money coming into a business from its activities.

Loss The difference between income and expenditure where income is less than expenditure.

Solvent The term used for a business that is capable of paying its costs.

Over to you

* Have you ever heard the phrase 'a business has become insolvent'? If so, when and what do you think it means?

* Why do you think a business might become insolvent?

Personal, Learning and Thinking Skills

This activity will help to provide evidence of Creative Thinker and Independent Enquirer.

Over to you

Think of a product or service that you use in the sport and active leisure industry. How is it marketed? Include in your answer:

* How is the product or service made attractive to you?

* Is the cost appropriate?

* How easy is it for you to buy this product or service?

5.6 Business problems

Being successful in business is very challenging as the UK has a highly competitive economy. Anyone running a business in the sport and active leisure industry faces daily challenges, initially to make their business successful and then to maintain its success as it grows.

Financial problems

For most businesses the main aim is to make a **profit**. All businesses have to pay out **costs** in order to run an activity or provide a service or product, which then makes money (**income**). If a business makes more money than it spends (ie when income is greater than costs) it makes a profit. If a business spends more money than it makes (ie costs are greater than income) it makes a **loss**. The other key financial measure for businesses is cash flow. Cash flow measures the amount of money coming into and going out of a business over a given period. Successful cash flow management ensures that there is always enough cash available to pay bills, wages etc. Cash flow determines how **solvent** a business is.

A business plan should always be at the heart of any new business. The business plan sets out how a business will be financed and ongoing financial planning ensures that it remains solvent as it operates. One of the purposes of business planning is to anticipate potential problems before they arise and put actions in place to avoid them. But however good the planning is in an organisation, unforeseen problems will arise and managers need to identify these and come up with solutions. Some examples of the kind of financial problems businesses may face are:

* not generating enough income (revenue) to pay the bills

* not generating a profit (making a loss)

* failing to identify when items for the business need to be bought, resulting in an unplanned loan or overdraft.

Marketing problems

All businesses have something to sell. This could be a product (something physical, like clothing), a service (like the use of a gym), or both. Marketing is the processes and activities involved in promoting a product or service. In order to sell their products or services, businesses need to find someone willing to buy them. The group of people the business expects to sell to is called the target market. In a sport and active leisure business, marketing is based on the four Ps:

* **Product**: What they will sell.

* **Promotion**: How the product/service is made more attractive to customers.

* **Price**: How much they will charge.

* **Placement**: Where the product/service is available for customers to buy.

If any aspect of marketing is carried out incorrectly it will impact on how well the product or service sells.

Staff problems

Businesses need staff in order to operate. The number of staff required, and the ability, qualifications and skills they need, will differ between organisations. Staff can be paid or voluntary. Most businesses employ staff and pay them an agreed wage, but some use voluntary staff who work for free. There will always be legal requirements that the business must fulfil, including things like insurance and staff checks such as CRB (Criminal Records Bureau) checking.

Staff effectiveness and efficiency

Staff need to be employed on the basis of the value they bring to the business. Lower-skilled staff may be cheaper to employ but may not be efficient or effective enough to make the business successful. Efficiency can be defined as 'doing something correctly with very little wasted money and time,' for example, completing work using the least resources and in the shortest time. Effectiveness can be defined as 'doing the right thing'. This means carrying out the right activities and applying the most appropriate strategies for the business. Training staff to be efficient can be relatively easy. However, higher-level skills may be required for staff to be effective, particularly in service-based businesses where success largely depends on how staff interact with customers.

Staff should always aim to keep the customers satisfied.

Customer satisfaction

Once a business attracts customers to buy the products/services offered, customer satisfaction becomes important. In simple terms, were customers happy with the product/service received for the price? It is usually easier to get repeat business from existing customers than to find new ones, so it is in a business's interest to put time and effort into keeping customers happy. This includes the quality of the product/service, how it was delivered, whether payment was processed smoothly and whether staff were polite. But, however hard an organisation tries, there will always be times when a customer is unhappy . If this happens it is important to try to repair the situation and satisfy the customer. There may be a cost or it may just involve making an apology. Staff need good communication skills to resolve things professionally.

Customer types and behaviour

Successful organisations collect data on customer behaviour, including the products or services customers buy and how often, how much they spend, and what combination of products and services they buy. This is called customer profiling and helps the organisation to find out more about the types of customers that are using their services or buying the product(s).

Just checking

Select a business in the sport and active leisure industry and answer the following questions:

* How does the business market its products or services?
* Do you think they have a good marketing strategy?
* Does the business provide customer satisfaction?
* Do you think the staff provide a good service?
* What types of customer use this business?
* Do you think this organisation has much repeat business?

Starting Point

What do you think are the problems associated with a business that does not plan and review its activities?

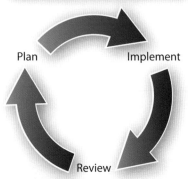

Plan   Implement

Review

The planning cycle.

Personal, Learning and Thinking Skills

This activity will help to provide evidence of Creative Thinker, Independent Enquirer and Self Manager.

Over to you

* Find out what your school or college mission statement is.
* Carry out research to find out the mission statement of three sport and active leisure providers.
* Explain whether you think each mission statement actually describes what the organisation is all about, its values and what it is trying to achieve.

5.7 Implementing best practice

Some aspects of business practice are common across all businesses. A well planned business avoids many of the problems that an unplanned business encounters. Planning is at the heart of a successful business enterprise.

To enjoy long-term success, businesses must be strategic. This means following a strict pattern of planning, implementing the plan, reviewing outcomes and then feeding the review back into the plan in order to do things better next time. This is called the planning cycle.

Setting objectives and monitoring achievement

Part of the planning process is the setting of objectives. Objectives are like the rudder of a ship. Without them, however much effort is put in, it is unlikely that the business will go in the right direction.

Business strategy

The strategy of a business is its game plan. Strategy helps a business to work out the best way to work in order to be successful. It can be seen as the process by which a business outsmarts its competitors. There are different strands to business strategy, and some common tools to identify the right strategy for any situation. A common theme of successful strategy is the development of a mission statement. The mission statement defines what the organisation is all about, what its values are and what it is trying to achieve.

SWOT analysis

SWOT analysis framework is one way for businesses to assess their business and start to develop a strategy that suits their needs. SWOT analysis looks at:

Strengths	**W**eaknesses
The attributes of a business that help it achieve its objective(s). In other words, what it is good at.	The attributes of a business that prevent it achieving its objective(s). In other words, what it is not good at.
Opportunities	**T**hreats
These are the external conditions that are helpful in achieving the objective(s), eg identifying a group of customers.	These are the external conditions that could damage the objective(s), eg a competitor.

Financial strategy

Organisations need to plan and manage their finances to ensure that they can meet their financial commitments in a planned manner and as **economically** as possible. Financial strategy should include long-term profit plans and shorter-term cash flow planning.

Sales and marketing strategy

The sales and marketing strategy identifies who the organisation is going to sell its products or services to and how it is going to do this. The sales and marketing strategy must identify the products or services to be sold, the target markets and any competitors.

Human resources strategy

The human resources strategy is concerned with ensuring that the organisation has the appropriate people in place to deliver its objectives. This will cover recruitment and retention of staff, staff terms and conditions and staff training.

Implementing strategy

Once a business has set its strategy it must implement it. To do this well the business must manage its costs and resources effectively. There are several techniques that businesses use to achieve this, including:

* budgeting

* forecasting

* managing cash flow.

Budgeting: This is basic financial planning and involves working out how much a business will need to spend in a given period, and how much income and money in the bank it will have to meet this expenditure.

Forecasting: This is the process of predicting when a business will get orders so that it can foresee demand for products or services and ensure it is able to meet customers' expectations.

Managing cash flow: Cash flow determines the solvency of a business, and is the cash coming into and out of the business's bank account. Businesses need to ensure that money transactions are planned for, as unplanned overdrafts or loans can be expensive. A business that does not have enough cash can become insolvent because it cannot pay its bills.

Over to you

Select a sport or active leisure business. Research it and then carry out a SWOT analysis on the business.

Businesses must think about their financial strategy.

Just checking

Choose a business in the sport and active leisure industry and carry out research to find out the following information. If possible, try to interview a person within the sport and active leisure industry who is involved in creating and implementing business strategies.

* What is their mission statement?
* What are the business's objectives?
* How do they assess their business?
* What are the main strategies that they are focusing on at the moment?
* How do they budget?
* How do they forecast?

Starting Point

If you were faced with a business problem, how would you find a solution? Make a list of the possible ways of trying to find solutions.

5.8 Developing and implementing solutions

Once business problems have been identified, solutions need to be found. However, before solutions can be put into practice, the problems must be fully considered and managers need to find creative ways to solve them.

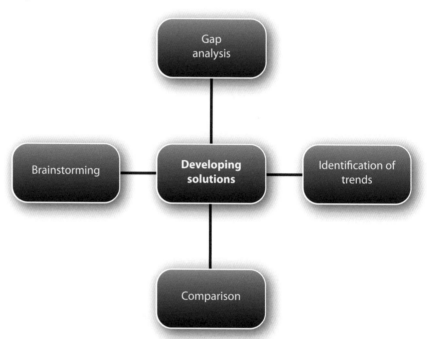

Developing solutions

A solution will dependent on the problem. There are different methods of identifying solutions that can be applied to most business-related problems. These include:

* **Gap analysis** is the process of identifying where there are gaps between what a business needs to achieve to meet its objectives and what it expects to achieve.

* **Brainstorming** is the process of coming up with solutions or ideas without judging them. The objective is to get as many ideas as possible and make sure they are as creative as possible. Once this part of the process has been completed, the ideas can be analysed and filtered so that the most appropriate are identified.

* **Comparisons** can be made with other organisations to identify best practice within the industry. This is known as benchmarking and can be done using case studies, articles from newspapers or journals, trade bodies or by working in partnership with other businesses.

* **Identification of trends or patterns** within the business can be helpful. In order to be effective, the business must ensure that accurate data is gathered and stored so that meaningful comparisons can be made. Trends in sales, costs, profit, cash flow, customer habits etc can be identified, and measures put in place to reduce any negative effects or ensure the resources are available to cope with peaks of demand.

Over to you

Carry out research into a sport and active leisure business. Find out what business problems they have had to deal with in the last six months and why these problems arose. Also try to find out how the business produced solutions to these problems.

Solutions to problems

When problems are fully understood, business managers should identify solutions. Managers operate in an environment where only certain things can be controlled or changed by them. For example, if the problem is that the cost price is too high, a solution might be to get suppliers to sell stock at a lower price. However, this may not be something the supplier will negotiate on, so it would then be out of the manager's control (though it is always worth trying). However, reducing costs within the business is within the control of the management. This might involve cutting staff costs and reducing marketing spend.

Change sales prices: If sales are low, one option might be to change the price of the product or service. Generally speaking a lower sale price will result in higher sales, but lower percentage profits. A business needs to consider the effect of this on its long-term profitability.

Marketing: Marketing campaigns can be used to try to bring in additional business, though there will be a cost to any additional marketing activity with no guarantee of results.

Human resource structure and roles: Making changes to staffing might be another way to improve business performance. This could involve changing the organisational structure, improving the performance of employees by training them better, or finding ways to improve their motivation through incentives or skilful leadership.

Case study: Stephanie's pre-school

Stephanie is the manager of a private pre-school for children aged between two and five years. The pre-school sessions run from 9.30am to 12.30pm. She has eight members of staff working with her, one of whom is the deputy manager. The pre-school usually has between 25 and 30 children at each session. Children aged two to three need to have a ratio of one member of staff per four children and children aged four to five need to have a ratio of one member of staff per eight children. The pre-school has recently not been making a profit as there has been a drop in the numbers of children attending each session. It is attached to a primary school and is not used before or after pre-school sessions. Stephanie is trying to think of ways in which she can increase income and decrease costs.

1 What could Stephanie do in order to find a solution to her business problem?

2 What are the pros and cons of carrying out the following:

   a changing the cost of the pre-school sessions

   b increasing the marketing for the pre-school

   c changing the staffing structure or roles?

3 How else could Stephanie try to increase her income?

Personal, Learning and Thinking Skills

This activity will help to provide evidence of Independent Enquirer, Creative Thinker and Self Manager.

Just checking

Suggest two methods that a health and fitness club could use in order to compete with another health and fitness club in the area.

Starting Point

* What presentations have you observed that you think went well?

* What sorts of things did the presenter or presenters do that were successful?

* What presentations have you observed that did not go so well?

* What sorts of things did the presenter or presenters do that could be improved?

5.9 Presentation skills

In many jobs in the sport and active leisure industry there will come a time when you need to deliver a presentation to one or more people. A presentation requires you to get the attention of an audience and maintain their interest in the information you want to give them. When you are presenting information there are some key skills that you need to learn and practise to help you deliver a good presentation. This topic helps you explore these skills and develop your existing presentation skills.

Preparation

Many people feel anxious at the prospect of delivering a presentation to an audience. One of the best ways of calming your nerves is to ensure that you are properly prepared for the presentation and to practise the presentation skills described below.

Eye contact

When you are delivering a presentation, try to look up from your cue cards or PowerPoint® presentation and make eye contact with people in the audience. By making eye contact you are establishing a rapport with the audience. This helps make them feel that you are talking personally to them, which helps to engage them and maintain their interest in what you are saying. By making eye contact you are also able to gain feedback from your audience – you will see if they are listening, and other reactions such as nodding or smiling too.

When you are giving a presentation try to use eye contact and open body language in order to communicate effectively with your audience.

Open body language

Body language can communicate a lot about what we are really thinking. Open body language should be used in presentations as this helps the audience to see you as an open, accepting and friendly person, as opposed to closed body language, which can make you look reserved and unwelcoming. When delivering a presentation you need to consider how you can use open body language with your facial expressions, gestures and stance. These factors impact on how well you connect with your audience and how well they receive the information. Keep your facial expression open by smiling easily but not all the time. Try not to cover your body – keep your arms unfolded, avoid touching your face and try not to hold anything in front of you. When answering a question, turn your whole body and feet to face the person who has asked it. Try to keep the palms of your hands open – don't clench your fists.

Speaking

How you speak is very important in a presentation. The aim of a presentation is to convey information to an audience, so you need to ensure that you can be heard. To help you speak audibly, practise speaking more loudly than you are used to. You could also practise your presentation whilst someone is sitting at the back of the presentation room so they can let you know if you can be heard. You should express yourself clearly in terms that your audience can understand. If you need to use **jargon**, make sure it is familiar to the audience – if not it should be explained it to them. Speak fluently without long gaps between words or sentences and try not to say 'umm' or 'err'.

Use of appropriate media

To maintain the interest of the audience, many presenters use a form of media such as PowerPoint® software. PowerPoint® allows you to include colourful slides, photographs, animation, video clips and web links in your presentation. A presenter using PowerPoint® needs to know how to use the software to produce an effective presentation. If PowerPoint® is not available, overhead slides can be used on an overhead projector to help provide visual aids such as text, tables or diagrams. Some tips to help you to prepare overhead or PowerPoint® slides include:

* Ensure that the font is the correct size so the whole audience can read it. There must be enough contrast between the colour of the text and the colour of the background to make it readable.

* Don't include too much information on a slide. Each should convey a single point with a few lines of text and maybe an image.

* The presentation should be structured with a clear beginning, middle and end. The beginning should introduce the presenter and the aims of the presentation. The middle should cover the main facts of the presentation, and the end is a conclusion that reinforces the message and allows time for questions and answers.

Audience

Make sure that the content of the presentation is appropriate for your audience. The audience may include your tutor, peers or people from the sport and active leisure industry.

Over to you

* Imagine that you have an audience that you are speaking to.

* Look in a mirror or use a video camera to talk about a subject of your choice.

* Check to see what sort of body language you are using.

* Repeat the process, this time trying to use open body language wherever possible.

JARGON BUSTER

Jargon Language used by specific groups of people that is not in common use.

Just checking

* Prepare a presentation using appropriate media.

* Practise your presentation, making sure that you speak audibly and fluently and use open body language. Practise looking up from your cue cards so that you can make contact with the audience.

Case study: Harry's company

Harry is the centre manager for a residential outdoor pursuits centre based in the Lake District. The centre runs lots of different activities including sailing, windsurfing, kayaking, climbing, mountain walking and potholing. It is a private limited company and Harry and his wife, his parents, his brother and his sister all own shares.

The outdoor pursuits centre has a lot of customers during the spring, summer and autumn months. These customers include schoolchildren on school residential holidays, university and college students learning to instruct in outdoor and adventurous activities and independent groups such as groups of ramblers. However, the winter months are relatively quiet due to the cold weather and short days, which mean activities have to finish early. They make very little profit during this period.

Harry has saved up a fairly large amount of money to invest in the centre. He is thinking about investing in some indoor facilities, which could help bring in customers during the winter months, but he is not sure what sort of facility to invest in. He is also aware that there is a large market for businesses running team-building days in the outdoors that he does not currently attract, and he thinks that this is would be a good area to focus on. He is also considering bringing in franchises to operate in his centre in order to provide products and services to his customers, as well as provide an increased income to the centre.

1 What are the benefits of having a private limited company?

2 What sorts of indoor facilities would you suggest Harry invests in to help attract customers to his centre? Explain why you made these selections.

3 What sorts of things could Harry do to try and attract the corporate market?

4 What sort of franchises could Harry bring in to his centre? Why do you think these would be a good idea?

For your project

This unit has explored different types of businesses in the sport and active leisure industry. You have examined success indicators for sport and active leisure businesses and are aware of the different sorts of business model and the benefits and problems associated with them. You have covered how these different types of businesses can interrelate within the sport and active leisure industry, and you should also be familiar with the management skills needed in order to run a successful sport and active leisure business.

Volunteers are important to many sport and active leisure organisations and this unit has covered the impact they can have and the importance of keeping volunteers motivated. It has also introduced you to the problems that businesses may face and methods used to develop and implement solutions. In addition you have learnt about implementing best practice in business. Finally, you have had the opportunity to develop your presentation skills, which will be valuable to you in your future career.

The following diagram gives some ideas for what you might decide to do your project on, based on the content of this unit.

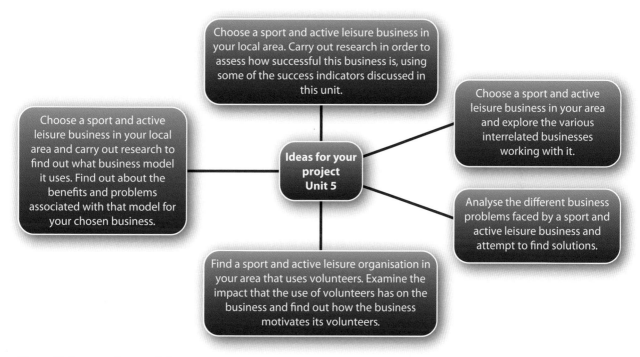

Choose a sport and active leisure business in your local area. Carry out research in order to assess how successful this business is, using some of the success indicators discussed in this unit.

Choose a sport and active leisure business in your area and explore the various interrelated businesses working with it.

Choose a sport and active leisure business in your local area and carry out research to find out what business model it uses. Find out about the benefits and problems associated with that model for your chosen business.

Ideas for your project Unit 5

Analyse the different business problems faced by a sport and active leisure business and attempt to find solutions.

Find a sport and active leisure organisation in your area that uses volunteers. Examine the impact that the use of volunteers has on the business and find out how the business motivates its volunteers.

Possible project titles

* How can a leisure centre increase the number of customers using the centre between 1pm and 3pm in order to increase its profits?

* How can a self-employed mountain leader increase the amount of business they get during the winter months?

* How effective are volunteers in providing good customer service in a sport and active leisure business?

* How do good management skills help to motivate staff?

* What are the problems associated with poor management skills?

Assessment guidance

This unit is assessed by one internally-set assignment. You will have a period of 16 hours to generate evidence for your assessment. In your assessment you will need to show that you:

* know how to describe successful business models that operate in different sectors in the sport and active leisure industry

* know how sport and active leisure businesses interrelate with other businesses

* are able to use evidence to reach appropriate conclusions on the impact of volunteers

* know about impacts upon the effectiveness, profitability and success of a business

* are able to demonstrate your understanding of the core features of the management skills required to contribute to a successful sport and active leisure business

* are able to identify business problems that have been encountered by sport and active leisure businesses and their causes

* are able to assess how best practice can be implemented in sport and active leisure businesses

* are able to develop solutions to business problems in sport and active leisure

* are able to present solutions to business problems to an audience or industry representative.

Time management

* Although you have 16 hours to generate evidence for this assignment, this time frame does not include time spent researching the topic area.

* The internal assessment will be split into different tasks. You will be given set times to generate evidence for each task whilst being supervised by your tutor or your employer.

* Your tutor may give you ideas for resources to use to help you carry out research before you attempt the task. Aim to make time to read this information and carry out research for the set task so you have a good understanding of the subject area.

* Your tutor may give you formative assessments, which are similar to the actual task. Make time to complete these 'trial' assessments as these will help to prepare you for the real task. Your tutor will give you feedback on the areas that you have completed well and any areas for improvement.

Useful links

Work experience within the sport and active leisure industry will enable you to talk to members of staff and find out about:

* different business problems that the sport and active leisure provider may be facing and the ways in which they are trying to deal with them

* the interrelationships of the business with other types of business models, eg by talking with staff who are self-employed such as aerobics instructors or personal trainers

* how organisations use volunteers and how effective and reliable they are.

Some television programmes look at different aspects of business and different business models. An example of one such programme is *The Apprentice*, where people are set different business tasks and have to make a product or find a solution for each particular task.

There are lots of useful websites that will help you with your research for this unit. For details of how to access these sites see the **Hotlinks section** – Introduction, page xi.

How you will be assessed

For your Unit 5 assessment, you need to make sure that you can meet all of the assessment criteria for the five learning outcomes, as shown in the table below.

Learning outcome	Assessment criteria
LO1: Know about successful business models used in the sport and active leisure industry	**1** Describe successful business models which operate in different sectors of the industry.
LO2: Know how different types of businesses interrelate in the sport and active leisure industry	**1** Describe how sport and active leisure businesses interrelate with other businesses in the industry.
LO3: Understand the impact of volunteers on the effectiveness, profitability and success of sport and active leisure businesses	**1** Provide conclusions, using evidence of the impact of volunteers on the effectiveness, profitability and success of businesses.
LO4: Know the management skills that contribute to successful sport and active leisure businesses	**1** Describe the management skills that contribute to successful sport and active leisure businesses.
LO5: Be able to develop solutions to business problems	**1** Identify business problems that have been encountered by sport and active leisure businesses and their causes.
	2 Assess how best practice can be implemented in sport and active leisure businesses.
	3 Develop solutions to business problems of sport and active leisure businesses.
	4 Present solutions to business problems to an audience or industry representatives.

Introduction

The media and the sport and active leisure industry have a very important relationship. The media is used to promote different sports and influences the uptake of sports by the public. The sport and active leisure industry uses the media to promote its initiatives. There are different types of media and many of these are explored in this unit. By learning about these, you will develop the skills needed to help you to create your own promotional campaign.

What will you learn?

In this unit you will cover the following learning outcomes:

LO1: Know how the sport and active leisure industry benefits the media

LO2: Know how the sport and active leisure industry promotes its own initiatives in the media

LO3: Understand why the sport and active leisure industry promotes its own initiatives in the media

LO4: Understand how media stories influence public perceptions of the industry

LO5: Understand the effectiveness of promotional campaigns for sport and active leisure

LO6: Be able to plan promotional campaigns for sport and active leisure

LO7: Be able to implement promotional campaigns for sport and active leisure

The following table shows how these seven learning outcomes are covered by this unit.

Topic	Pages	Learning outcomes covered
6.1 Types of media	162–163	LO2
6.2 How the sport and active leisure industry benefits the media	164–165	LO1
6.3 How the sport and active leisure industry promotes its initiatives in the media	166–167	LO2
6.4 Ways that the media can be used to promote or influence the sport and active leisure industry	168–171	LO2
6.5 Why the sport and active leisure industry promotes its initiatives in the media	172–174	LO3
6.6 How media stories influence public perceptions of the industry	175–177	LO4
6.7 Reviewing promotional campaigns for sport and active leisure	178–179	LO5
6.8 Implementing a promotional campaign in sport and active leisure	180–183	LO7
6.9 Planning a promotional campaign	184–187	LO6

THINKING POINTS

* What sorts of media are used to promote sports and active leisure events?

* How is media used in sports and active leisure events to promote other, unrelated products and services?

Functional Skills

Personal, Learning and Thinking Skills

This unit offers various opportunites to develop functional skills and personal, learning and thinking skills. Where appropriate, activities are signposted with the relevant skills that you can develop.

Diploma Daily

Ban on Booze Adverts

A new policy prevents the promotion of alcoholic drinks during sport and active leisure events. The government is trying to tackle teenage drinking and binge drinking as death and injury rates soar from alcohol abuse. The government believes that any association of sport and active leisure with alcohol should be removed by introducing this blanket ban. Alex Brown, the Rugby United captain, says, 'We have enjoyed a very good relationship with our sponsor Caveniss. Their funding has certainly helped us to get to where we are today but with the enforced removal of this sponsor I really don't know what is going to happen to our sport.'

1 What sport and active leisure events do you know of that advertise alcoholic drinks?

2 Why do you think alcoholic drinks are advertised at these events?

3 Do you think it would be a good idea to have a ban on advertising alcoholic drinks at sport and active leisure events? Explain your answer.

How you will be assessed

This unit will be assessed by one main assignment based on you planning and implementing a promotional campaign for a sport or active leisure purpose, followed by a review of the effectiveness of promotional campaigns in sport and active leisure. You will need to present evidence of the following in your assignment:

* An analysis of the strengths and weaknesses of promotional campaigns in sport and active leisure. One of the campaigns will need to focus on raising awareness of a social agenda.

* A plan for a promotional campaign for a sport or active leisure purpose.

* A signed learner observation record form from your tutor, confirming that you collaborated with others to implement the promotional campaign.

* Written evidence or video/audio recordings of the three promotions you used in your campaign.

Unit links

This unit links closely to Level 2, Unit 2: Encouraging participation in sport and active leisure.

Case study: Sponsorship for Ellie's team

Ellie is 18 years old and plays netball at a high level. She would love to train and play netball full time, but gets very little income from playing – occasionally she gets some prize money if the team does well in a competition. She has a full-time job to pay for her living and travel expenses and spends time after work training with her team. At the weekends she is involved in competitions. The rest of her team also have full-time jobs. Their coach has got a sponsor interested in paying for the team's travel expenses, in return for them wearing the sponsor's logo on their tops and posing in a calendar produced by the sponsor.

1 Why do you think this team receives very little money from playing their sport?

2 What types of netball media coverage have you seen?

3 Do you think the sponsor is offering a good deal to Ellie's netball team? Explain your answer.

4 If Ellie and her team did not have to work, how do you think it would affect their netball performance?

At one time, the only way sport and active leisure events could be accessed was by attending in person. Today, most of your experiences of these events will probably be via media coverage. Media coverage has played a central role in extending the reach of sport and active leisure activities around the world. Today you have access to a huge range of media, including television, written press, and online and digital resources. This topic provides an introduction to each of these types of media.

Types of media

Broadcast

Many people today experience sport events by watching them on television.

Broadcast media includes television and radio. Television is broadcast in three different ways:

1. Terrestrial: distributed via radio signals and received by aerials.

2. Satellite: distributed using satellites and received by a satellite dish.

3. Cable: distributed by cables and requires a physical connection to the cable via a cable box.

Initially, the only television programmes that were broadcast were from the BBC. Today, you can receive programmes from a huge range of channels, most of which are broadcast nationally. Some of these national channels also carry local broadcasts such as local news bulletins.

There are also many different radio channels. Some broadcast across the nation, but many only broadcast in their local area. For local radio, the show can only be received within a certain area.

Written press

Media in the form of written press include:

* national newspapers
* local newspapers
* magazines/journals.

National newspapers: Newspapers are printed daily; however, sales of paper copies of newspapers have recently fallen. To try to combat this, the more popular newspapers also produce online editions. There are two main types of national newspaper:

* broadsheet (or 'quality') newspapers, eg *The Independent*, *Telegraph* etc
* tabloid (or 'popular') newspapers, eg *The Sun*, *The Mirror* etc.

Broadsheet newspapers used to be printed on much larger sheets of paper than tabloids. However, as many of these newspapers are now printed in a more compact form, the distinction between 'broadsheets' and 'tabloids' has lost some of its meaning and the terms 'quality' and 'popular' are starting to be used.

Quality newspapers report their stories in a factual way and focus on **'hard' news** such as political and economic issues. Popular newspapers have more photographs and there is a greater emphasis on **'soft' news** stories such as celebrity news.

Local newspapers: Local newspapers often have a similar format to national newspapers; however, the news stories are usually related to the local community. Most local newspapers are printed on a weekly basis and some are free.

Magazines/Journals: Magazines and journals are usually printed weekly, monthly or quarterly throughout the year. Various sport and active leisure activities have magazines dedicated to them – some have more than one.

Online media

Online media is accessed through the internet. Examples of online media include:

* national governing body websites
* sport-specific websites
* news websites
* blogs
* e-zines
* podcasts
* social networking sites, eg Facebook and Twitter.

Digital resources

Digital resources require electronic devices in order to access the information. Examples of these resources include:

* digital videos
* e-books
* gaming systems
* CD-ROMs.

E-books are becoming a popular digital resource.

Personal, Learning and Thinking Skills

This activity will help to provide evidence of Independent Enquirer and Reflective Learner.

Over to you

* Examine a quality paper and a popular paper.
* Compare the newspapers – what are the differences between the two?
* Try to find a sport and active leisure-related news story that is in both newspapers.
* Read both stories and then describe the differences in how the papers report the story.

Personal, Learning and Thinking Skills

This activity will help to provide evidence of Independent Enquirer, Creative Thinker and Reflective Learner.

Over to you

* What types of digital resources do you have access to?
* How can you use these resources to access information about sport and active leisure activities?

Just checking

* What types of media do you use on a regular basis?
* Why do you use these types of media most?
* Why don't you use other types of media as much?

Starting Point

When you watch a sport and active leisure activity on the television or see photos of a sports event, what advertising do you notice on the players' kit or in the venue?

JARGON BUSTER

Commercial Advert played between programmes to advertise a product or service.

Target audience Specific group of people that companies selling a product or service want to advertise to.

Personal, Learning and Thinking Skills

This activity will help to provide evidence of Independent Enquirer, Creative Thinker and Reflective Learner.

Over to you

* Watch a sport and active leisure programme that has commercial breaks.

* Make a note of the types of commercials that are shown during the breaks – what products and services are they promoting?

* What types of people would use these products or services?

* Why do you think the companies have targeted that particular activity to advertise their product?

6.2 How the sport and active leisure industry benefits the media

Sport provides good content for the media as it creates lots of different stories and has a wide range of sporting characters, including heroes, villains and fools. These provide compelling content for coverage in newspapers, TV shows and websites. The sport and active leisure industry therefore provides a range of benefits for the media, which are explored in this topic.

Advertising income

The main reasons for advertising are to make people aware of a product or service and to make it seem desirable so that people want to buy it. Advertising income comes from companies paying for television or radio time or an advertising space to promote their product or service.

Commercials

The BBC does not permit **commercials** (it makes its money from viewers paying a licence fee and by selling its programmes abroad) but all other channels have commercial breaks. Companies pay for time slots in the commercial breaks during which they can promote their product or service.

Commercials are played during coverage of sport and active leisure events on TV and the radio, usually whilst the activity has stopped such as at half time in football games. Businesses pay more to advertise during major events, as these attract large audiences. The annual American Football Super Bowl, for example, attracts up to 90 million viewers and charges around $2.7 million for a 30 second advert! Sporting events are very popular and TV companies can make a lot of money from selling advertising time during them. Around 25% of the money spent on advertising goes on commercials.

Written press

Over 65% of the money spent on advertising each year is spent on advertising in the written press. This is because adverts in the written press can be directed more easily at an advertiser's **target audience** (and are cheaper than TV adverts).

Sales of newspapers

People are keen to read about sport and active leisure events, so newspapers provide detailed coverage to help to sell their paper. Many have a regular separate 'pull-out' section dedicated to sport and active leisure, for example *The Times* has a regular section on football called 'The Game'.

Sales of sports magazines

Sports magazines are designed for a **niche market** and usually cover just one sport or leisure activity such as 'Country Walking'. They have a specific audience who are passionate about this activity. Companies that supply a product or service for people who participate or who are spectators at this activity will advertise in these magazines, as they are able to reach their target audience directly.

Which sports magazines do you enjoy reading?

JARGON BUSTER

Niche market A small group of people who share a particular interest – a product or service is especially designed for them.

Personal, Learning and Thinking Skills

This activity will help to provide evidence of Independent Enquirer, Creative Thinker and Reflective Learner.

Over to you

* Examine three different newspapers.
* Where are stories related to sport and active leisure found in each newspaper?
* How much of the newspaper is dedicated to sport and active leisure coverage?
* Which sports get the most coverage? Why do you think this is?
* Now look at one full week's coverage from one newspaper that has sport and active leisure stories.
* How does the content of the sport and active leisure stories differ through the week?
* Why do you think there is this difference?

Just checking

* Why do you think the Indian Premier League (IPL) cricket tournament was designed to have a 30-second break between overs?
* How do the sports or activities being shown influence the types of commercials during breaks?
* Explain why companies would be willing to spend money on commercial breaks during the coverage of two different current sport and active leisure events.

Starting Point

* How do you find out when sport and active leisure events that you want to watch are taking place?
* What sport and active leisure events do you like taking part in?
* What made you interested in taking part in this activity in the first place?

Personal, Learning and Thinking Skills

This activity will help to provide evidence of Independent Enquirer, Creative Thinker and Reflective Learner.

Over to you

Carry out research to find out what sports stadiums have to do to follow these acts:

1 Safety of Sports Grounds Regulations (1987).
2 Fire Safety and Safety of Places in Sports Act (1987).

6.3 How the sport and active leisure industry promotes its initiatives in the media

The sport and active leisure industry benefits from the media in many ways. Newspapers, radio and television have enlarged the audience for sports and enriched the experience of following sport. The industry uses the media to help promote events and influence the public to buy its products. Media stories and coverage of events in sport and active leisure have also influenced changes in legislation within the industry.

Provision of copy for newspapers and magazines

The sport and active leisure industry works closely with the media. This relationship is clearly seen with newspapers and magazines. Sport provides these with copy and content, which means that a person from the sport and active leisure industry writes an article about their sport or activity that the newspaper or magazine then prints – this is called 'provision of copy'. The sport and active leisure organisation benefits as it can generate interest in the activity and promote specific events. The newspaper or magazine also benefits as it has an article written by an expert to add to its content.

How the media influences legislation in sport and active leisure

Sport and active leisure stories covered in the media have helped to increase awareness of health and safety issues. This has resulted in significant pressure on decision makers, which has influenced legislation concerning the sport and active leisure industry. Key areas in which the media has influenced legislation in sport and active leisure include:

* safety in sports grounds
* outdoor activities
* working with children.

Safety in sports grounds

Two sports stadium disasters, the Heysel Stadium Disaster and the Bradford City Fire Disaster, received heavy coverage in the media. The Heysel Disaster occurred when a wall collapsed in the Heysel Stadium in Brussels before the start of the 1985 European Cup Final – 39 people were killed and 600 injured. The Bradford fire tragedy in 1985 occurred during a league match between Bradford City and Lincoln City; 56 people died. The severity of these disasters combined with the media coverage led to the introduction of the Safety of Sports Grounds Regulations (1987) and the Fire Safety and Safety of Places of Sport Act (1987).

After the Hillsborough Stadium Disaster at the FA Cup semi-final between Liverpool and Nottingham Forest in 1989, where 96 people died, more legislation was brought in to increase the safety of spectators at sports events. This included the Safety of Sports Grounds (Accommodation of Spectators) Order 1996 and the Football Spectators Act 1989. The Football Licensing Authority (FLA) was also created; its main role is to ensure the safety and effective management of football supporters inside stadiums.

Outdoor activities

The Lyme Bay Disaster in 1993, in which four teenagers drowned whilst kayaking on a school trip, was widely covered in the media. Shortly after this, the Adventure Activities Licensing Authority (AALA) was set up to inspect activity centres and other outdoor and adventurous activity providers to ensure the safety of outdoor activity provision.

Working with children

Stories in the press about sport and active leisure coaches abusing children led to a range of child protection legislation. These acts ensure that there are consistent standards of care for children and that anyone wishing to work with children must have a **CRB check** first to prevent unsuitable people working in these jobs.

> ## JARGON BUSTER
>
> **CRB check** Carried out to check if a person has had any prior convictions, been cautioned, or given a reprimand or warning for a criminal offence.

This sports coach will have undergone a CBR check.

> ### Just checking
>
> * What other legislation are you aware of that affects the sport and active leisure industry?
> * Why do you think media pressure can influence legislation in sport and active leisure?

Starting Point

Select a sport or active leisure activity. How does the media promote your chosen activity?

6.4 Ways that the media can be used to promote or influence the sport and active leisure industry

The media plays a huge part in sport and helps to create great sporting moments. The well known phrase, 'They think it's all over … it is now!' was broadcast during the 1966 World Cup final as England scored their fourth goal to beat Germany. People all over England, many of whom were not even born then, know and use this phrase. Moments like this create strong media-sport relationships and illustrate their importance.

Advertising or branding of products or services

Sport and active leisure attracts huge audiences and creates memorable moments, so it also attracts a lot of money from businesses trying to promote their products and services. There are different ways in which businesses can do this, including:

* advertising

* branding

* sponsorship.

Advertising

Some companies pay to place adverts around the perimeter of the arena in which a sports event is taking place. Another relatively new method of advertising is for companies to paint their logo or brand onto the pitch. People see these adverts whilst watching the sport, and companies will pay a lot more if the event is shown on TV as their adverts reach a bigger audience.

Personal, Learning and Thinking Skills

This activity will help to provide evidence of Independent Enquirer, Creative Thinker and Reflective Learner.

Over to you

* Watch three different types of sport and active leisure activity.

* Make a note of the advertising that is shown within the actual venue – is there perimeter board advertising and/or pitch advertising?

* What types of products or services are being advertised?

* Why has the company selected this sport and active leisure event to advertise their product or service?

Perimeter board advertising at the Pierre Cornelis Stadion in Belgium.

Branding

This is where a brand name, sign, symbol or slogan is used by a business to promote its product or service. In sport and active leisure, players may help advertise sports clothing or products. They wear the clothing or use the product during games and interviews, which helps to advertise the brand.

Sponsorship

This is when a business pays the costs of a sport and active leisure event or helps fund a team. The money from the business may go to the national governing body of the sport, the organisers of the event, or to pay for sports equipment and sports kit for the teams. This money is given in exchange for the business promoting their product or service during the event or the team's matches. For example, players may have the logo of their sponsor company on their sports kit, which will be seen by their supporters. If the team's games are regularly shown on TV, the company will pay more as their logo will get more '**airtime**' and be seen by more people. Companies can also arrange sponsorship deals so that they are included in the name of the event and are therefore mentioned by TV presenters whenever they introduce it (eg 'Welcome to the Barclays Premier League…').

Personal, Learning and Thinking Skills

This activity will help to provide evidence of Independent Enquirer and Creative Thinker.

Over to you

* Select five different brands and write or draw their sign, symbol, name or slogan.
* Design your own brand for a sport and active leisure product or service. Give it a name and a logo (a sign or symbol).
* Explain why you have come up with your selected logo.

JARGON BUSTER

Airtime Amount of time that something is shown on the television.

Jonny Wilkinson promoting a pair of Adidas® boots.

Businesses also sponsor individuals who excel in their sport. Examples include David Beckham, Jonny Wilkinson and Venus Williams. These people are paid large sums of money by sponsors to wear or use their product – for example, watches or branded clothing. The sponsored sportsperson will be contracted to wear the product whilst participating in their sport or during media interviews, and this promotes the product as these sports events and interviews will be watched by large audiences. Newspapers can gain exclusive interviews with sponsored individuals in exchange for including a by-line to promote the sponsor. However, there are strict guidelines that business and television programmes must follow to ensure that they do not contain overt branding or advertising. For example, a presenter can only mention the sponsors of a sport and active leisure event a certain number of times per programme. A watchdog body called Ofcom ensures that these guidelines are adhered to.

Coverage of sport and active leisure events on television

The sporting events broadcast on television can help to increase interest in the sport and active leisure activity and lead to increased participation in the activity. If you take a look at a list of television schedules, you will find that sport and active leisure events are on television at most times of the day. There is even a Sky sports news channel that provides 24-hour coverage of sports-related news! Television coverage of sport and active leisure generates money for the sport, which can help improve the quality of the performance. This additional money can be used to improve facilities and equipment and help players train and improve.

Raising awareness of issues or social agendas through promotional campaigns

Sport and active leisure can play an important social role by raising awareness of issues or social agendas. On an international scale, the 1995 Rugby World Cup was hailed as an event of historic social significance. It was the first major sporting event to take place in South Africa following the end of **apartheid**. Before this event, rugby had always been perceived in South Africa as an elite sport played by the minority white population. Black South Africans would actively support the opposition when the national side played. However, all this changed in 1995 when the recently-elected President, Nelson Mandela, actively supported the South African rugby team and appeared at the final wearing a rugby shirt with the team captain's number on the back. This act, and the fact that South Africa won the competition, had a huge impact in terms of unifying the nation through sport.

Nelson Mandela congratulating the South African captain, François Pienaar, on winning the 1995 Rugby World Cup.

In the UK, the media help to promote social agendas including increasing participation in sport and active leisure activities to help prevent bullying, crime, binge drinking, drugs and obesity, and promote community spirit. A number of well-known sports stars have been involved in campaigning to increase the participation of children in PE and sport and active leisure. For example, Ian Wright has been leading the Fitter Schools UK Challenge and Dame Kelly Holmes has been appointed the first National School Sport Champion.

Other media campaigns to raise awareness of social agendas involving sport include the Rugby Football League signing up to the Stonewall campaign to raise awareness of lesbian, gay and bisexual equality and tackle homophobia. In football, the Kick Racism Out of Football campaign has helped to reduce racism in football. The Children's Play initiative is also being promoted in the media, which aims to develop free play opportunities in the areas of greatest need in the UK. The initiative also supports Play England. The aims of Play England are for all children and young people in England to have regular access to free, inclusive, local play provision and play space.

Personal, Learning and Thinking Skills

This activity will help to provide evidence of Independent Enquirer and Creative Thinker.

Over to you

* What social campaigns are you aware of that are being actively supported by people in the sport and active leisure industry?
* Why do you think people involved in sport and active leisure can have a big influence on social agendas?

Just checking

* Find an interview with a sports player in a newspaper. Is the player sponsored by a business? How can you tell?
* Why are there campaigns to increase children's participation in PE and sport and active leisure?
* How does the coverage of sports events affect your own participation in sport and active leisure?

Starting Point

* How do players behave when they are being interviewed by the media?
* Why is their behaviour important?

Personal, Learning and Thinking Skills

This activity will help to provide evidence of Independent Enquirer, Creative Thinker and Reflective Learner.

Over to you

* Name three professional sport and active leisure teams from different sports.
* Name three amateur sport and active leisure activities or teams from different sports.
* How much media coverage does the amateur sport and active leisure activity have compared to the professional?
* Why do you think these differences exist?

6.5 Why the sport and active leisure industry promotes its initiatives in the media

The media benefits from the popularity of sport and active leisure, but sports teams and clubs are usually very happy to appear across all forms of media too. As well as helping them financially, this exposure allows a sport to gain its own voice and promote its initiatives. Almost all professional teams employ media officers to liaise with the media outlets on their behalf. These media officers carefully control the image of the club and its players. All managers and players are given media training to help them learn how to behave in the public eye.

Why the industry promotes its initiatives in the media

Raising the profile of sport and active leisure activities

Intense public interest in sport means that certain sports are guaranteed coverage to some extent. As you have seen, the national newspapers fill the back pages with sports stories. Individuals and sports authorities can use this provision to promote themselves and their initiatives through press conferences and interviews.

Raising awareness of sport and active leisure agendas

The media can help to raise the profile of key government initiatives that involve the sport and active leisure industry. Top of the social agenda at present is increasing participation to combat social issues such as obesity, drug and alcohol misuse, anti-social behaviour and crime. The sport and active leisure industry also benefits from the media by increasing awareness of other social issues that affect it, such as the effects of pollution on athletes during the 2008 Beijing Olympics.

Professionalising sport

Professional sports are sports in which athletes are paid a wage for their performance. This means that the athlete does not have to do other work to earn money and therefore allows them to devote all their working time to training and competition. This helps the athlete to improve their performance in their selected sport, which in turn helps to increase the popularity of the sport. The media has helped to professionalise many sports because some of the money generated by the media attention goes to pay professional athletes their wages

Benefits of promoting sport and active leisure through the media

Promoting sport and active leisure through the media has clear benefits for the industry. Some of these include:

* increased audience and spectator numbers for events
* increased awareness of sport and active leisure activities or events
* increased sponsorship opportunities for athletes and coaches.

Increased audience and spectator numbers for events

If a sport and active leisure team are successful, they are more likely to receive coverage in the media. This coverage helps to increase public interest in that team or in the sport or activity. This increased interest and associated rise in spectator numbers increases the potential income to the sport from sponsorship and advertising, which in turn attracts even more attention from the media!

Consider the success story of England's Rugby World Cup victory in 2003. This benefited English rugby enormously. There was a sudden surge of interest in rugby, which helped the Rugby Football Union earn large sums of money, for example from increased gate revenue at Twickenham. Jonny Wilkinson, who performed a starring role with a breathtaking drop goal just seconds from the end, was suddenly everywhere, appearing in newspaper and magazine interviews, billboard adverts and TV commercials. Record numbers turned up to see Wilkinson play for his next club, Newcastle Falcons.

Increased media coverage can help to attract larger audiences to a sporting event.

Increased awareness of sport and active leisure activities or events

When sporting events take place and are covered in the media, it can increase participation in that particular sport or activity. When Wimbledon is on people are encouraged to participate in tennis, and when the Tour de France is taking place suddenly the roads seem to have lots more cyclists on them! After the success of England in the Rugby World Cup the greater public awareness helped increase participation in rugby, which benefited small, local rugby clubs around the country. All this helps to direct additional revenues into a sport, to help governing bodies grow the sport even more.

Increased sponsorship opportunities for athletes and coaches

Athletes and sports coaches who are successful stand to gain a lot of money from an increase in sponsorship opportunities. Sponsors will pay lots of money to have their product or service associated with success.

Celebrity status

Successful sportspeople can become celebrities in their own right. Public interest in top sports performers generates stories for all forms of media, including newspaper columns, specialised magazines, television programmes and websites. These record both the professional sporting achievements of the individual and details of their personal lives. The sport and active leisure industry encourages this attention to some degree, as it helps to expand audiences and therefore increase income. For example, David Beckham is a brand in himself, which has been referred to as the 'Beckham Brand'. A large number of people admire David Beckham because of his lifestyle and sporting ability and want to be like him. By buying the product or service that Beckham is promoting, his fans gain an association with him.

Personal, Learning and Thinking Skills

This activity will help to provide evidence of Reflective Learner.

Over to you

* How does watching a sport or active leisure event affect your participation?
* Have you ever tried a new sport or activity because you have seen it on TV or read about it?

173

Positive images and role models

Successful sport and active leisure participants can provide positive images for media campaigns and become role models that people look up to and admire.

Acquisition of TV rights for certain sporting and active leisure events

Television companies pay lots of money to buy TV rights to some sport and active leisure events. This money can be used for different purposes, including paying for the costs of the event, paying participants, prize money and giving money to the national governing body for that sport or activity. High profile events that are guaranteed a large audience attract high bids from lots of TV companies. The TV company that secures the rights to the event is then able to generate a large income by selling time slots for commercials to be aired during the breaks in the broadcast. Sky pays around £1.4 billion for the rights to Premiership football, and the income from Sky has completely changed high-level football in England.

Ellen MacArthur brought increased public interest to sailing after breaking the world record for the fastest solo sail around the world.

6.6 How media stories influence public perceptions of the industry

The media play a significant role in influencing how people think and feel about sport. The sport and active leisure stories that the media pick up can turn sports players into heroes or villains and shape our ideas about these people and the sport in which they participate.

Negative, biased or critical media stories

Biased or critical reporting

National broadcasting and print media tend to be biased in favour of their national team. For example, you will find that most UK newspapers reporting on international games involving UK teams will be biased towards the UK team. This is to appeal to their readers, who will mainly be from the UK and so more likely to agree with stories written by reporters who are sympathetic to the UK team.

Drug abuse in sport, particularly cycling and athletics, has received highly critical reporting. In the 1988 Olympics, Ben Johnson 'won' the 100 m sprint but was stripped of his medal after he was found to have taken banned drugs. More recently, other athletes such as Marion Jones have found themselves at the centre of a media storm after producing positive drugs tests. The media has been responsible for driving the investigation of drugs scandals such as the Balco Labs case in the USA, which led to the downfall of Marion Jones and others. These reports have tainted the public image of athletics and decreased public interest in it, therefore reducing media coverage.

At times the media can be particularly critical of individuals or teams that are perceived to be underperforming. Some of the tabloid press in the UK have even depicted football managers as turnips and players as donkeys after poor performances.

Misrepresentation of the sport and active leisure industry by the media

Some sport and active leisure activities can be misrepresented by the media, in that stories relating to them tend not to be an accurate reflection of that activity or the people who take part in it. For example, in football some elite players' personal lives make headlines in the papers mainly when they are behaving badly, such as by taking drugs or drinking excessively, which can give the public the impression that all football players behave in this manner in their personal lives.

Ignoring minority interest sport or active leisure activities

Sports that do not attract large audiences receive little interest and support from the media. There is very little income created by broadcasting or writing about these minority interest sports and active leisure activities. As a result, they are often largely ignored by the media, especially by commercial channels that rely on advertising revenue for their income. Public broadcasters such as the BBC do cater

How does the media respond to stories of sports stars behaving badly?

Personal, Learning and Thinking Skills

This activity will help to provide evidence of Independent Enquirer, Creative Thinker and Reflective Learner.

Over to you

* Watch a sports match in which your team is playing.
* Now imagine you are the commentator for that match.
* How is your commentary affected by the fact that you support one team over the other?
* Do you challenge decisions made by the officials? If so, which ones?

Ben Johnson set a new world record in the 100 m sprint at the 1988 Olympics. After he failed a drugs test, Johnson's record became invalid.

175

Over to you

* Try to watch a television programme called 'Transworld Sport' which is shown on Channel 4. This contains lots of stories on different sport and active leisure events, many of which are not often reported on in the media.
* Make a list of all the sport and active leisure events that are included in one programme.
* How many of these events are not shown regularly (if at all) on TV or written about in the media? Why do you think this is?

Over to you

* Select two successful sport and active leisure participants who are poor role models.
* What have they done to make them poor role models?
* How do you think this behaviour could affect people who look up to them?

to some degree for minority sports, as they do not rely on advertising revenue for their income and have a legal responsibility to cover certain sports.

Many of the sports that are underrepresented in the media are female sports such as netball, women's football and women's hockey. This is because the majority of people who attend sporting events, read about sport in the media and watch it on TV are men, who are perceived to be less interested in women's sport. However, many females are also more interested in watching male sports rather than the female equivalent, perhaps because they are more heavily publicised and are easier to access.

Negative images and poor role models

The media, especially newspapers, are always on the lookout for a story that will attract readers. Newspapers have to fill their columns with a certain number of stories every day. When a newspaper has negative information on a sports celebrity, for example about them taking drugs or having extramarital affairs, they will try to find out as much as possible about it to build up the story. This may involve paying people involved with the sports celebrity a lot of money to tell their story and expose the celebrity. These stories help to fill the paper and attract a lot of public interest.

Some people in the sport and active leisure industry are poor role models because of how they behave in competition or in their private lives. For example, consider how participants in some sports behave towards officials. Those who are not respectful to the officials are giving other people the impression that this is acceptable behaviour.

Excessive focus on elite sport

Elite sport attracts large audiences, which in turn attracts lots of media coverage and generates a large income. As a result, the media choose to focus mainly on elite sport, such as Premiership football. In 1992, Sky bought the rights to the upper tier of English football and formed the Premier League. As a result, the Premiership became a hugely profitable product and has a global audience. However, this has resulted in some negative impacts. Many longstanding fans of Premiership teams have been priced out of the game as they are not able to afford the ticket prices. Football clubs further down the league receive very little or no income from media coverage, so can't attract top players to their team. This means that most lower-league football clubs will never get to enjoy the financial benefits of being in the Premier League.

Portrayal of countries hosting major events

Some countries that have hosted major sport and active leisure events have been portrayed in negative ways by the press. Before the 2008 Beijing Olympics, for example, there was a sudden increase in negative portrayals of China due to its human rights record. Before the 2010 FIFA World Cup in South Africa, the English and German media ran lots of stories about the crime rates and the poor infrastructure of the country. The Vancouver Winter Olympic Games in 2010 also received a lot of negative press coverage in the UK for being poorly organised.

Influence of negative, biased or critical media stories

Scheduling of sporting and active leisure events

The scheduling of major events, such as the 100 m sprint in the Olympics and the football World Cup finals, is influenced by the access of the audiences to these events. For most sporting events, the access for American and European audiences is considered the priority. Therefore, major events tend to be scheduled at times when these audiences are likely to watch them. On weekdays in the UK, virtually all football matches are played in the evening between 7pm and 9pm, as this is peak viewing time – the majority of the audience is not at work and has free time to watch the match.

There are even times when the athletes' needs seem to be placed behind attracting the maximum audience. In the Olympic Games in Athens in 2004, the marathon race was scheduled to take place during the hottest part of the day so that it could be shown at a time that would attract the largest audience.

Image of women in sport

Over a set period, the Women's Sport and Fitness Foundation examined national newspapers in the UK and discovered that just 2% of articles and 1% of images in the sports pages were devoted to female athletes and women's sport. When females are featured on the back pages of national newspapers, it is often for the wrong reasons. Successful sportswomen featured in newspapers are often depicted as glamorous women rather than as athletes. For example, the media attention given to women's beach volleyball is disproportionately high. However, as female sport and active leisure participants and teams improve their performance and achieve more success, they are beginning to receive more coverage from the media. For example, the women's FA Cup final is now regularly televised.

The England women's football team celebrate a win against the Netherlands in the UEFA Women's Euro 2009 semi-final.

Perceived lack of safety in outdoor activities

Outdoor and adventurous activities receive large amounts of media coverage when a person gets injured or dies whilst participating in the activity. For example, articles about skydiving only tend to appear in newspapers when a person's parachute fails to open, and people taking part in expeditions are usually only newsworthy if they get lost and their lives are in danger. This media coverage can prevent people from considering taking part in outdoor and adventurous activities, because the only time they hear about them is when things go wrong.

Invasion of privacy

Elite sportsmen and women are followed in both their public and private lives. For example, the indiscretions of Tiger Woods were heavily publicised by the media when news of his alleged extramarital affairs broke in December 2009. Tiger Woods is one of the highest-earning sports stars of all time and has helped to bring golf to a wider range of people. The public 'outing' of his alleged affairs resulted in Woods taking a break from professional golf.

Just checking

* Watch an international sporting event in which a team from the UK is competing. Do you think the presenter is biased? Explain your answer.

* Explain why minority sports are not widely publicised in the media.

* Do you think all sport and active leisure stars enjoy being in the media spotlight? Explain your answer.

* Do you think women's sport will gain more exposure from the media in the future? Explain your answer.

Starting Point

What sort of factors do you think you need to consider when reviewing a campaign?

6.7 Reviewing promotional campaigns for sport and active leisure

In order to help you to understand the effectiveness of a campaign it is a good idea to spend time reviewing campaigns that have run in the past and campaigns that are currently running. You will be able to learn from this to help you to plan your own sport and active leisure campaign later on in this unit.

Analysing campaigns

Examining the strengths and weaknesses of the campaign

Take time to consider the different parts of the campaign, such as the aims, the media approaches used, who the target audience was, whether the campaign was appropriate to that audience, the timing of the promotional activities and the roles and responsibilities of the team. In which of these areas do you think the campaign went well? For example, a particular campaign may have selected a good media approach because it was accessed by a large proportion of their target audience. Also consider the areas in which you feel that the campaign did not do so well. For example, perhaps the campaign did not use appropriate images to reach the target audience.

Effectiveness of message content

The aim of a campaign is to communicate a particular message. You can review the effectiveness of a message by asking the target audience questions such as:

* What do you think this campaign is trying to say?

* Did the campaign make you react in any particular way?

If the target audience can correctly identify the main points of your message and reacted positively to it, such as by wanting to attend the event or to try to stop smoking, then you know the content of this message was effective.

The way that the message is communicated

You should consider the media approaches that were used and how they were used. For example, were these approaches appropriate for the target audience? If the campaign used posters, were they placed in areas where the target audience would see them? Did the campaign use appropriate language and images for their target audience? To help you review these features of the campaign, it is a good idea to gain feedback by questioning individuals in the target audience.

It is a good idea to question the target audience of a campaign to find out what they think about it.

Reviewing the campaign using measurements of success

The success of a campaign can be measured in many ways. It may not have to affect a large number of people in order to be successful. For example, if the campaign was to reduce anti-social behaviour by increasing participation in sport and active leisure and it reached one person who now participates regularly and no longer engages in anti-social behaviour, this can have a big impact upon the community but may not be reflected in the numbers of crimes committed before and after the campaign. Other methods of measuring success could include the money that was made, the number of participants, the number of people participating regularly in sport and active leisure activities, the number of people stopping smoking, or the amount of weight lost by a group of people.

Surveying effects of the campaign

Carrying out a survey with people affected by the campaign will also help you to review a campaign. You could devise short questionnaires that people can complete anonymously, ensuring that you provide opportunities for them to give both positive and negative feedback. Alternatively you could verbally survey people by asking them questions to gain their feedback.

Using qualitative and/or quantitative data

Quantitative data is data that you can measure, such as the number of people who participated in an event or the amount of profit that was made. If large numbers of people participated in the promoted event or a large profit was made, the campaign could be called successful. Qualitative data is data that takes into account people's thoughts and feelings. For example, positive verbal or written feedback from people who saw the campaign would indicate that it was a success.

Starting Point

* Why do you think promotional campaigns are important?
* What current promotional campaigns are you aware of?

Personal, Learning and Thinking Skills

This activity will help to provide evidence of Independent Enquirer.

Over to you

* Examine promotional material for a local event.
* Who is the target audience?
* Do you think the material will attract its target audience?
* Does the promotional material contain all the required information?

Marketing campaigns can help to increase participation in sports and active leisure activities.

6.8 Planning a promotional campaign

There are many things to consider when you are planning a promotional campaign. Allow yourself plenty of time for the planning stages of your campaign to ensure that it is appropriate and will meet your aims.

Aims of campaign

When you are planning a promotional campaign, one of the first things to consider is the aims of the campaign. Campaigns may be aimed at:

* promoting an event
* promoting a sport or active leisure product or service
* influencing public perceptions
* raising awareness of social agendas
* encouraging or increasing participation in physical activity.

Promoting an event

If you are aiming to promote an event, one of the main aims of the promotion will be to attract more participants to enter the event or to attract spectators to watch it. The main aims of the promotional material will therefore be to communicate the following information: the benefits of attending for a target group or groups; the date, time and location of the event; any costs, such as admission charges.

Promoting a product or service

The main aims of this type of campaign are to attract a target audience and communicate the benefits that it can gain from using the product or service. You need to let the target audience know where they can buy the product or service and the costs involved. Usually the lowest possible cost of the product or service is highlighted in the promotional materials, eg 'Prices start from £19.99'.

Raising awareness of social agendas

This type of promotion needs to appeal to its target audience, provide information on the issues associated with a particular social agenda, then give information about what can be done to try to combat the problem.

Encouraging or increasing participation in physical activity

These campaigns will usually target specific groups of people who have been identified as not participating in enough physical activity. The campaign will need to identify with its targeted audience, provide information on the benefits of participation and/or the health problems associated with not participating and provide information on how people can increase their participation.

Marketing principles for your media campaign

Your media approach should include the key marketing principles covered by the acronym AIDA:

* **A**wareness: The media used should make the intended customers aware of your product or service.

* **I**nterest: Get your customer interested in the product or service by explaining its benefits or features.

* **D**esire: Make the customer feel that they want to own the product or use the service.

* **A**ction: The promotional material should encourage the customer to take action and buy the product or service.

Media approaches

Once you have considered the aim or aims of the campaign, you can begin to consider the media approach that you will take to reach your target audience. Different types of media approach include:

* an article in a student or local paper

* posters

* local radio adverts

* flyers

* television/video adverts

* intranet web page

* internet

* sponsorship.

An article in a local paper

This allows you to advertise to a wide audience in your local area. This is perfect if your campaign targets people in the local area, such as if you are promoting a family fun day event. However, it could be difficult to attract a reporter to do a piece on a smaller event, and taking out an advert could be expensive. An easier and less expensive option might be to place an article in your student paper. This will be suitable if your target audience are students, such as if you are promoting a five-a-side football tournament for people aged between 16 and 19.

Posters

These need to be eye-catching and appeal to their target audience. They will need to be placed in areas where the target audience will see them.

Local radio stations

These can be used to advertise products and services. The product or service needs to be suitable for local people, and the radio show on which it is broadcast would need to appeal to your target audience. For example, if your target audience were teenagers it would be better if your advert was broadcast during a popular music radio show than a classical music show.

Posters need to be eye-catching and include relevant information for the campaign.

Cycle to School Day

April 1st is our Cycle to School Day

Instead of taking the bus or getting a lift, get on your bike for a healthier and **greener** way to get around

All cyclists will receive a free £5 voucher to spend in the local cycle shop

Flyers

These are a good, inexpensive way to advertise a product or service. They inform people about the product or service and the recipient can keep the flyer so that they can refer back to it later should they decide to buy the product or service. The text in a flyer should be kept to a minimum and it should have some eye-catching pictures that will appeal to your target audience.

Television/video

You may decide to produce a campaign using television or video. This will allow you to use visual aids and verbal communication to help to convey your message. You might then upload your video to a website, as showing it on TV would be very expensive.

Intranet

Your school, college or sport and active leisure provider may have an intranet site where you can post details of your sport and active leisure product, service or event.

Internet

Other ways of promoting your sport and active leisure product or service involve using the internet, for example by advertising on social networking sites such as Facebook or MySpace, sending emails, or using a website text reporting service.

Sponsorship

You could sponsor a local sports team or event as part of your campaign. Most sponsors provide some form of resource or money to the organisation that they are sponsoring. You could consider offering your skills rather than cash, such as by helping to run children's activities, manning the refreshment stand or stewarding during the event, in return for your campaign being promoted at the event.

Different types of promotion can be used to advertise the same product or service to help reach all of your target audience. If you are working in a team, decide the best methods of advertising for your resources, budget and each team member's skills.

Identified audiences

When planning your campaign you need to identify who your target audience is. Factors to consider when deciding on your target audience include their age, gender, religion, social class, culture and possibly political interests. Once the target audience has been identified, you can plan your promotional materials so that they appeal to your audience and attract their attention. Your target audience will influence the language and images that you use and your method of advertising.

Materials and equipment needed

Once you have an idea of the media approach that you plan to use, you need to make sure you have access to all the materials and equipment that you need – for example, a video recorder and a computer with appropriate software for designing posters or flyers.

Roles and responsibilities in the team

Within your group you must decide who is going to perform each of the roles required to plan and implement the promotional campaign successfully. It is a good idea to assign a role to each member of your team so that they know what they are responsible for. Once you have worked out the basic requirements of each role, you can determine which role each person is most suited to. Some people in your team may need to take on more than one role in order to meet all the requirements. If one person does need to take on more than one role, it is important that they take on the roles with slightly less responsibility.

Timing of promotional activities

Timing is crucial for your promotional campaign. If you are advertising an event, ensure you give people enough notice about the date and time so that they can leave this time free to participate or watch. You then need to provide promotional reminders nearer the time so that your audience don't forget about your event.

Case study: Badminton tournament

Alfie, Harjinder, Karl and Anita are working together to promote a mixed pairs badminton tournament that they are organising. The tournament is aimed at students in their college aged between 16 and 18 years and is due to run in the last week of the summer term. They need to work out what types of media would be best to use in order for most students in the college to find out about the tournament. They are planning to charge an entry fee and then use some of this money to buy prizes for the winners and runners-up; the rest of the money will go to charity.

1 What types of media approach do you think would be best in order to reach the target audience?

2 Explain why you have selected these approaches and why you think they are suitable.

3 How far in advance of the tournament do you think the group should start promoting the event? Explain your answer.

4 What sorts of materials and equipment will the group need to:
   a promote the event
   b run the event?

Just checking

* What are the aims of your promotional campaign?

* Who are your target audience?

* What media approaches do you plan to use for your promotional campaign?

   Explain why you selected these media approaches.

* What equipment and resources will you need for this promotional campaign?

* What are your roles and responsibilities within your team?

Starting Point

What problems do you think you may come across when implementing your promotional campaign?

6.9 Implementing a promotional campaign in sport and active leisure

Once you have thoroughly planned your promotional campaign, you need to work well with the rest of your team to put this plan into practice. In this topic you will learn how to work well with the rest of your team and how to clearly promote your message.

Importance of team work and working together

You will be working with other people during the promotional campaign. The people that you work with may be a combination of those who have media skills and people who are based within the sport and active leisure industry. You need to work well together to get the best results. Make sure each person is assigned roles so that they know exactly what is expected from them. There should be a person nominated to make decisions and ensure everyone in the team has carried out their job role.

Working well as a team will help you to achieve success with your campaign.

Coordinating different media approaches

You may be using more than one media approach – for example, posters and a podcast – to reach your target audience. Make sure that all forms of media approach are clearly linked and completed in good time, before the campaign is due to be launched.

Contacting individuals or organisations to be involved

You may find that businesses and organisations are willing to help you promote your campaign if you put your request to them politely, for example by agreeing to put up your posters around their building. They may help in other ways too, such as by providing sponsorship or resources. A local company may be interested in demonstrating its support by sponsoring you to help promote its products and services. For example, if you were running a volleyball tournament, you could suggest that the sponsor has their business logo clearly written at the top of the programme and on any promotional posters in return for help with expenses or equipment. Some businesses may even provide resources to help you with your event, such as sporting equipment or refreshments, without being a formal sponsor. It is usually expected that the business will still get a mention of thanks in some way, such as 'Thank you to Craghill Sports Stores for supplying water bottles for all participants' written on any literature handed out during the event. This helps the business to be seen to be supporting local causes and helps to promote their product or service.

Promotional messages

There are some key elements to address when implementing your promotional message. Your promotional campaign should:

* have a clear message or idea

* include the use of persuasion

* provide information

* give information on a **unique selling proposition** (USP) or benefit.

Clear message

Your promotional campaign should aim to send a clear message to its target audience. The use of visual images helps to portray a clear message, as these are often recognised and understood more quickly than text.

Use of persuasion

All campaigns aim to try to encourage their target audience to do or buy something. Therefore, the language and images used need to be persuasive.

Provide information

You will need to include details of what people need to know if they are going to respond to your campaign by buying the product you are advertising or attending an event you are promoting. Information such as the date, the time, the costs, what activities will be there etc should all be included in the promotional message.

Unique selling proposition or benefit

Include in your campaign why people should take action after seeing your promotion.

JARGON BUSTER

Unique selling proposition
Something that you can offer that is unique to the product or service you are advertising and makes it stand out from competitors.

Personal, Learning and Thinking Skills

This activity will help to provide evidence of Independent Enquirer, Creative Thinker and Reflective Learner.

Over to you

Consider the two examples below:

1 Come and join us at our Sports Day.

2 Don't miss the sporting event of the year!

* Which message do you think is the most persuasive?

* Why do you think this is?

* How can you use persuasion in your campaign?

* What is your USP or benefit going to be in your campaign?

Examine the poster below.

April 1st is our Cycle to School Day

Instead of taking the bus or getting a lift, get on your bike for a healthier and **greener** way to get around

All cyclists will receive a free £5 voucher to spend in the local cycle shop

1 Who do you think this poster is aimed at?

2 Do you think that the image used is suitable for this audience?

3 What do you think is good about this poster?

4 What do you think could be improved?

Communication skills

When you are implementing your promotional campaign, the whole process is about communicating a message to your target audience, so good communication skills are essential. You will also need to consider how you will communicate with the rest of your team.

Verbal

If your campaign involves verbal promotion, such as an advert on a local radio show or a podcast, you need to make sure that the language you use is appropriate for your audience. For example, if your target audience is teenagers then it may be acceptable to use **slang** words that are popular amongst this group. However, you should never use swear words as these are offensive to many people.

You need to speak clearly and fluently. You will also need to consider how long your verbal message is so that it is long enough to pass on all the necessary information but not so long that they lose interest.

Written

Any written communication in a campaign needs to be of a suitable length. Too much written text will put people off reading the message at all, but it must communicate all the required information such as dates, times and costs if you are promoting an event.

Visual

The use of visual images helps to portray a clear message. Images are recognised and understood more quickly than written text, so you need to carefully consider which images you will use to ensure that they attract the attention of your target audience.

JARGON BUSTER

Slang Informal language, often containing words that are mainly used by specific groups of people, for example, 'cool', 'wicked' or 'innit'.

It is much easier to demonstrate how a piece of equipment works than to explain it in words.

Meeting the intended aims

You need to consider how you will measure the success of your campaign. You could consider setting yourself SMART targets. SMART stands for:

✳ Specific

✳ Measurable

✳ Achievable

✳ Realistic

✳ Timely.

When these targets are met you will know that you have achieved some or all of your aims. For example, rather than stating, 'The aim of the campaign is to increase participation in sport and active leisure activities,' you could say, 'The aim of the campaign is to increase participation by 14–16-year-old females in lunchtime aerobics classes. We aim to increase participation by 15% within two months of starting the campaign.'

There are other ways that you could measure the success of your campaign. These include recording:

✳ the numbers of participants at an event

✳ the sales income or profit from an event or product

✳ feedback on an event or a new product or service

✳ effects on social agenda – for example, has there been a reduction in binge drinking or an increase in physical activity participation amongst the target groups?

Case study: Matt's rugby club

Matt is 18 years old and has recently qualified as a junior rugby coach. He is keen to start a junior rugby club in his local village for children aged between 8 and 10 years. However, the local community already has junior football and netball clubs for children of this age group, so he is worried that he may not get sufficient support to get the rugby club up and running.

Matt has decided to start the promotion of his rugby club during the rugby Six Nations competition, with the club due to start just as the Six Nations finishes. He has designed posters that include images of England rugby players and information about where and when the rugby classes are due to start. He is also trying to think of a catchphrase or slogan that will grab people's attention to put on his posters.

Matt plans to place the posters on notice boards around the local community and in the local primary school. He has also spoken with the school's head teacher, who has given him permission to give a 'rugby taster session' in the PE lessons of children in Years 4 and 5.

1 Who do you think the target audience is for this campaign?

2 Think of a catchphrase or slogan that Matt could include on his campaign posters. Why do you think this is appropriate for the campaign?

3 What do you think about the images that Matt has used on his posters? Do you think they are appropriate?

4 What other images could Matt use?

5 What other methods could Matt use to reach his target audience?

6 Why do you think Matt has timed his campaign to coincide with the Six Nations?

7 How could Matt assess whether his campaign has been successful?

For your project

This unit explores the importance of the relationship between the media and sport. Sport is covered in all forms of the media and helps to sell media products. Businesses also use sport to advertise their products and services and in return give money to sport and active leisure organisations and players, and the media assists in this process. There are times when the media provides significant support to sport and active leisure, which can increase participation and audience numbers, as well as create pressure to influence legislation. However, there is also a negative side to the relationship between the media and sport, where biased, negative or critical reporting can influence the public's perception of the sport and active leisure industry.

This unit has also introduced you to promotional campaigns, which are used in sport and active leisure by the media to promote products and services. They are designed to reach a target audience and influence that audience into action.

The following diagram gives some ideas for what you might decide to do your project on, based on the content of this unit.

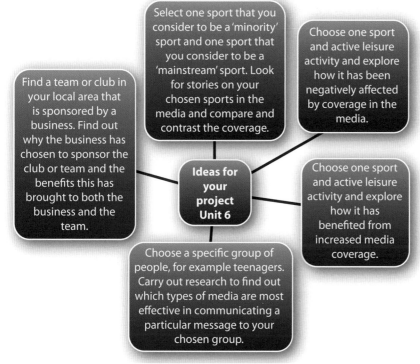

Select one sport that you consider to be a 'minority' sport and one sport that you consider to be a 'mainstream' sport. Look for stories on your chosen sports in the media and compare and contrast the coverage.

Choose one sport and active leisure activity and explore how it has been negatively affected by coverage in the media.

Find a team or club in your local area that is sponsored by a business. Find out why the business has chosen to sponsor the club or team and the benefits this has brought to both the business and the team.

Ideas for your project Unit 6

Choose one sport and active leisure activity and explore how it has benefited from increased media coverage.

Choose a specific group of people, for example teenagers. Carry out research to find out which types of media are most effective in communicating a particular message to your chosen group.

Possible project titles

* How does the media affect participation in minority sports?

* To what extent is the media starting to pay more attention to women's sport?

* How can different types of media reach different target audiences?

* How does the sport and active leisure industry help to promote participation?

* How does a particular company promote their product or service through sport and active leisure events?

Assessment guidance

This unit is assessed by one internally-set assignment. You will have a period of eight hours to generate evidence for your assessment. In your assessment you will need to show that you:

* are able to provide a description of how the sport and active leisure industry benefits the media

* know how the industry promotes its own initiatives in the media

* know the different ways that media can be used to promote or influence sport and active leisure

* understand why the sport and active leisure industry promotes its own initiatives in the media

* are able to examine benefits of promoting sport and active leisure through the media

* are able to assess how negative, biased or critical media stories can influence public perceptions when reporting on the industry

* can identify aims for promotions

* can identify media approaches that match target audiences

* are able to organise your time and resources

* are able to design promotional messages that convey benefits

* are able to communicate promotional messages to sport and active leisure audiences that meet the intended aims of campaigns

* are able to provide an analysis of the strengths and weaknesses of promotional campaigns in sport and active leisure

* are able to collaborate with others to implement a campaign.

Time management

* Although you have eight hours to generate evidence for this assignment, this time frame does not include time spent researching the topic area.

* The internal assessment will be split into different tasks. You will be given set times to generate evidence for that task whilst being supervised by your tutor or your employer.

* Your tutor may well give you ideas for resources to use to help you to carry out research before you attempt the task. You should aim to make time to read this information and carry out research for the set task so that you have a good understanding of the subject area.

* Your tutor may give you formative assessments that are similar to the actual task. You should make time to complete these 'trial' assessments, as these will help to prepare you for the real task. Your tutor will be able to give you feedback on the areas that you have completed well and areas for improvement.

Useful links

To help you understand this unit, it is a good idea to spend time watching sports-related programmes that are broadcast on the BBC and on commercial channels. This will help you to understand a number of aspects relating to this unit, including:

* advertising
* critical and biased reporting
* positive role models
* scheduling of events
* image of women in sport.

You should also examine both national and local newspapers so that you can see how sport and active leisure events are reported in the press and the differing amounts of exposure that different sports receive.

Work experience will help you to see how the business that you are placed with promotes its products or services and give you ideas for your campaign.

There are lots of useful websites that will help you with your research for this unit. For details of how to access these sites see the **Hotlinks** section – **Introduction**, page xi.

How you will be assessed

For your Unit 6 assessment, you need to make sure that you can meet all of the assessment criteria for the seven learning outcomes, as shown in the table below.

Learning outcome	Assessment criteria
LO1: Know how the sport and active leisure industry benefits the media	**1** Describe how the industry benefits the media.
LO2: Know how the sport and active leisure industry promotes its own initiatives in the media	**1** Describe how the industry promotes its own initiatives in the media. **2** Describe the different ways that media can be used to promote or influence sport and active leisure.
LO3: Understand why the sport and active leisure industry promotes its own initiatives in the media	**1** Explain why the industry promotes its own initiatives in the media. **2** Examine the benefits of promoting sport and active leisure through the media.
LO4: Understand how media stories influence public perceptions of the industry	**1** Assess how negative, biased or critical media stories can influence public perceptions when reporting on the industry.
LO5: Understand the effectiveness of promotional campaigns for sport and active leisure	**1** Analyse the strengths and weaknesses of promotional campaigns in sport and active leisure.
LO6: Be able to plan promotional campaigns for sport and active leisure	**1** Identify the aims for promotional campaigns. **2** Identify media approaches to use with target audiences. **3** Organise time and resources to implement media approaches.
LO7: Be able to implement promotional campaigns for sport and active leisure	**1** Collaborate with others to implement campaigns. **2** Design promotional messages. **3** Communicate promotional messages to sport and active leisure audiences to meet the intended aims of campaigns.

Introduction

In the sport and active leisure industry the customer is extremely important. It is therefore necessary to ensure that, wherever possible, customer expectations are met or surpassed. In this section you will explore ways in which a sport and active leisure provider can improve access for different types of customer to help improve their participation in sport and active leisure. You will learn about a range of customer service skills that will help you to work with the public effectively and efficiently.

What will you learn?

In this unit you will cover the following learning outcomes:

LO1: Know the requirements of participants in sport and active leisure

LO2: Know how to improve access to participation in sport and active leisure

LO3: Know the management and leadership skills needed to improve sport and active leisure provision

LO4: Know the customer service skills required in the sport and active leisure industry

LO5: Be able to meet the customer service needs of sport and active leisure participants

LO6: Be able to propose improvements to access to sport and active leisure for different groups

The following table shows how these six learning outcomes are covered by this unit.

Topic	Pages	Learning outcomes
7.1 Participant requirements in sport and active leisure	194–195	LO1
7.2 Improving access to participation in sport and active leisure	196–199	LO2
7.3 Management and leadership skills	200–202	LO3
7.4 Customer service skills	203–205	LO4
7.5 Customer service issues	206–207	LO4
7.6 Communicating effectively with customers	208–211	LO5
7.7 Factors affecting access for different groups of people	212–213	LO6
7.8 Reviewing and improving access	214–215	LO6

THINKING POINTS

* When have you been impressed with the customer service that you received?
* What do you think made this customer service so good?
* When have you been disappointed with the customer service that you received?
* What could the person have done to improve their customer service skills?

Functional Skills

Personal, Learning and Thinking Skills

This unit offers various opportunities to develop functional skills and personal, learning and thinking skills. Where appropriate, different activities are signposted with the relevant skills that you can develop.

Diploma Daily

Equal Access for All?

A new sport and active leisure centre has opened in the south-east, which will only allow females, people from ethnic minorities and people with disabilities to use the centre's facilities. The manager of this centre says, 'This restricted access is due to the fact that these groups of people are underrepresented in sport and active leisure activities. We want to increase participation opportunities for these groups. By having a centre that only allows access to specific groups of people we can provide facilities and activities that are tailored to meet their needs.'

1 Do you think centres with this type of restricted access are a good idea?

2 What are the problems that may be associated with this type of centre?

Unit links

This unit links closely to Level 2, Unit 2: Encouraging participation in sport and active leisure, Unit 4: Working in the local sport and active leisure Industry, Unit 5: Businesses in the sport and active leisure industry and Unit 6: Media in sport and active leisure.

How you will be assessed

This unit will be internally assessed by one main assignment that requires you to:

* review current access to sport and active leisure for different participant groups

* show that you can meet the customer service needs of two different participants in sport and active leisure in a realistic work setting, using your communication and presentation skills.

In your assignment you need to provide evidence of the following:

* A review describing current access to local sport and active leisure for two different participant groups, with suggestions of how to improve access to local sport and active leisure for a specific population.

* A signed learner observation record form from your tutor or work experience/work placement supervisor, commenting on your demonstration of communication and presentation skills with at least two different customers.

Case study: Football focus

Hassan is a 15-year-old Muslim. He enjoys playing football in PE lessons and would like to take part in more football outside school. His friends play once a week after school at a local sport and active leisure centre and he would like to join them. Hassan would need to take two buses to get to the leisure centre and would have to pay for this as well as contributing to the cost of pitch hire. His family is living on a limited budget and so would struggle to cover these costs. Hassan also has regular prayer times throughout the day and he does not know if the centre provides access to a quiet prayer room.

1 What are the access problems that Hassan has to deal with in order to take part in football after school?

2 How could the sport and active leisure provider help Hassan overcome these problems?

Starting Point

* What sort of requirements do you think you have for participation in sport and active leisure?

* How do your requirements differ from those of your parents or grandparents?

7.1 Participant requirements in sport and active leisure

Participation in sport and active leisure is important for everybody, but different people have different requirements. When you are working in the sport and active leisure industry you need to understand these differing requirements so that you can help to ensure that every customer's needs are met.

Participant groups and their requirements

The different participant groups that you may work with include:

* people of different ages
* people of different **socioeconomic** backgrounds
* people of different cultures and religions
* people with disabilities
* people with health conditions
* people with learning difficulties
* injured people
* females
* obese people
* males
* families.

The descriptions of each of these groups and benefits of participation for them are covered in Unit 2, Topic 2.1. In this topic you will explore the differing requirements of each group.

People of different ages

Children: Children should be active for at least an hour a day. They need lots of supervision and varied activities that require minimal skills. A parent/guardian will usually stay with children aged five or under. Children are unable to focus for long periods of time, so varied activities help to keep their attention. Activities need to be enjoyable so that they want to take part. Examples include obstacle courses, role play (eg pretending to be animals) and games like stuck in the mud. The main aim when working with children is to keep the majority of them active at any one time.

Young people: This group have some sporting skills, require less supervision and will have formed preferences for certain activities. In many cases young people take part in activities with the same gender. There is often a social element attached to participation.

Older people: For many activities older people will need minimal supervision. The main requirements are that they keep active through aerobic exercises, some strengthening exercises and balance exercises. This helps keep their body fit and strong enough to cope with everyday activities. There is also a strong social element to participation.

People from different socioeconomic backgrounds – there is currently a divide in participation rates based on socioeconomic background. People from poorer backgrounds tend to have lower activity levels than people from richer backgrounds. Requirements for people from poorer socioeconomic groups may include reducing costs of activities and improving access to free activities such as cycling and walking routes.

JARGON BUSTER

Socioeconomic To do with social status and how wealthy a person or group is.

Rehabilitate Undertake activities to help with the recovery of an injury.

People from different cultures and religions may require information leaflets and signs written in different languages. Their religion or culture may have strict guidelines on dress, such as females wearing a hijab (head scarf) or males wearing turbans, which must be permitted during an activity. Some cultures do not allow females to be seen by males in swimming costumes, so female-only swimming sessions would need to be provided.

People with learning difficulties may require qualified additional support to help them whilst they are taking part in a sport and leisure activity. This support ensures they understand what they need to do and helps to guide and supervise them through the activity.

People with disabilities may require additional qualified support or resources to help them participate in sport and active leisure activities. For example, a person who is in a wheelchair will need support to get safely into a swimming pool and may require equipment such as a hoist.

Obese people should take part in any physical activity that can help them to get fit and lose excess body fat. Many obese people feel self-conscious about going to a gym so sessions that are specifically designed for obese people may help to encourage participation.

People with injuries and health conditions require activities to help them **rehabilitate**. They may need specialised equipment and qualified staff to supervise and ensure that they do not endanger their health. For example, a person with high blood pressure should not lift very heavy weights.

Females and males – sport and active leisure facilities must provide single sex or private individual changing facilities and single sex toilets. Females tend to prefer class-based activities where they can socialise and/or activities that target specific areas of fitness. Women with young children may need access to crèche facilities. Males often prefer competition-based sports and activities like football or squash. Working males and females require access to facilities in the evenings or at lunchtime.

Families require activities in which they can all participate together, such as tennis, or a range of activities in which different members can participate within the same centre. A crèche facility may be required to allow adults and older children to participate whilst a young child is cared for. They need changing and toilet facilities that cater for adults and children of all ages.

Egypt's Aya Medany competing in the 2009 Modern Pentathlon World Cup in a hijab.

Personal, Learning and Thinking Skills

This activity will help to provide evidence of Independent Enquirer.

Over to you

How does your local sport and active leisure centre provide for the needs of people from different cultures or religions?

Just checking

Visit a local sport and active leisure provider or look at their website to find out how they meet the requirements of the following participant groups:

* children
* older people
* people with physical disabilities
* obese people
* families.

Starting Point

Why do you think it is important for all people to have access to sport and active leisure?

7.2 Improving access to participation in sport and active leisure

The Department of Culture, Media and Sport states that, 'Everybody should have the opportunity to participate in sport and physical activity regardless of sex, age, race or disability'. A range of policies and legislation are in place to allow equal access for all people to sport and active leisure facilities and activities. In this topic, some of these policies will be examined to help you assess how well your local sport and active leisure providers are following them.

Equal opportunities legislation

There are a number of Acts of Parliament in place to protect people from discrimination and ensure they have access to equal opportunities. These include:

* **Sex Discrimination Act 1975:** Makes it unlawful for an employer to discriminate on the grounds of sex or marital status in recruitment, promotion and training.

* **Race Relations Act 1976:** Makes it unlawful for an employer to discriminate on the grounds of race, colour, nationality or ethnic or national origin.

* **Disability Discrimination Act 1995:** Makes it unlawful for an employer to discriminate on the grounds of disability and places a duty on employers to make 'reasonable adjustments' to premises or working practices to allow the employment of a disabled person.

* **Human Rights Act 1998:** Ensures that all people are entitled to have their rights respected in everyday life and when being held in custody.

* **Equality Act 2006:** Set up an Equality and Human Rights Commission to encourage and support the development of a society that has the following beliefs and values:

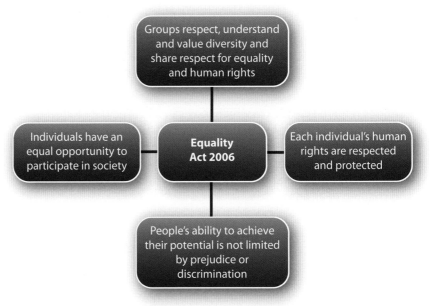

Groups respect, understand and value diversity and share respect for equality and human rights

Individuals have an equal opportunity to participate in society

Equality Act 2006

Each individual's human rights are respected and protected

People's ability to achieve their potential is not limited by prejudice or discrimination

New pieces of legislation are sometimes adapted. For example, the Equality Act (2006) is due to become the Equality Bill. The aims of this Bill are to give individuals greater protection from unfair discrimination and set a new standard for those who provide public services, so that they treat everyone with dignity and respect. The Bill is planned to prevent discrimination based on age, disability, gender reassignment, marriage and civil partnership, pregnancy and maternity, race, religion or belief, sex and sexual orientation.

Making reasonable adjustments to provision

A disabled person is defined as someone who has a physical or mental impairment that has an effect on their ability to carry out normal day-to-day activities. In England there are 11 million people who are disabled. It is important to remember that disabled people are a diverse group and have different requirements. The Disability Discrimination Act means that a sport and active leisure provider is bound by law to make reasonable adjustments to its provision to ensure it is allowing equal access for disabled people. One key area in which a provider is expected to make these adjustments is helping disabled people overcome a physical barrier. This can be carried out by removing the barrier, altering the barrier, avoiding it or providing services by alternative methods.

Examples of how a provider could make reasonable adjustments to overcome a physical barrier include: widening doorways; providing ramps as well as or instead of steps for wheelchair users; and providing tactile buttons in lifts that can be found easily by a visually impaired person. The sport and active leisure provider should try to pre-empt the needs of disabled customers and have services ready for them should they be requested. For example, they could have information leaflets in Braille available in case a blind person requests one or have adapted gym equipment in place for people with specific disabilities. Other aspects of the business such as marketing and publicity should also be involved, to ensure that any information they provide clearly states that the sport and active leisure provider has access and provision for disabled people.

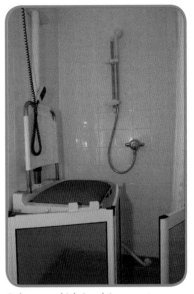

A shower cubicle in a leisure centre that has been adapted for the needs of disabled customers.

Not discriminating against certain groups

All groups of people should have equal access to the facilities of a sport and active leisure provider. By law, a centre cannot actively discriminate against certain groups by restricting their access. However, the services and activities that they provide may still discriminate against certain groups unintentionally. For example, if the facility does not have a crèche then this is a form of discrimination against parents with young children, as they will not be able to participate in activities if they have a young child to look after. If there are no female-only swimming sessions supervised by female staff, then this could be classed as a form of discrimination as it restricts the access of female Muslims.

Different methods of complying with the legislation

A sport and active leisure provider can demonstrate different methods of complying with equal opportunities law. These include:

* Provision of suitable facilities for different groups – such as equipment suitable for disabled people, access to a prayer room, or provision of a crèche for childcare.

* Provision of activities for different groups – such as exercise classes specifically designed for older people, female-only swimming sessions, or qualified staff and activities for people with learning difficulties.

Using skills to ensure participation

To help to encourage participation, people working within the sport and active leisure industry should have good interpersonal, motivational and leadership skills. This will help to provide the customer with confidence and help them to take the first step and participate in a sport and active leisure activity. It will also help motivate them to continue to participate.

Promoting activity through targeted media

In order for a sport and active leisure provider to encourage equal opportunities, they must ensure that they are promoting the activities they have on offer to everyone in their local community. It is therefore necessary to find out how different groups of people receive promotional materials. For example, groups such as teenagers tend to have ready access to different types of technology like mobile phones and the internet, so promotions using these forms of media would be appropriate for this age group. However, older adults would be more likely to receive promotional material through reading printed information such as posters, local papers or village magazines.

Over to you

What methods could you use to promote activities designed to encourage participation in the following groups of people:

* partially-sighted people
* Muslim women
* teenage girls
* full-time mothers?

Teenagers could be targeted via websites and social networking sites.

Working with community leaders

A sport and active leisure provider can help ensure that it caters for the needs of the local community and provides equal opportunities by forming links with community leaders. Most communities have some form of leadership. Community leaders may be from a religious background (such as a priest or imam) or from an education background (such as a school head teacher). If a centre can work with these people it will gain an understanding of that community and become aware of any cultural or religious beliefs that may affect the community's needs.

Frameworks of good practice by trade bodies

An 'Equality Standard for Sport' was launched in 2004. It is a collaboration between sports councils and UK Sport and is supported by:

* CCPR (Central Council of Physical Recreation)
* The Women's Sports Foundation
* The English Federation of Disability Sport
* Sporting Equals.

This is a framework for helping sports organisations to widen access and reduce inequalities in sport and physical activity for individuals, groups and communities that are **under-represented** in this area in the UK. These groups have been identified as women and girls, ethnic minorities and disabled people. The main aims of the Equality Standard are to develop sport and active leisure provision in order to increase participation at all levels of sport.

The CCPR is an organisation that represents the national governing and representative bodies of sport and recreation in the UK. Its aims are to promote, protect and develop sport and recreation at all levels in the UK, and it is independent of government control.

The Women's Sports Foundation is part-funded by Sport England. It is the main organisation working to promote, improve and increase opportunities for women and girls in sport and other physical activities in the UK.

The English Federation of Disability Sport (EFDS) covers six National Disability Sports Organisations. The EFDS is the national body responsible for developing sport for disabled people in England and has helped to develop frameworks such as the 'Playground to Podium' initiative. 'Playground to Podium' is designed to increase the participation of disabled people in sport and help disabled people progress from PE and community sport to high-level performance and competition.

Sporting Equals is an organisation that promotes ethnic diversity across sport and physical activity. It works with national organisations and sports governing bodies to promote racial equality in sport and active leisure. Its work includes administering the Sport for Communities Project, which provides funding grants to help increase participation in sport by ethnic minorities, migrants and refugees, and helping local authorities to plan, develop and promote racial equality through all their sports provision and services.

Community leaders can help to ensure that sport and active leisure initiatives are appropriate for their local area.

JARGON BUSTER

Under-represented In a smaller proportion than would be found in the general population.

Just checking

* Choose a sport and active leisure provider in your local area and explain how they use different media to promote their activities. Do you think the message reaches all of the local community?
* Who do you think are the community leaders in your local area? Are any of these people involved with improving access to participation in sport and active leisure?
* How does your local sport and active leisure centre provide access for disabled people?

* How have managers or leaders influenced your participation in sport and active leisure?

* Think about where you live. What skills do you think a manager or leader should have in order to help improve local sport and active leisure provision?

7.3 Management and leadership skills

People working in the sport and active leisure industry need to have good management and leadership skills in order to improve provision. These skills are examined in the following topic.

Being a role model

Participants frequently look up to a manager or leader as a source of inspiration and knowledge, and children and young people often imitate their behaviour. Therefore, leaders must have good self-management skills and demonstrate proper personal and professional behaviour at all times, such as by being punctual, fulfilling promises and having good personal presentation standards. Some leaders also use other role models to help influence behaviour and encourage good practice. Role models who have excelled, such as players from the England rugby team, often run workshops to promote their sport. Participants can easily identify with these role models and are motivated to learn from them and participate in sport and active leisure.

Personal, Learning and Thinking Skills

This activity will help to provide evidence of Independent Enquirer, Creative Thinker and Reflective Learner.

Over to you

* Who is your role model?
* What qualities does this person have?
* Why do you think sporting role models can help to improve sport and active leisure provision?

JARGON BUSTER

Prejudice When an unfair judgement is made about someone. Prejudices are often negative views about people because of their religion, race, gender or personal choices.

Stereotyping Generalising about a person or a group of people rather than treating everyone as individuals.

Recognising prejudice and stereotyping

Any leader or manager should make it clear to all participants that **prejudice** and **stereotyping** will not be tolerated in any form. They are types of discrimination and must be recognised and dealt with swiftly. To help people understand the full implications of prejudice or stereotyping, a leader might provide information leaflets to help identify unacceptable behaviour and attitudes.

Using motivational strategies with participants

A leader needs to motivate participants to help them meet their goals and continue to participate. Motivational strategies include:

* **Active encouragement:** Using praise when something is done well.

* **Delegation:** Giving others some sort of responsibility, such as leading the warm-up. This helps give them a sense of importance and develop confidence in their own abilities.

* **Positive reinforcement:** Actively rewarding good practice, for example by providing praise or awarding certificates, to encourage participants to repeat good behaviour.

* **Recognising achievement:** When people, especially children, work hard, they like to have their achievements recognised. Several schemes award badges or certificates when participants achieve a certain level of skill or ability.

* **Goal setting:** Working with groups or individuals to decide on short-and long-term goals to help them progress.

Prioritising different customer needs

A manager or leader can't deal with all the needs of their different customers all the time. They should place these needs in order of priority. The most important should be dealt with quickly and the less important left until later on.

Over to you

'Football is for boys and netball is for girls'.

* What do you think about this statement?
* How is this statement stereotyping males and females?

Arsenal Women's Football Team celebrate after winning the 2005 FA Women's Cup final.

Over to you

Imagine you are a sport and active leisure centre manager in your local area. Place the following different customer needs in order of importance and explain why.

* timetabling an older adults' exercise class
* getting a broken access ramp to the facility fixed
* installing a baby changing facility in the male changing area (already available in the female changing area)
* timetabling 'Mother and Baby' yoga classes
* timetabling female-only swimming sessions.

Personal, Learning and Thinking Skills

This activity will help to provide evidence of Independent Enquirer, Creative Thinker and Reflective Learner.

Understanding key health and safety issues

The manager or leader of a facility or activity is responsible for the health and safety of all participants. They must provide a safe environment and minimise any risks. They must also ensure that they and all participants follow any relevant health and safety legislation.

Over to you

* How does your local sport and active leisure provider create a suitable physical environment for its customers?
* What sort of hospitality does this centre provide?
* Do you think the physical environment of this centre could be improved?

Taking active leisure into specific communities

Before introducing any new form of active leisure into a community, a leader or manager should have as much information as possible about the needs of that community. They should ideally meet with leaders of the community and start to build relationships, as these people can help to encourage participation. Once the leader has a full understanding about what sorts of things the community needs in order to take part in sport and active leisure, they can try to ensure everything is in place from the start. For example, if the community the leader is working with need to be able to pray at a certain time in the activity session, this can be scheduled into the activity session so that it meets the community's needs. This will help the community that the leader is working with trust them and accept that they have an understanding of the needs and requirements of that community.

Creating a suitable physical environment for customers

The physical environment is important and facilities must meet the specific needs of customers. Cleanliness is vital, especially in toilet and changing areas. In most sport and active leisure facilities there are also areas where people can buy refreshments and meet socially.

Just checking

* What types of prejudice or stereotyping are you aware of in sport and active leisure?
* Why is it important for a manager to be able to prioritise different customers' needs?
* What ideas could you give a leader trying to introduce active leisure into your community?

7.4 Customer service skills

In the sport and active leisure industry you will work with customers on a daily basis. To do this successfully you need a good knowledge of **customer service** skills and must be able to apply them to different situations to ensure that customers are satisfied and return. In this topic, customer service skills will be examined to prepare you for your career in the sport and active leisure industry.

Customers

A customer is a person who buys or uses a particular service or product. Within sport and active leisure there are two types of customer, external and internal.

External customer: This is someone from outside the organisation who pays to use a service or buy a product. External customers may visit a sport and active leisure provider to make general enquiries about what the facility has to offer in order to decide if they wish to use the product or service.

External customers visiting a sport and active leisure centre to find out about membership deals.

Internal customer: This is someone working within the organisation that a team member must deliver a service to, such as a co-worker, supervisor, supplier or maintenance contractor. For example, a receptionist making bookings for a class taken by a visiting instructor.

Skills

Communication techniques

Both verbal and non-verbal communication techniques can be used to communicate with customers. However, the way that you communicate with a customer will differ depending on the type of customer you are dealing with.

Starting Point

Do you think that all customers should be dealt with in the same way? Explain your answer.

Personal, Learning and Thinking Skills

This activity will help to provide evidence of Independent Enquirer, Creative Thinker and Reflective Learner.

Over to you

* How would you adapt your verbal communication to speak to the following groups of people:
    - people who have English as their second language
    - older adults
    - large groups of people in a sports hall?
* How do you think a customer would feel if they were talking to a member of staff who was looking around with a bored expression on their face and fiddling with a pen?

Verbal communication: Always be polite and address the customer appropriately. Many adults prefer to be addressed as Mr, Mrs or Ms, for example 'Hello, Mrs Smith' if you know their name, or 'Excuse me, Sir/Madam' if you don't. When addressing individuals, verbal communication should be used in a conversational manner, but in larger groups you will need to speak louder so that the whole group can hear. How you communicate with different individuals or groups will vary to some degree. For example, when working with children use a softer tone so that they are not intimidated.

Written communication: This can include signs, notices, promotional material and websites. The language used in written communication should be appropriate to the audience and must not contain any language or pictures that may offend customers. In locations with a large number of ethnic minorities or visitors from overseas for whom English is a second language, information in different languages should be used to help communicate effectively with all customers.

Please remove outdoor shoes before entering the swimming pool changing area.

Proszę zdjąć obuwie zewnętrzne przed wejściem do przebieralni na terenie basenu.

Veuillez enlever vos chaussures avant d'entrer dans le vestiaire de la piscine. Merci.

Por favor quitase los zapatos antes de entrar en la zona de la piscina.

Va rugam, nu intrati incaltati in sala de schimb.

プール更衣室には靴を脱いでお入りください。

Producing signs which translate information into different languages can help sport and active leisure facilities to communicate effectively with customers.

Interpersonal skills

Active listening: This plays a significant role in communication and should be used when a customer is talking to you. Active listening means that you make eye contact with the customer and react to what they have said, for example by nodding or verbally agreeing with them. This is followed up with questions to show that you have understood what the customer has said or need clarification.

Empathy: Empathising with customers is very important. **Empathy** is the ability to understand the needs of others. If you can understand why the customer is feeling the way they are, you are more likely to be able to deal with them appropriately.

Attitude: Whenever you have contact with a customer they will form an impression about your attitude. If you have a positive attitude you are happy to take on the tasks involved in meeting their needs and make every effort to provide a high level of service. A negative attitude will result in poor customer service and dissatisfied customers.

Personal, Learning and Thinking Skills

This activity will help to provide evidence of Independent Enquirer, Creative Thinker and Reflective Learner.

Over to you

* Give examples of how a person demonstrates that they have a positive attitude to their work.
* Give examples of how a person demonstrates that they have a negative attitude to their work.

Sensitivity related to physical contact

Although some customers may appear to need physical assistance – for example, someone with resricted mobility climbing steps – you should not automatically take their arm to assist them. Of course, they may appreciate a steadying arm, but you should always ask first whether they require help. Thre are different ways of dealing with those situations, such as pointing the customer in the right direction of a lift or an escalator.

Personal presentation

Customers will form an impression about you within a few seconds of meeting you. It is therefore important to portray a professional image by taking care of your personal presentation. If you look smart, have clean, ironed clothing and have taken care over your personal hygiene and grooming, the customer is more likely to form a positive opinion of you and the rest of the facility.

Ability to work in a team

The ability to work in a team is essential to providing good customer service. You also need to understand the different job roles in your organisation so that you can contact the most appropriate person to help with customer questions or requirements.

Ensuring new and repeat business

The sport and active leisure industry is very competitive, so good customer service skills are vital in gaining new business and maintaining repeat business. If a customer is happy with the service then they are more likely to continue using your organisation. A happy customer is also more likely to generate new business by recommending you to others.

Awareness of different buying personalities

People have different personalities, and the way in which they buy products or services will differ depending upon what kind of buying personality they have! For example, there are some customers who like to be the first to own a new product; these are known as competitive shoppers. Spontaneous shoppers will be attracted to products or services that are discounted or where there is only limited stock available. Methodical shoppers like to research a product thoroughly before they buy it. Lastly there are the humanistic shoppers, who are influenced by what other people say about a product or service.

Promoting opportunities for all

Good customer service involves providing facilities and activities for everyone in the local community. You need to know how to help different groups of people to meet their requirements and promote opportunities for everybody in sport and active leisure.

Being people-focused

A person who is people-focused is concerned with how others feel and does all they can to ensure people's needs are met. This means that they have excellent customer service skills.

Just checking

* How might your customer service skills differ when dealing with internal and external customers?
* Why are good customer service skills essential for anyone working in the sport and active leisure industry?
* What do you think you could do to practise your customer service skills?

Starting Point

* Have you ever paid for a product or service that you were not happy with?
* What sort of customer service did you receive when you complained about the problem?
* Were you happy with this customer service or not?

7.5 Customer service issues

As the saying goes, 'You can please some people some of the time but not all people all of the time!' At some point in your work in the sport and active leisure industry you will probably need to deal with a customer who is not happy with the service or product that they have received. You should manage this so that both of you feel satisfied that the issue has been resolved successfully.

Dealing with a difference of opinion with a customer

How you deal with a difference of opinion with a customer is very important. Whenever a customer is unhappy and there is a difference of opinion, there is always the likelihood of this leading to conflict. It is therefore very important that you follow basic guidelines for dealing with differences of opinions with customers in order to avoid conflict. You should respect the customer and listen carefully to what they have to say. Ensure you give an apology such as 'I'm sorry you feel that way,' even if the organisation or product is not at fault. Remain calm and don't argue with the customer. Where possible, try to find a solution to the difference in opinion. If a solution cannot be agreed on, or if you feel the discussion may be leading to conflict, involve your manager. Once a solution has been agreed, it should be followed up to ensure that what has been promised actually happens.

Over to you

Examine the situations shown below.

* In which situations do you think the member of staff dealt with the situation well?
* In which situations do you think they did not deal with the situation well?
* What could the member of staff have done better?

Situation 1

Customer: I bought this resistance band six weeks ago and it's starting to tear. I'm afraid it will break.

Employee: Can I take a look at the band please? Thank you. What exercises have you been performing with this band?

Customer: I've mainly been using it for upper body strengthening.

Employee: How have you stored the band?

Customer: Rolled up in a cupboard at my house.

Employee: Do you have a receipt?

Customer: Yes, here it is.

Employee: Thank you. It appears that there may have been a fault with the production of this band – would you like to have a full refund or shall I replace the band for you?

Customer: A new band would be great – thank you very much.

Employee: You're welcome; sorry for your inconvenience.

Situation 2

Customer: There's no toilet paper in the ladies' and one of the toilets seems to be blocked.

Employee: Sorry, that's nothing to do with me. You'll have to find someone else to help you.

Situation 3

Customer: The air conditioning isn't working in the fitness studio again.

Employee: Yeah I know; it's a bit annoying isn't it?

Customer: It's been broken for weeks now. I don't pay my membership fees for this kind of service.

Employee: Well, you know what it's like. We've been waiting for a part to get it fixed.

Customer: How much longer will it be like this?

Employee: Not really sure, another few days or a week maybe?

Customer: So I'm expected to pay £100 a month and go to exercise classes in the height of summer with no air conditioning?

Employee: Calm down love, you could always go to a different gym.

Recognising, addressing and resolving issues

A careful approach must be taken to dealing with customer complaints.

When a customer is not happy with a service or product there may be conflict between the customer and members of staff. It is good practice to discuss the problem with them in a quiet area so other people cannot overhear and the conversation remains confidential. Conflict can then be avoided by using the following approach:

* Listen carefully to what the customer has to say – this will empower them as they will feel that they are being taken seriously.

* Ask questions to gain a full understanding of their complaint.

* Summarise the complaint so they are clear that you understand their issue.

* Remain impartial, avoid taking sides between your employer and the customer, and aim for a no-blame approach.

* Show that you recognise that they have a genuine complaint and take ownership of the complaint by apologising. (It may not be your fault, but you are representing your organisation and are apologising on behalf of the organisation.)

* Suggest a solution and make sure that the customer is happy with it.

* Follow up to ensure that the agreed solution has been delivered to the customer.

You may sometimes have to deal with customer issues that you can't resolve or are not qualified to deal with. In these situations you need to know how and when to bring in a more senior person to deal with the issue.

Just checking

* Why is it important that all members of staff who work with customers have training in how to deal with customer service issues?

* It has been said in business that if a complaint is dealt with well, the customer will tell more people about it (which will generate more business) than if they had never had a complaint. Do you think this is true? Explain your answer.

Starting Point

What are the different methods used to communicate with customers in the sport and active leisure industry?

7.6 Communicating effectively with customers

To meet the needs of customers in sport and active leisure, good communication skills are essential. No matter how much you know about customer service skills and the facility in which you work, they will be of little use if you have not mastered good communication skills. This topic explores the different methods that you can use to communicate effectively with customers in the sport and active leisure industry.

Communicating effectively

To communicate effectively you need good communication skills and a thorough knowledge of the facility in which you work, including an understanding of the different job roles in the organisation. Other key factors to help you communicate effectively are outlined below.

Providing information or referring to an appropriate source

If a customer requires detailed information, such as exercise class timetables, you should be able to find the appropriate leaflet, timetable or information sheet to give them or else direct them to where they can get the information themselves. For example, 'If you go to the reception desk at the entrance of the building, the exercise class timetables are located on the reception front desk.'

Good communication skills are important in the sport and active leisure industry.

Providing accurate information

When a customer has requested information, you must make sure you provide an accurate answer. For example, if they asked what time lane swimming was available and were given an incorrect day and/or time, they would be unhappy if they arrived to find they had wasted their time and money travelling to the facility and were unable to participate in the activity.

Use of appropriate language

Use language that can be easily understood by the customer. For example, the language you use to communicate with a child is different from the language you use with an adult. Do not use language that may be offensive. Swear words are never acceptable when working with customers in the sport and active leisure industry.

Speaking clearly

Always speak clearly rather than mumbling so that the customer can understand what you are saying. Speak at the appropriate volume so you can be easily heard. This could mean raising your voice over background noise, such as music or noise from other customers. Use the correct tone of voice to indicate to the customer that you are happy to talk to them.

Adapting communication style to meet different needs

How you address different customers depends on the individual that you are dealing with. When speaking to children you should aim to look friendly and may bend down so that you can see and hear each other properly. Use a pleasant tone of voice and make sure that the language you use is appropriate for a child to understand. When addressing older adults it is a good idea to call them Mr, Mrs or Ms, at least at first – they may be offended if you address them by their first name as this can be perceived as a lack of respect.

As a customer enters a sport and active leisure facility you have your first opportunity to demonstrate your customer service skills. A simple greeting with a smile as the customer arrives through the door gives the impression that you are pleased to see them and makes them feel welcome.

Using appropriate body language

Ensure your body language is portraying the intended message. Body language includes the following.

* Your facial expression helps reinforce what you are saying. For example, if you are encouraging a customer to reach an exercise target or goal you should smile so that they can see that you are pleased with their progress – this will encourage them to continue. Try not to frown or look annoyed when dealing with situations where you feel uncomfortable, as this can make the customer feel ill at ease too.

* Your posture will communicate to your customers how you are feeling and how seriously you are taking them. If you stand up tall with a straight posture it will make you look alert and interested in what they have to say. A slouched posture gives the impression that you are not interested or can't be bothered.

* The gestures that you use can help to reinforce what you are communicating to a customer. For example, if you are directing them somewhere then it might be helpful to raise your arm and point in the direction of where they need to go.

Personal, Learning and Thinking Skills

This activity will help to provide evidence of Independent Enquirer, Creative Thinker and Reflective Learner.

Over to you

How would you verbally communicate with the following people:

* a group of children in a sports hall
* an older person who has difficulty hearing
* a female teenager?

In your answer include how you would greet them, how you would address them, the language that you would use and the volume and tone of your voice.

* All cultures have an accepted distance that they stand from other people when communicating with them. This is known as 'personal space'. When talking to a customer, stand close enough that they can hear you clearly but try not to 'invade' their personal space by standing too close, as this will make them feel uncomfortable.

What message do you think this fitness instructor is communicating to her class through her body language?

Presentation skills

How you present information to your customers is also a very important factor in meeting the customer service needs of sport and active leisure participants. The key areas in presentation skills include:

* **Audibility**
  How you speak is very important in a presentation. The aim of a presentation is to convey information to an audience so you need to ensure that you can be heard by everyone. To help you to speak audibly you may need to practise speaking more loudly than you are used to. You could practise speaking whilst a person is sitting in the back of the presentation room to check if you can be heard.

* **Clarity of expression**
  Express yourself clearly in terms that your audience can understand. If you need to use jargon, make sure it is familiar to the audience – if not it should be explained it to them.

* **Fluency**
  Aim to speak fluently with no long pauses between sentences. Try not to say 'err' as this can be off-putting for an audience.

* **Open body language**
  Body language can communicate a lot about what we are really thinking. Open body language should be used in presentations as this helps the audience to see you as open, accepting and friendly, as opposed to closed body language, which makes you look reserved, distant and unwelcoming. Open body language includes open facial expressions, keeping your arms and legs uncrossed, keeping the palms of your hands open rather than clenching your fists, and turning your whole body to face a person who is asking you a question.

JARGON BUSTER

Jargon Language used by specific groups of people that is not in common use.

Open body language should be used when delivering a presentation.

* **Eye contact**
  When delivering a presentation try to make eye contact with people in the audience. Eye contact helps to make the audience feel that you are talking personally to them, which helps to engage them with what you have to say.

* **Quality of presentation content or instructions**
  Ensure that the presentation you deliver is at the right level for the audience and contains the correct information.

* **Use of aids such as visual aids**
  Use visual aids such as a PowerPoint® presentation or an overhead projector to help maintain your audience's interest. These allow you to present information in different forms such as tables, diagrams or photos. You may also choose to use equipment from the sport and active leisure industry as visual aids, especially if you are referring to them in your presentation.

Just checking

* Explain how you have demonstrated effective communication skills, either with customers in the sport and active leisure industry or with other people.
* When have you delivered a presentation? What do you think are your strengths and areas for improvement in terms of your presentation skills?

Starting Point

In what ways does your local sport and active leisure provider aim to provide access for everyone in your community?

Personal, Learning and Thinking Skills

This activity will help to provide evidence of Reflective Learner, Creative Thinker and Independent Enquirer.

Over to you

* What are the American College of Sports Medicine (ACSM) guidelines for physical activity for adults? (Look back to Topic 1.2, **Over to you**, page 6).

* Suggest ways in which an adult can meet these requirements using the facilities of a sport and active leisure centre near you.

People with disabilities should not have any physical barriers when accessing sport and active leisure facilities.

7.7 Factors affecting access for different groups of people

This topic explores the access requirements of different groups. Access is not just about the physical requirements that allow people to enter sport and active leisure facilities; it also takes into account the types of facilities and activities provided. Different groups may have differing access requirements and if these are not met, it can prevent participation.

Access requirements for different groups of people

Health conditions

People with health conditions are often encouraged to increase their participation in physical activity. Examples of such health conditions include high blood pressure, type 2 diabetes and coronary heart disease. However, people with health conditions need to be supervised by appropriately qualified staff. These staff must design exercise programmes for individuals following specific guidance related to their condition and then regularly review the programme.

Disability

According to the Disability Discrimination Act, sport and leisure providers cannot have any physical barriers to disabled people accessing and using their facilities. The facility should provide planned activities for people with disabilities, such as wheelchair basketball, blind golf, wheelchair hockey or Goalball, with suitably qualified coaches leading sessions.

Age

People of all ages should be able to access a sport and active leisure provider. However, people of different ages have differing requirements and tend to prefer different types of activities. For example, a street dance class would usually attract both male and female teenagers, whereas bowls tends to attract older adults. A facility should aim to offer activities for people of all ages, including parent and baby, parent and toddler, children, teenagers, young adults and older adults.

Barriers to participation

There are a range of barriers that can prevent people from participating in sport and active leisure activities. These barriers can be divided into two groups:

1 physical barriers

2 perceived barriers.

A physical barrier is a real factor that will have to be overcome in order for a person to participate. Examples of physical barriers include:

* not being able to afford to use the facilities

* no public transport to the provider

* lack of culturally-accessible facilities such as women-only sessions

* lack of time

* home and family responsibilities

* lack of facilities for disabled people.

Perceived barriers are barriers that people assume are there but that may not really exist. Examples of perceived barriers include:

* Lack of time – some people think they have no free time for sport and active leisure activities, but find that they do have time to watch TV. This time could be better spent taking part in physical activities.

* Feeling self-conscious – for example an obese person may think that they are being looked at and judged in a gym where they are surrounded by other people who are 'slim and fit'.

* Parental concerns about neighbourhood safety – this can prevent children from taking part in outdoor activities.

* Health conditions – for example older adults may not know about support that sport and active leisure providers can provide to help people with health conditions.

Lack of suitable activities

If a sport and active leisure centre does not provide suitable activities for a person, then this would be classed as a physical barrier. For example, if a health and fitness centre only provided exercise classes that are suitable for very fit people then they are not providing suitable activities for people new to exercise or obese people.

Discrimination

If a person feels that they are being discriminated against in a sport and active leisure facility it is a physical barrier to participation and will affect their access. To prevent discrimination, the provider needs to ensure that its facilities and activities don't discriminate between different groups of people and that all of the staff are trained so that they are aware of the needs and requirements of different groups of people.

Lack of customer service

Lack of customer service is a perceived barrier to participation. If a person does not feel that they are receiving appropriate customer service it will affect their access to sport and active leisure. Qualified staff should be provided to deliver effective and appropriate services for different groups of people, and all customer-facing staff must be trained to meet the needs of every customer.

Personal, Learning and Thinking Skills

This activity will help to provide evidence of Independent Enquirer and Reflective Learner.

Over to you

Go to your local sport and active leisure provider(s) and make notes of how the centre provides:

* physical access to and around the facility for people in wheelchairs

* access to and around the facility for people who are visually impaired.

Find out and list the types of activities that are provided for people with different impairments.

Personal, Learning and Thinking Skills

This activity will help to provide evidence of Independent Enquirer, Creative Thinker and Reflective Learner.

Over to you

What sorts of sport and active leisure activities do you think the following groups of people would generally like to take part in?

* adult males

* young female adults

* older females

* teenage males and females.

Just checking

* What are your physical barriers and perceived barriers to greater participation in sport and active leisure?

* Explain different strategies that a sport and active leisure centre could use to help remove two physical barriers to participation.

* How does your local sport and active leisure provider motivate its customers?

Starting Point

How can sport and active leisure providers carry out reviews to ensure that they are encouraging access for all people in the local community?

7.8 Reviewing and improving access

Now that you know about the requirements of different groups, you can review how your local area provides them with access to sport and active leisure. You can then assess how well your local area provides participation opportunities and suggest any areas for improvement.

Reviewing access

There are various websites and surveys that will help you review access trends across the nation.

The Active People Survey

This is carried out by Sport England and is the largest survey of sport and active recreation in the UK. The survey is carried out annually and you can also view updates published four times a year. This survey provides information on how participation varies from place to place and between different groups in the UK. The survey measures NI8 to show how many adults are meeting recommended weekly exercise guidelines. It also measures such aspects of sports participation as volunteering, club membership and overall satisfaction with provision.

Over to you

* Go to the Active People Survey webpage on the Sport England website and click on the results from the most recent survey. For details of how to access this website see the **Hotlinks** section – **Introduction**, page xi.
* Make a list of the main findings of the survey.
* What does this information suggest about participation in sport and active leisure across the UK?

Hotlink

Specific information about the participation of under-represented groups in sport and active leisure can be found on the following websites: Sporting Equals, The Women's Sport and Fitness Foundation and The English Federation of Disability Sport. For details of how to access these websites see the **Hotlinks** section – **Introduction**, page xi.

Over to you

* Visit one of the websites listed in the **Hotlinks** box using the link given on page xi.
* Why do you think that group of people is under-represented in sport and active leisure participation in this country?

Interviewing people

To review the provision of and access to sport and active leisure in your area you can carry out interviews with local people. They will be able to tell you their thoughts on whether they have enough access and if the types of activities and facilities provided meet their needs.

Current or potential participants: To assess current participants, you can interview customers of a sport and active leisure provider. Potential participants are those who are not currently participating but may do so in the future. You will need to search for people to interview who don't take part regularly now.

Using industry information

Some centres will regularly review their provision and may carry out interviews to determine if customers' needs are being met – ask a manager if they do this and if you can access their information. They may also use questionnaires to assess customer satisfaction. If the provider has a membership scheme they may have information on their members, including details of gender, ethnic background and any disabilities. If you are able to access this information you will have a good picture of the groups of people that use the facility.

Identifying strengths and weaknesses of provision

Once you have accessed enough information about a sport and active leisure provider and the different groups in your local community, you can identify the areas in which the facility is meeting equal opportunities requirements and providing access for different groups and the areas in which it is not. Check to see if the provider is complying with equal opportunities legislation too. For example, is there sufficient access and provision for disabled people?

Suggestions to improve access

By reviewing the access for different groups to a facility, you may find areas where the centre can improve. Examples of methods to improve access include:

Offering family-friendly activity sessions is one method of improving access.

* Promoting activities through targeted media and ensuring that the promotional materials can be seen by different groups of people. For example, posters and information leaflets could be placed in playgroups and schools to attract women with children.

* Working with community leaders to gain information on requirements of the local community and to encourage participation.

* Offering single-sex activity sessions supervised by female staff.

* Ensuring that the facility takes into account religious needs, for example providing quiet prayer rooms.

* Making public transport available to and from the facility.

* Ensuring under-represented groups are included on a facility's staff.

* Increasing training for employees on meeting the needs of disabled people.

* More information about provision for people with health conditions.

* Using media showing role models from under-represented groups excelling in sports.

* Allowing a wide range of clothing choices.

* Providing crèche facilities for parents with young children.

Just checking

* How is a local sport and active leisure provider trying to improve access for under-represented groups?

* How is this provider complying with equal opportunities legislation?

* What could they do to help improve access?

Case study: Access for Marc

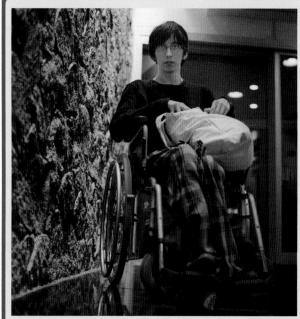

Marc is 18 years old. Two years ago he was in a car accident and injured his spine; he now has to use a wheelchair as he is unable to use his legs. He still has full movement in his arms and upper body. Before the accident Marc took part in lots of different sport and active leisure activities. He now feels ready to try and find out more about sports in which he can take part whilst in a wheelchair so that he can meet new people and find new sports that he enjoys.

Marc visits his local leisure centre for the first time and finds the access into the centre very easy – they have ramps for wheelchair users and wide doorways. However, he finds that the reception desk is quite high up and he struggles to see and hear the receptionist when they are talking. He asks about what sorts of sports are available for disabled people and is directed to some information leaflets. The information leaflets are placed on shelves and again he struggles to reach the leaflet that he is interested in.

After reading through the leaflet, Marc finds that the leisure centre can only really offer swimming for him. He can also use some equipment in the gym that has been specially adapted for people in wheelchairs. He has a look around the centre and spots a poster on one of the notice boards that is advertising wheelchair tennis in a private health and fitness club not too far away. He takes down the phone number and plans to find out more later that day.

Marc decides to go swimming at the centre. Once he is changed he asks a member of staff to help him get into the pool. He has to wait for five minutes while they find a member of staff who is able to use the hoist to transfer Marc safely into the pool. Once Marc has finished swimming, a member of staff is ready to assist him out of the water.

1 Do you think the leisure centre that Marc visited was accessible for wheelchair users?

2 What activities did the centre provide that were appropriate for Marc?

3 In what ways do you think the centre could improve its provision for disabled people?

For your project

This unit explores ways in which sport and active leisure centres can provide equal opportunities to access their facilities and allow every person to participate in sport and active leisure activities. It also examines the skills needed by employees in the sport and active leisure industry in order to ensure that all customers have a good experience and continue to participate. These skills may be very important to you in your future career.

There are a range of different groups of people that are under-represented in sport and active leisure participation. This unit has introduced you to various strategies that have been put in place to help improve participation in these groups.

The following diagram gives some ideas for what you might decide to do your project on, based on the content of this unit.

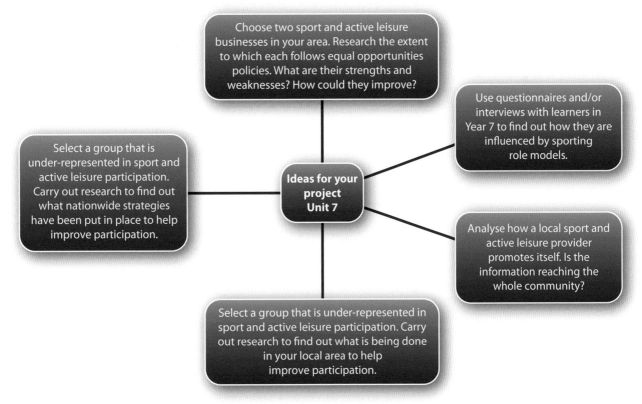

Choose two sport and active leisure businesses in your area. Research the extent to which each follows equal opportunities policies. What are their strengths and weaknesses? How could they improve?

Use questionnaires and/or interviews with learners in Year 7 to find out how they are influenced by sporting role models.

Select a group that is under-represented in sport and active leisure participation. Carry out research to find out what nationwide strategies have been put in place to help improve participation.

Ideas for your project Unit 7

Analyse how a local sport and active leisure provider promotes itself. Is the information reaching the whole community?

Select a group that is under-represented in sport and active leisure participation. Carry out research to find out what is being done in your local area to help improve participation.

Possible project titles

✳ Are disabled people given sufficient access to sport and active leisure provision in my local area?

✳ What are the best methods of using media to promote participation for older people?

✳ How can a local health and fitness provider improve their access for people with health conditions?

✳ How are the needs and requirements of Muslim women met by a local sport and active leisure provider?

✳ Are people working in the sport and active leisure industry given sufficient customer service skills training?

Assessment guidance

This unit is assessed by one internally-set assignment. You will have a period of 10 hours to generate evidence for your assessment. In your assessment you will need to show that you know:

* how to describe the requirements of different participant groups in sport and active leisure

* how sport and active leisure organisations comply with equal opportunities legislation to meet different participant needs

* the management and leadership skills required to improve provision of sport and active leisure activities

* how to engage with customers through customer service

* how to avoid and resolve customer service issues

* the level of current access to the industry for different groups

* ways to improve access for specific populations to local sport and active leisure

* how to assist customers and provide them with valid information

* how to adapt your communication style to meet the needs of different customers

* how to convey information or instructions clearly using presentation skills

* how to show initiative in the resolution of customer complaints.

Time management

* Although you have 10 hours to generate evidence for this assignment, this time frame does not include time spent researching the topic area.

* The internal assessment will be split into different tasks. You will be given set times to generate evidence for each task whilst being supervised by your tutor or your employer.

* Your tutor may well give you ideas for resources to use to help you carry out research before you attempt the task. You should aim to make time to read this information and carry out research for the set task so that you have a good understanding of the subject area.

* Your tutor may give you formative assessments that are similar to the actual task. You should make time to complete these 'trial' assessments, as these will help to prepare you for the real task. Your tutor will be able to give you feedback on the areas that you have completed well and any areas for improvement.

Useful links

Work experience within the sport and active leisure industry enables you to talk to members of staff and customers to help you understand equal opportunities and how the centre where you are based complies with equal opportunities legislation. Work experience also allows you to observe staff dealing with different customers so that you can see customer service skills in action and how they are adapted to meet the needs of different customers.

Some television programmes look at different aspects of access for different groups of people in sport and active leisure provision. Many of these programmes are documentaries based on studies of local communities such as Panorama or Horizon.

Keep up to date with research information from nationwide surveys such as the Active People Survey, or try to find out about local surveys carried out in your area.

There are lots of useful websites that will help you with your research for this unit. For details of how to access these sites see the **Hotlinks** section – **Introduction**, page xi.

How you will be assessed

For your Unit 7 assessment, you need to make sure that you meet all of the assessment criteria for the six learning outcomes, as shown in the table below.

Learning outcome	Assessment criteria
LO1: Know the requirements of participants in sport and active leisure	**1** Describe the requirements of different participant groups in sport and active leisure.
LO2: Know how to improve access to participation in sport and active leisure	**1** Describe how sport and active leisure organisations comply with equal opportunities legislation to meet different participant needs.
LO3: Know the management and leadership skills needed to improve sport and active leisure provision	**1** Describe the management and leadership skills required to improve provision of sport and active leisure activities.
LO4: Know the customer service skills required in the sport and active leisure industry	**1** Describe how to engage with customers through customer service.
	2 Describe how to avoid and resolve customer service issues in selected situations.
LO5: Be able to meet the customer service needs of sport and active leisure participants	**1** Provide customers with valid information.
	2 Adapt communication style to meet the needs of different customers.
	3 Convey information or instructions clearly using presentation skills.
	4 Show initiative in the resolution of customer complaints.
LO6: Be able to propose improvements to access to sport and active leisure for different groups	**1** Describe current access to local sport and active leisure for different participant groups.
	2 Suggest how to improve access for specific populations to local sport and active leisure.

YOUR PROJECT

Introduction

This unit provides you with guidance and information to help plan and complete your project for your Diploma qualification. You will also see ideas for the project at the end of each unit in this book – these will help to get you thinking about what you could do for your project. This unit includes advice on selecting an appropriate topic, help with planning the project, ways in which you can carry out research for your project, how to review your project and finally different methods of presenting your project.

What is the project?

The project is an exciting part of your Diploma qualification as it involves investigating a topic that you are interested in so that you can extend and expand your understanding. You will have between one and two years to complete your project. You will probably have a tutor who is assigned to help you with your project and check on your progress.

What do I need to do to complete the project?

* Your project can be carried out as part of a group or individually. If you are working in a group, each person must have a clearly identified role and produce their own evidence for the entire project.

* Identify a question or brief that clearly states what you are going to do and come up with some aims and objectives to help you do it.

* Produce a plan of how you intend to achieve your aims and objectives.

* Carry out research for your project using appropriate techniques such as questionnaires, fitness tests or interviewing people.

* Use sport and active leisure equipment or techniques safely and effectively. This means that you need to follow health and safety advice and ethical guidelines.

* Demonstrate your ability to see your project through to completion.

* Share the outcome of your project, which must include a review of your own learning and performance with others using appropriate communication methods. This means that you need to be able to reflect on what you think went well and what you would do differently if you were to carry out the project again.

How your project will be assessed

The assessment process is based on your ability to plan, manage, complete and review your project. You need to provide the following pieces of evidence for your project assessment:

* a project proposal

* an activity log

* records of information accessed/researched

* the project outcome and any supporting information that you have created

* recordings, observations or witness testimony for any parts of the project that have required you to be observed

* a project review.

What is covered in the rest of this unit?

Think carefully about the topic you select for your project – this is the first step in achieving success.

* **Choosing your project topic**: This section gives you ideas on how to select a project topic.

* **Planning your project**: This helps you to develop your project aims and objectives and to complete your project proposal form.

* **Researching your project**: This section helps you to find information about your chosen topic from various secondary sources such as books and websites.

* **References and bibliography**: Help on how to reference your work and write a bibliography.

* **Research methods**: This section provides you with suggestions on how to carry out your own research.

* **Ethics and health and safety**: This covers what you need to do to ensure the health and safety of your project participants.

* **Reviewing and presenting your project**: This section deals with what should be included in your review and ways in which you can present your project.

Choosing your project topic

Your project topic will either be related to sport and active leisure or help you to progress onto further education or employment. Choosing your project topic can be quite difficult as you will probably have lots of different areas of interest in sport and active leisure.

Top tips for choosing your project

Some top tips to help you choose your project title include:

* make sure you choose something that is of interest to you

* make sure you talk through your choice with your tutor so that they can help you work out if it is a suitable topic

* don't choose a topic just because your friend is doing something similar.

Helping you choose a topic

A good starting point to help you choose your project is to make a list of some or all of the following:

* the units that you have especially enjoyed while studying for your Diploma

* subject-specific areas within sport and active leisure that most interest you, eg physiology, psychology or biomechanics

* the sport and active leisure activities that you enjoy taking part in or watching, eg football, basketball or volleyball

Think about the sport and active leisure activities you enjoy.

* careers that you are interested in within the sport and active leisure industry, eg sports journalism, working with children or sports therapist.

Think about careers in the sport and active leisure industry that you are interested in pursuing.

This will give you an overall picture of the areas that you enjoy and you can then start to think about how you can link up the areas to come up with a project topic.

For example:

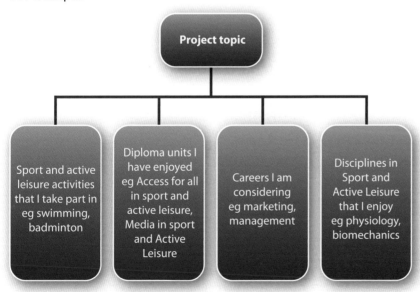

You could use this information to come up with a project topic that incorporates three of these areas of interest. For example, you could do your project on methods of using media (area of interest 1) to promote access for all (area 2) in swimming (area 3). An alternative would be to focus on just two areas of interest and examine biomechanics (area 1) in swimming (area 2).

Over to you

Make a list of the following:

* the sport and active leisure activities that you enjoy taking part in or watching
* the units that you have especially enjoyed in your Diploma study
* careers that you are interested in within the sport and active leisure industry
* disciplines in sport and active leisure that you are interested in.

Planning your project

Once you have chosen a project and talked it through with your tutor, the next stage is to plan what you need to do and how you are going to do it. These are your aims and objectives. When you have considered your aims and objectives you need to complete a project proposal form that must be approved before you can continue.

Aims and objectives

Once you have your general idea for the project, you need to consider your aims and objectives.

Aims

An aim is a statement of what you are going to do. You should try to be quite specific when describing your aims. Consider these two examples:

1 The aim of this project is to see if yoga increases flexibility.

2 The aim of this project is to assess if participation in a weekly yoga class for six weeks increases flexibility in males.

Objectives

You need objectives as well as aims. An objective is what you are going to do or study to help you achieve your aims. These objectives can then be broken down into smaller tasks, which help you to plan how you are going to find out the information you need. For example:

* describe what flexibility is

* explain how yoga affects flexibility

* identify suitable flexibility tests

* carry out flexibility tests before and after yoga participation

* identify whether flexibility has increased after six weeks of participation in yoga classes.

Project Proposal Form

When you have decided on your aims and objectives, you then need to complete a Project Proposal Form. This must be checked by your tutor to ensure that your project is appropriate and that you have carried out all the necessary planning.

Section One

Title or working title of your project: This should be in the form of a question, for example, 'Does participation in a weekly yoga class increase the flexibility of males?'

Project objectives: These consist of the tasks that you need to complete and the information that you need to find out in order to answer your project question.

Form of project outcome: In this section you need to include information on how you plan to present the project, such as in a written report or a presentation.

Over to you

* Which of these two aims is clear and specific?

* What information does this aim include that makes it clear and specific?

* For the first aim there are lots of possible things to test – can you give examples of what could be explored?

You will need to think about how you will measure felixibility if this is one of your objectives.

224

Your role and responsibilities (group projects only): If you are working in a group you need to make it very clear what your roles and responsibilities will be. For example, 'I will be carrying out research to find out about the participation of males in yoga classes.'

Section Two: Reasons for choosing this project

Include in this part how the project topic relates to sport and active leisure or how it will help you to progress onto further study or employment.

Section Three: Activities

Include in this section the activities that will need to be carried out during the project. List the things you will need to do and the order in which you will do them. For example:

* find information on flexibility in males and how yoga affects flexibility
* find a suitable yoga class
* find six males aged between 18 and 20 who have not tried yoga classes before and are willing to take part in the study
* carry out flexibility testing for each male – sit and reach, shoulder flexibility and calf flexibility tests
* ensure participants take part in a weekly yoga class for six weeks
* repeat flexibility testing.

Within this section are details on milestones:

* milestone one: Target date (set by tutor-assessor)
* milestone two: Target date (set by tutor-assessor).

These milestones will be set by you and your assessor to help your assessor to monitor your progress and ensure the project is completed on time. For each milestone a target date is set and you will need to try and ensure you have completed the work required before or on that date. Examples of milestones could be:

* completion of testing, for example, completing the pre- and post-yoga participation flexibility tests
* producing a first draft of your findings.

After each milestone is completed you will need to talk to your tutor so that they can check if the milestone has been achieved. If the milestone has not been achieved, they may work with you to come up with an action plan to help you to achieve the milestone.

Section Four: Resources

In this section you need to list the main resources that you will need, which will depend on the project that you have chosen. For example, information resources such as textbooks or journals might be needed to provide background before you can start the project. You might also need physical resources such as fitness testing equipment and human resources such as the participants.

The remaining sections of the Project Proposal Form are for your tutor and proposal checker to complete.

What physical resources will you need?

225

Researching your project

You will need to use various information sources to help you research your project. There is a huge range of information sources available, and as part of your project you must be able to locate at least three different sources of appropriate information for yourself.

Sources of information

You will probably have access to a wide range of information sources. Some examples are shown below:

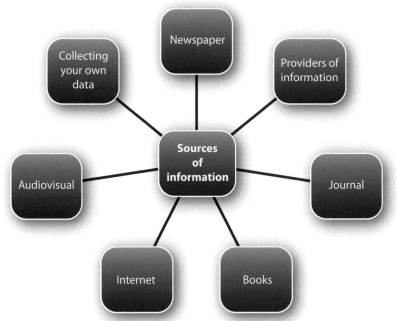

Books

Books provide you with information about specific topics. They are a reliable source of information as they are usually written by subject specialists. You can access textbooks at your school or college library, at public libraries, via the internet (eg Google books) or by buying a copy from a bookshop. Try to use books written within the last five years so that you can be sure the information is up to date and relevant.

Internet

The internet contains a huge amount of information and is updated regularly. Not all internet sites are written by subject experts so you cannot always be certain that the information provided is accurate. However, some sites provided by recognised organisations such as the British Nutrition Foundation or national governing bodies will contain accurate information as these are written by specialists.

Journals

A journal or magazine is published frequently, eg weekly, monthly or quarterly, and will contain accurate, up-to-date information on specific subject areas. You can access journals at your library and some can also be accessed via the internet, but you may need to pay a subscription charge.

Newspapers

National newspapers are published daily and local papers are usually published weekly. They will contain information on all sorts of topics, though it can be time-consuming to find the information that is relevant to your project.

Think about how you can use a variety of information sources to help you research your project.

Audiovisual

These types of sources include DVDs, CDs, CD-ROMs, television programmes and films.

Collecting your own information

You may need to collect your own information for your project, such as by using questionnaires, interviews, fitness testing etc. There is more information on this later in the unit.

Providers of information

Some public bodies provide information that you may find useful for your project research, for example:

* The Department of Health
* The National Health Service
* Sport England.

For details on how to access the websites of these organisations, see the **Hotlinks** section – **Introduction**, page xi.

Primary and secondary information

Information that you measure or have found out yourself is called primary data. When you have used information that has been produced by someone else it is called secondary data.

Over to you

Look at all the different types of information listed above. Which types are primary and which types are secondary?

References and bibliography

You are actively encouraged to carry out research as this is a necessary part of your project. You must also understand how to reference your work properly. If you do not reference your sources then it will look like you have plagiarised the work. Plagiarism means someone has copied work from another person or source and passed it off as their own. It is a form of cheating. As you are carrying out research for your project, make a note of all the sources of information as you use them so that you can include this information in your bibliography.

How to reference your work

Any information that you want to use in your project and write out word for word is called a quote. You need to include details of the source of the quote in the bibliography, which goes at the end of the project, as well as indicating in the text where the quote is from. A quote is identified by placing the words taken directly from the source in speech marks. For example, 'Plagiarism means someone has copied work from another person or source and passed it off as their own. It is a form of cheating.' After the quote you must include brief details of the source, so that the reader knows which of the sources in the bibliography you are quoting from. In this case you would put '(Stafford-Brown, 2010)'. If you use a diagram or picture from another source, for example if you cut and paste it from the internet, you must reference it in the same way, as you have not produced it yourself.

If you want to write a summary of information that has come from one or more textbooks, then you can write the summary in your own words with no speech marks and reference the author or authors at the end of the paragraph. For example, 'Flexibility is a measure of the range of movement around a joint. Flexibility decreases as a person gets older as their ligaments become less elastic (Stafford-Brown et al, 2007; Wesson et al, 2006).' Here you will see the words 'et al'. This is used when there is more than one author and it means 'and the rest'. You must include all the authors in the bibliography.

What is a bibliography?

A bibliography shows that you have used a range of sources of information for your research. It consists of an alphabetical list (by author surname) of all the different sources of information that you have used for your project. You need to provide enough information to allow another person to find the sources you have used for themselves. There are different ways of writing different entries in the bibliography depending on the type of source that you have used. Most people use the Harvard referencing system, which is outlined below.

Books

To include a book in your bibliography you will need to make a note of:

* the name of the author or editor – surname first followed by their initial; for books with more than three authors, give the name of the first author, followed by 'et al' (and others)

* year of publication – this is usually found somewhere on the first few pages of the book

* title of the book – this is usually written in italics in your bibliography

* the edition number if it is not a first edition

* the city the book was published in

* the publisher – the company that published the book.

So for this textbook you would write in your bibliography:

Stafford-Brown, J (2010) *Level 2 Higher Diploma Sport and Active Leisure Student Book*, Harlow, Pearson Education

Journals

To include a journal in your bibliography you need to make a note of:

* the name of the author

* the year of publication

* the title of the article

* the name of the journal (in italics or underlined)

* the volume and/or issue number of the journal

* the page numbers of the article.

For example:

Wilding, A (2010) 'Perceptions of sport psychology within track and field athletics', *The Sport and Exercise Scientist* 22: pp12–13

Websites

To include a website in your bibliography you need to make a note of:

* the author

* the year – this can usually be found at the bottom of the page

* the web page title

* the full address of the website

* the date you accessed the page.

For example:

NHS Direct (2010) 'Common health questions', www.nhsdirect.nhs.uk (accessed 9 March 2010)

Newspapers

To include a newspaper in your bibliography you need to make a note of:

* the author

* the year

* the article title

* the newspaper name (in italics)

* the day and month the article was written

* the page number(s) of the article.

For example:

Kessel, A (2010) 'Chambers and Ennis strike gold', *The Observer*, 14 March, p16

Over to you

Find a suitable source of information for your research project from each of the following:

* a book
* a website
* a newspaper
* a journal.

Write a bibliography entry for each in the correct way so that they can be added to your bibliography.

Research methods

Collecting your own information is known as primary research. There are lots of different methods that you can use to collect information. You need to consider what information you want to find out and the best way of obtaining it.

Types of research method

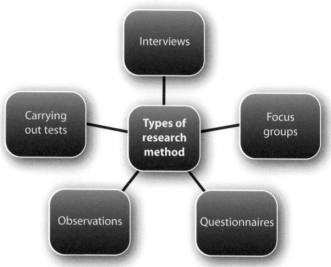

Interviews

This is where a researcher asks someone a series of questions. The researcher can ask the questions face to face or over the telephone. You need to record what the person being interviewed says, either with a voice recorder or by using a pen and paper and writing the answers down. However, writing the information down can take time and you may miss important pieces of information whilst carrying out the interview.

When carrying out an interview, consider the following points:

* Have a list of questions ready beforehand that you plan to ask in the interview. Run these questions by your tutor first to check that they are appropriate.

* Make sure that the person you are interviewing is clear about the purpose of the interview so that they understand why you are asking the questions.

* Try not to have too many questions that require just a 'yes' or 'no' answer, eg 'Do you like taking part in swimming?' Instead phrase the question so that the interviewee can provide more information, such as 'Why do you like taking part in swimming?'

* If you have not understood an answer, ask for more information or ask the person to explain what they mean.

* Try to keep the interview short.

* Remember to thank the interviewee at the end for their time.

Conducting an interview can be a good way of finding information.

Focus groups

A focus group is a group of people who provide information on a particular subject. They are often used to help companies find out what their customers want, for example if a new TV programme will be popular. The people involved in a focus group session may have an interest in the subject being considered or may just be selected at random. A researcher will guide the session to explore people's ideas on a particular topic. As with interviews, information can be recorded and/or written down and then analysed after the event.

A focus group in action.

Observations

During an observation session, the researcher observes a person or group in a particular situation. Observations can be made in a variety of situations, for example, observing the performance of a football player when they are playing at home and away, or observing how staff in a sport and active leisure centre offer support to disabled people.

Questionnaires

Questionnaires are used to carry out a survey of people's opinions or habits. A questionnaire consists of a series of questions that must be carefully considered to ensure you will gain the information you need for your project. You can use closed or open questions in a questionnaire.

A closed question requires the person to answer by picking from a choice of options, for example:

What physical activities do you like to take part in?
Choose from:

team games	☐	swimming	☐
racket games	☐	walking	☐
exercise classes	☐	other	☐

An open question leaves the person free to answer in any way, for example:

What physical activities do you like to take part in?

Make sure you check your questions with your tutor before using them for your research.

Carrying out tests

You may need to carry out different tests to provide information for your project. Examples of physical tests include health tests (blood pressure, BMI, resting heart rate), fitness tests (flexibility, strength, cardiovascular fitness), skills tests (agility, reaction time) and biomechanics (lever length, velocity, acceleration). You need to make sure you know the **protocol** of each test and how to record and analyse the results.

Over to you

* What type of research method would be best for your project?
* Explain why you have chosen this method of research.
* Could you use any other types of research method for your project?

JARGON BUSTER

Protocol The method that you need to follow in order to carry out the test accurately.

231

Ethics and health and safety

Whilst carrying out research for your project you may need to work with different people and possibly have people participate in your research, especially if you are collecting data. When you are working with other people you must follow ethical and health and safety guidelines, which are in place to protect people's rights and protect them from harm.

Ethics

Ethics are concerned with protecting people to ensure that they are not frightened, embarrassed, harmed or negatively affected in any way as a result of your research. If you are collecting data from people by carrying out physical tests, they must complete an informed consent form. An informed consent form provides:

* an accurate description of the procedures that the participant will be expected to follow

* details of any discomfort that the participant may feel whilst taking part in the test (for example, in a multistage fitness test where they are encouraged to exercise until exhaustion)

* details of any risks to the participant

* details of the benefits you are expecting from carrying out the research

* information explaining that the participant is free to stop the test at any point.

The informed consent form should also explain to the participant that they are free to ask questions about any part of the testing process.

Asking participants to complete an informed consent form is an essential part of the physical testing process.

Confidentiality

All information that you collect from physical testing, interviews or questionnaires should be kept confidential. The Data Protection Act (1998) states that any information collected from participants for research must be kept confidential. To help maintain the confidentiality of your participants, give each participant an identification letter or number (or both) and refer to them by this in your written reports, for example 'Participant A'. This will ensure that anyone reading the information will not recognise who the participants are.

Health and safety

Make sure that the research methods you use are safe and will not cause harm to other people. For example, if your participants need to take part in a form of exercise as part of your research, they should complete a PAR-Q (see page 25), which checks that it is safe for them to participate.

The questionnaire on the next page gives examples of the types of question participants may be asked.

An example of a PAR-Q:

1. Has your doctor ever told you that you have a bone or joint problem, such as arthritis, that might be made worse by exercise? **Yes/No**

2. Do you have high blood pressure? **Yes/No**

3. Do you have low blood pressure? **Yes/No**

4. Do you have diabetes mellitus or any other metabolic disease? **Yes/No**

5. Has your doctor ever told you that you have a heart condition and that you should only do physical activity that is recommended by your doctor? **Yes/No**

6. Have you ever felt pain in your chest when doing physical exercise? **Yes/No**

7. Are you currently taking prescription drugs or medication? **Yes/No**

8. Do you suffer from unusual shortness of breath when at rest or with mild exertion? **Yes/No**

9. Do you have a history of coronary heart disease in your family? **Yes/No**

10. Do you ever feel faint, have spells of severe dizziness or lose consciousness? **Yes/No**

11. Do you drink more than the recommended maximum amount of alcohol per week (21 units for men and 14 units for women)? **Yes/No**

12. Do you smoke? **Yes/No**

13. Do you exercise regularly (three times a week or more) or do a job that is physically demanding? **Yes/No**

14. Are you, or could you possibly be pregnant? **Yes/No**

15. Do you know of any other reason why you should not participate in a programme of physical activity? **Yes/No**

If you answered YES to any of these questions, please give details

_____

_____

_____

_____

_____

_____

_____

I hereby state that I have read, understood and answered honestly the questions above:

Participant's name:
Participant's signature:
Date:

If the participant has answered YES to one or more questions, they should consult their doctor before taking part in your research. If they have answered NO to all the questions then you can be reasonably sure that they have no underlying health conditions that may be affected by taking part in physical activity for your research.

Also bear the following in mind:

✳ You should not use any chemicals or substances that may be harmful to health, such as alcohol, in your project.

✳ When conducting interviews, make sure you are safe by carrying out the interview in a public place and not knocking on the doors of people that you do not know.

✳ Check all your planned activities are safe and appropriate with your project supervisor before you begin.

Presenting and Reviewing your project

Once you have gathered all the information you need for your project, you need to develop ideas to show that you have understood the topic that you are investigating. You will also need to present your project and include a review of the results and analyse the project's outcomes. You can then present your project's outcome and your review in the way that you outlined in your proposal.

Developing ideas

To demonstrate your understanding of the topic that you have investigated, you will need to examine the information that you have collected and carry out some form of analysis to interpret what this information means. For example, what happens to the values you are measuring? Do they go up, down, stay the same or vary? Are there any differences, similarities or relationships in the data that you have found? Are the results that you have found what you expected? For example, you may have carried out an investigation into how increased participation in sport and active leisure affects people's health. If you had taken resting heart rates before and after a six-week programme of increased participation you would need to find out how the resting heart rates had changed – this could be carried out by finding out the average resting heart rate of all people who had taken part in the investigation and comparing the before and after heart rates. You will then need to be able to explain these results and state what you have found and give a reason or reasons as to why you think this occurred. In this instance you would expect the resting heart rates of this group to go down as participation in sport and active leisure makes the heart stronger and lowers the resting heart rate.

Reviewing your project

Your review should cover the following points:

* The conclusion that you have drawn from your project, eg weekly participation in yoga classes does increase flexibility in males, particularly in the lower back and hamstrings.

* The project objectives that were or were not achieved and the reasons for this success or lack of success.

* What you have learnt and the skills that you used in the project.

* How well you performed – this can include feedback from other people, such as the participants you tested as part of your project.

* What you would do differently next time – for example, attend the yoga class yourself to ensure that the participants were attending.

* Ideas for follow-up work that you could do in the same or other areas of study and interest.

Methods of presenting your project

There are two main ways of presenting your project:

* written text, such as a report

* an oral presentation.

Written projects

For written projects, ensure that you include at least the following information:

* what the project is about

* what you did

* the results

* a discussion which examines and explains what you have found out

* a conclusion to summarise and review your project

* a bibliography.

Try to ensure that your written information is presented in a logical order and that it is all clearly relevant to the project. Some features that will help you structure your written report include:

* a title page

* a contents page

* different headings and sections

* page numbers

* labels on diagrams or tables

* an appropriate font size and colour.

Make sure that you have used correct spelling and grammar and appropriate punctuation throughout.

Oral presentation

Factors to consider when you are preparing an oral presentation include the following.

* Length of time for presentation – practise delivering your presentation to ensure that it is not too long or too short.

* Will you use handouts? What information will you include?

* What visual aids will you use, eg PowerPoint®, overhead projector etc?

* The structure of your presentation – it should include:

    o an introduction

    o the main part of the presentation – what your project was about and what you found out

    o time for questions – allow the audience to ask questions about what they have heard.

Over to you

* Which method do you plan to use to present your project?

* Why have you selected this method?

* What factors do you need to consider when using this method of presentation?

Glossary

Airbrushed Using computer technology to improve the way someone looks in a photograph.

Airtime Amount of time that something is shown on the television.

Anatomy To do with the structure of the body.

Antagonistic muscle pair Muscles that work in partnership to produce movement.

Apartheid A system of enforced separation and segregation of black South African people and white South African people from 1948 to 1994.

Arthritis A group of conditions that damage joints, causing inflammation, swelling and pain.

Best value Councils have to get as much for their money as they can in order to improve their service.

Bioelectrical Impedance Analysis This measures body composition by sending a lowlevel electrical current through the body – the current will encounter resistance when passing through fat tissue. This level of resistance can be used to calculate a body fat percentage.

Blood lactate Lactic acid is produced by the muscles when they are exercising without any oxygen. Lactic acid is converted into lactate as it enters the bloodstream. The amount of lactic acid produced by the body is estimated from the amount of lactate in a person's blood.

Cartilage Tough elastic tissue.

Cholesterol Cholesterol is produced naturally by the body and is in some of the foods we eat. Having too much cholesterol in the body is not good for us as it sticks to the insides of our blood vessels. This reduces the space for blood to flow through, which results in an increase in blood pressure.

Commercial Advert played between programmes to advertise a product or service.

Contract When a muscle contracts it produces a force (and usually gets shorter) in order to give movement.

Costs Money that the business spends on its activities.

CRB check Carried out to check if a person has had any prior convictions, been cautioned, or given a reprimand or warning for a criminal offence.

Creatine sports drinks Creatine is a legal substance that is believed to help increase muscle strength and speed and to help muscles recover more quickly after exercise.

Customer service Assistance and courtesy given to the people who use or buy a product or service.

Degenerative conditions Conditions that get worse over time. They are related to ageing.

Dehydration When a person does not have enough water in their body.

Digressive activity An activity that gradually decreases in intensity.

Disposable income Money available to spend on non-essential goods and activities.

Durability The ability to last and resist wear.

Economically Without wasting any money.

Empathy The ability to understand the feelings of others.

Ergometer A piece of exercise equipment designed to measure the amount of work performed by a muscle or a group of muscles.

Franchisee An individual who buys the rights to use a company's name and successful business model for their own business.

Franchisor A successful business that other businesses can buy into.

Functional fitness The ability to carry out everyday tasks such as bending to tie shoelaces or walking to the shops.

Glycogen-loading sports drinks Drinks containing high levels of carbohydrates in the form of sugars.

GP referral Being referred by a doctor to a leisure centre or health club to begin a specialised exercise programme.

Graphite composite Material made from graphite mixed with other materials, like titanium and Kevlar.

Hard news News that deals with serious events or topics, such as political stories.

Health The state of physical, emotional and social wellbeing.

Hollow Having a space or gap – for example, a straw is hollow as it has a gap for drinks to be sucked up through it.

Income The money coming into a business from its activities.

Jargon Language used by specific groups of people that is not in common use.

Joint The place where two bones meet.

Lactic acid A chemical produced in the body when a person does anaerobic exercise (exercise without oxygen).

Laissez faire A French term that literally means 'let it be'.

Legislation Laws that cover people's rights and responsibilities.

Loss The difference between income and expenditure where income is less than expenditure.

Lubricating fluid Fluid that reduces the friction between two surfaces so that they can slide past each other more easily.

Mechanics of movement The study of how a sports performer carries out different movements.

Media Methods of communication that reach and influence lots of people.

Mental resilience The mental ability to cope with stress and recover from disappointments.

Midline An imaginary line that splits your body into a left-hand and right-hand side.

Moderate exercise Exercising at a certain level so that the activity raises your heart rate but you are still able to carry on a conversation, ie you are not out of breath!

NI8 This is a term used in the Active People Survey that represents the percentage of people aged 16 years or over in an area who have participated in sport and active recreation for at least 30 minutes at a moderate intensity on three or more days a week.

Niche market A small group of people who share a particular interest – a product or service is especially designed for them.

Paranoia Excessive anxiety and suspicion.

PAR-Q This stands for 'Physical Activity Readiness Questionnaire' and consists of a list of questions with 'yes' or 'no' answers that ask about someone's health. If a person answers 'yes' to any question they may need to visit a doctor and get their authorisation before exercising. See page 233 for an example of a PAR-Q questionnaire.

Physiology The physical and chemical processes involved in the functioning of the body.

Pliable Able to stretch and change shape.

Policy initiatives This phrase is used to cover a wide range of things that the government does to help it achieve its aims, such as new laws being passed, new schemes, new targets, or new rules on funding.

Prejudice When an unfair judgement is made about someone. Prejudices are often negative views about people because of their religion, race, gender or personal choices.

Profit The difference between income and expenditure (costs) where income is greater than expenditure.

Protocol The method that you need to follow in order to carry out the test accurately.

Psychological To do with the mind.

Rehabilitate Undertake activities to help with the recovery of an injury.

Rural An area in the countryside.

Self-evaluation Thinking about what you have done well and the areas that you need to improve.

Slang Informal language, often containing words that are mainly used by specific groups of people, for example, 'cool', 'wicked' or 'innit'.

Social To do with life with other people.

Socioeconomic To do with social status and how wealthy a person or group is.

Soft news News that deals with less serious events and topics, such as celebrity news and lifestyle features.

Solvent The term used for a business that is capable of paying its costs.

Stereotyping Generalising about a person or a group of people rather than treating everyone as individuals.

Sweet spot The best place on the racket head to hit the ball.

Target audience Specific group of people that companies selling a product or service want to advertise to.

Target participant group The group an activity is aimed at because it is something that they may enjoy or see as beneficial. For example, a 'bums, legs and tums' class might be targeted at adult females aged between 30 and 40 years.

Tendon Attaches muscles to bones.

Tone The pitch, level and sound of your voice, which can be used to express how you are feeling.

Torque A force that turns an object.

Under-represented In a smaller proportion than would be found in the general population.

Unique selling point Something that a business offers its customers that is exclusive to that business.

Unique selling proposition Something that you can offer that is unique to the product or service you are advertising and makes it stand out from competitors.

Urban An area that is built up such as a town or city.

VO2 max This is a measure of a person's aerobic fitness and is the maximum amount of oxygen that a person can take in and use.

Wellbeing People feeling good about themselves.

Pages given in *italics* indicate pictures and diagrams; pages given in **bold** indicate definitions of terms – more definitions can be found in the **Glossary** (pages 236-237).